How to Prepare for the Scholastic Aptitude Test

How to Prepare for the Scholastic Aptitude Test

Lester Hirsch, Ph.D

Western New England College

A Trafalgar House Book

McGraw-Hill Book Company

New York, St. Louis, San Francisco, Auckland, Bogotá, Düsseldorf,
Johannesburg, London, Madrid, Mexico, Montreal, New Delhi, Panama,
Paris, São Paulo, Singapore, Sydney, Tokyo, and Toronto

Printed in the United States of America

Trafalgar House Publishing, Inc.
145 East 52nd Street, New York, New York 10022

Library of Congress Cataloging in Publication Data

Hirsch, Lester M.
How to prepare for the scholastic aptitude test

"A Trafalgar House book."
1. Scholastic aptitude test. 2. Universities and colleges — United States — Entrance examinations. I. Title.
LB2353.57.H57 378.1'62'64 79-18438
ISBN 0-07-029041-5

Printing: 1 2 3 4 5 6 7 8 9 SM Year: 0 1 2 3 4 5 6 7 8

Contents

1.

Introduction

When you and nearly two million other students take the Scholastic Aptitude Tests, which are given on Saturdays in November, December, January, April, and June, you might not realize the years of planning and effort that have gone into creating them.

The concept of uniform objective testing for college entrance became a reality in November, 1900, when the first College Entrance Examination Board was organized at Columbia University. In the beginning, only a few eastern colleges, like Columbia and Harvard, were involved. The original objectives of the Board were to provide better communication between secondary schools and colleges and to create some uniformity in secondary school curriculums. The Board developed a test to determine the academic proficiency of college applicants and to find a more efficient method of selecting and placing college freshmen.

The first examinations were in essay form and tested the candidate's proficiency in subjects like English, French, German, Greek, Latin, history, mathematics, chemistry, and physics. Students in 1901 were expected to know these subjects before entering college; obviously, many changes have occurred in high school and college standards during the past eighty years.

Times changed, and so did the style and the content of the examinations. The first Scholastic Aptitude Test was added to the College Entrance Examination Board program, and was administered in June, 1926, to some 8000 candidates. During the next fifty years, the tests were modified still further–the subject matter was updated, altered, and standardized; achievement tests in individual subjects were developed; a scoring scale of 200 – 800 was established, and the test gradually began to assume the form it has today. The last important modifications took place in 1974, when the Standard Written English Test was added to the S.A.T. list and made a part of the present exams.

To apply to take the S.A.T.'s, you should ask your guidance counselor for the necessary application forms. If this is not practical, write directly to the College Entrance Examination Board, either at Box 592, Princeton, New Jersey 04540, or at Box 1025, Berkeley, California 94701. Fill out the application, list three colleges to which you're applying, and return the application form with the present fee of $6.50. This guarantees your admission to the tests and pays for sending copies of your scores to the admissions boards of the colleges you designated. If you are unable to pay, indicate your circumstances when you apply, and the Board will waive the fee.

After you've applied, you'll receive an ATP (Admissions Testing Program) form, an information packet, a personal information form, some data about the tests themselves, and instructions as to when and where the exam will be given. (Tests are given in several hundred centers throughout the United States, so you'll be tested at a center close to your home.) This material should reach you about two weeks before the actual testing date. Check it over carefully to make sure that all of the information is correct. If it isn't, or if you cannot take the tests as scheduled, phone the College Entrance Examination Board immediately to rectify the situation. Don't lose your ticket, because you cannot take the test without it.

A little advance preparation can reduce the anxiety produced by any testing situation. The questions in this book follow the same format and are written in the same style as the actual S.A.T. questions, so study them carefully. They could be considered a rehearsal of the actual test conditions. Your "score" will help you determine the subject areas in which you need review.

Since a good vocabulary is important for the Verbal Aptitude Test, enhance your knowledge of words from the review material in this book, and use a dictionary whenever you see an unknown word. Algebraic and geometric skills are necessary for the mathematics section of the S.A.T.'s, so review your math with the help of the sample questions. Reread your high school math notes, review the use of fractions, percentages, graphs, and ratios; and, most importantly, relearn the multiplication tables and methods of long division—especially if using a calculator has made you rusty. You won't be allowed to bring a calculator or a dictionary to the exams.

Before taking any exam, a good night's sleep is always more beneficial than an all-night cram session. The S.A.T.'s aren't designed to measure what you've memorized. They measure observation and reasoning abilities, and grade you according to how well you use the knowledge that you have. Staying awake all night trying to review a lifetime of learning skills won't result in a better S.A.T. score.

Above all, don't waste any time worrying about the test results. If you've used this book carefully and kept up with your schoolwork, you should have no trouble scoring well.

On the morning of the exam, try to arrive at the test center at least half an hour before the test is scheduled to begin. You should bring some form of identification other than your ATP ticket, and three or four extra pencils. Find a seat in a comfortable location, and relax.

The exams will last about three hours, usually from 9:00 A.M. until 12:00 noon. They normally begin with the Verbal Aptitude Test, in two parts of half an hour each; then the Standard Written English Test, which lasts for half an hour. Usually, after two hours of testing, you'll be given a brief rest, and then continue with the Mathematics Aptitude Test, given in two half-hour segments.

Once the tests begin, follow the proctor's instructions carefully, and read and follow all instructions in the test booklet. Since these are objective exams, you'll be expected to fill in blanks, complete sentences, match columns, complete mathematical equations, and answer multiple-choice questions.

Mark your answers in pencil on the separate answer sheet provided. Make certain that you use the correct answer sheet and that you answer the question in its correct space on the answer sheet. If you change an answer, erase the first mark completely and carefully. The S.A.T.'s are scored by mechanical process, so an incomplete erasure could be recorded as an incorrect answer.

Each question will be counted equally. Don't spend too much time on any one question; if you don't know an answer, skip it and answer the questions that you can. Then, if you still have time, go back and look over the unanswered blanks. Only a fraction of a point is deducted for each incorrect answer, so if you're completely unsure of the correct one, it's a good idea to take an instinctive guess. Once you've answered a question, don't erase it unless you're absolutely certain that your first choice was incorrect. Statistics prove that the first response to a multiple-choice question is usually the best one.

Follow the proctor's instructions carefully. Remember, each section of the S.A.T. lasts only half an hour–if you think it is necessary, bring a watch. Work as rapidly and as efficiently as you can, without rushing, and don't work too long on any one question. The practice questions in this book will help you to gauge your most efficient pace.

After the S.A.T.'s are over, go home and relax.

About six weeks after the exam, the College Board will send you an Admissions Testing Report, and will give you your S.A.T. scores and the scores of any achievement tests that you may have taken. These scores will also be sent to your high school and to the three colleges you designated when you applied. The Board will send your scores to any other colleges you choose, for a fee of $2.00 each. The college admissions boards will weigh your test results against those of other applicants and make their decisions in accordance with their admissions needs.

But let's put first things first. Study this book carefully, analyze your academic strengths and weaknesses, review the subject matter, and do your best on the S.A.T. — it can be a very important step toward your academic future.

Selecting a College

Selecting a college can be a perplexing decision. From hundreds of colleges, all in different locations, all with different academic and social opportunities, you must choose one that suits your abilities, your goals, and your budget.

How do you choose? First, decide exactly what interests you the most. Take a sheet of paper and a pen, and try to picture yourself ten years from now. Will you be working with books, with machines, with ideas, or with people? What part of the country do you want to live in? In a city or in the country? Will you be married? Will you be working for a corporation or for yourself? Picture yourself in various situations. Once you can bring your interests and your ideals into focus, you'll be ready for the next step–matching yourself with a suitable college.

If you feel that you might do well in several different fields, select a college with a curriculum broad enough to afford you a chance to explore some of your alternatives during your freshman year. You might feel yourself drawn to engineering or business, or to a liberal arts program in psychology, political science, linguistics, art, music, or history. The best general advice, then, is to choose a college that has the best offerings in any field you may wish to pursue.

At this point, your S.A.T. scores will help you narrow your choices. If you do well on the verbal tests, but not so well in the mathematical areas, and if you aren't interested in science or engineering, you obviously wouldn't want to attend a technological school. Follow your instincts and your common sense. You may be unsure of your future professional plans, but you'll always have the option of changing majors or changing schools. Exposure to a single exciting college course could completely change your academic direction.

Carefully consider the location and atmosphere of any prospective college or university. Geographic location might not seem very important when weighing educational values, but it can affect your social life and your academic performance. If you don't like cold winters, you'd never be happy attending a college in Maine. If you prefer a dry climate, choose a school in Arizona rather than one in Hawaii. Some students attending rural colleges complain about an unexciting social life, while some students at urban colleges complain about deteriorating neighborhoods, a higher cost of living, and noise. Environment can be a tremendous influence on the learning process, so check carefully on the location of any college to which you apply.

The size of the school and the campus atmosphere are important factors to consider. Would you prefer a large campus or a small one? Would you be happier attending a university with an enrollment of 25,000, or attending a junior college with only 400 students? Could you learn a subject taught by a graduate assistant in a 200-seat lecture hall? Would you be more comfortable in a college small enough to allow the students to know each other personally? Can you picture yourself in a socially oriented school – where parties and clubs and athletics are a substantial part of academic life? Or do you imagine yourself learning in a strictly intellectual atmosphere, where every student is aiming for graduate school? Or would a campus having an equal emphasis on work and on play be more to your taste?

Cost is a very important consideration when choosing a college. Financial problems have ended the education of many promising students, so try to limit your choices to schools that fit well within your budget. Some colleges charge more than $8000 yearly for room, board, tuition, and books, and extras will probably cost another $1000. Some state colleges, however, offer an excellent education, and cost about $3000. If the school is near enough for such an option, do you want to commute from your home? It isn't wise to force yourself or your family to sacrifice too much for an expensive and prestigious education if there is a less expensive and equally reputable college available.

Do you want to work while attending college? If you can afford it, don't work during your freshman year. You'll need the time to adjust to your new environment, to make friends, and to keep your grades up. If possible, wait until your sophomore year to take a job – and even then, don't try to work full-time. It's almost impossible to work forty hours a week and still carry a full academic course load.

Scholarships and financial aid programs are available at most colleges. Find a copy of *Barron's Handbook of American College Financial Aid* at your public or school library, or ask your counselor about these opportunities – but don't expect financial aid to cover your full educational costs. Carefully check the costs of the college you wish to attend, and realistically appraise whether you can afford it. Remember that tuition costs and living expenses are constantly climbing; even if you can afford your freshman year, succeeding years might become much more expensive. Work out your budget carefully.

There are several ways to learn more about colleges that you may wish to attend. College directories, such as *Barron's Profiles of American Colleges* or *The College Blue Book,* provide a fairly accurate compilation of different colleges throughout the United States. These books list the cost of each college, its strengths and weaknesses, its student profile, available majors, extracurricular activities, requirements for admission and graduation, and application deadlines. Your public or school library has a selection of college catalogues, or you can write directly to the college admissions offices and ask for pertinent details. Arrange to meet alumni from the colleges you have in mind, and talk with them. Visit the campuses, talk to the students and professors, and arrange to sit in on a few classes.

Your high school guidance counselor can offer invaluable help in selecting a college. He or she should have a record of your grades and your S.A.T. scores, and can give you objective advice about your chances of success at various colleges. Your counselor has your best interests in mind, so talk frankly when discussing your future college goals.

Choice of a college is an important decision and should be taken very seriously. Don't let well-meaning friends or parents talk you into a particular major because "there's a lot of money in that field." Don't let anyone talk you into a college because he or she went there ten years ago, or because the campus is so attractive, or because your best friend has decided to go there. Don't, however, let anyone talk you *out* of any particular college because the competition will be stiff or because the coursework will be difficult. Analyze your own goals and limitations, listen to what everyone else has to say, and then decide for yourself.

Your own motivation is the most important factor to consider. No matter how bright you are, no matter how well you did or will do on the S.A.T.s, if you're not interested in attending college right now, or if you're interested in a nonprofessional career that doesn't require a degree, there's no reason to rush into your freshman year. Remember, you can always change your mind and apply later. Many students go to college because they've been told that they "need a degree" – but they don't know what they need it *for.* Although college is an excellent way of finding out exactly what you want out of life, many students attend college simply from habit, or because of parental pressure; they have no academic interests and no goals, and they often graduate with a degree that they never use. The decision may be the most important one you'll ever make – but it is entirely *your* decision, so weigh it carefully.

When and if you do decide on a school you'd like to attend, send for an application. Then, look for alternative choices. Don't apply to only one college, even if it's your first choice. Select about five schools of similar merit that offer a curriculum and atmosphere suited to your needs. Many promising students put all of their academic arrows on one bow and apply to only one college. If, for any reason, you aren't accepted by your first and only choice, by the time you receive your rejection notice, it will be too late to apply anywhere else for the upcoming fall semester. Apply to three or four schools that meet your needs – then choose a final emergency alternative: a local junior college or a community college that you're absolutely certain will accept you. Then, if for any reason you aren't accepted by any of your first-choice colleges, you can still enroll in the fall. Keep your grades up for a semester, and then try to transfer to one of your first-choice colleges. The number of mid-year freshman applicants is much less than those applying the fall semester, so your chances of acceptance are even better.

Your senior year in high school is a crucial time for you. While deciding on a career and on a college, and while preparing for the S.A.T.s and other exams you may be taking, you should re-orient your attitude and learn a new set of academic habits–habits that will be easier to acquire while still in high school than during the rush of first-semester college life.

What can you do to prepare yourself more effectively for college? Take stock of yourself, of your assets and weaknesses, your interests, your finances, and your aspirations. In addition to these major personal assessments, pay more attention to the details of your academic activities. Keep careful notebooks; later, they might be useful for college review. Since so much of academic learning depends on the printed word, your reading skills will be of vital importance. Try to improve them while you're still in high school. Learn to use a dictionary whenever you see an unfamiliar word. Arrange an efficient work schedule, allowing enough time for classes, for homework, for outside reading, for relaxation.

Before you leave high school, try to become more familiar with the public and school libraries. Read books and articles on every possible topic that interests you, and read a few on topics you couldn't care less about. Learn how to extract information from printed sources. Learn how to use indices, guides, catalogues, concordances, and other reference books that can help you find answers to any questions you have – and then ask more questions. Your high school library may have resources sufficient for high school research, but your college library will be larger, more advanced.

and more specialized to enable you to produce the professional work that will be required of you.

Most importantly, learn to take your schoolwork very seriously. Most college professors are subject-centered, not student-centered. They won't have time to worry about your feelings or your ego. They're concerned with the students' knowledge of the subject they teach, and they grade accordingly. Since your professors will be experts in their fields of study, they might expect you to be as enthusiastic as they are; even if enthusiasm is impossible, try to take the subject matter as seriously as you can. You'll often have to learn material from texts that seem incomprehensible, and you may be tested on subject matter that the professor never covered in class. Most professors assume that college students are mature adults, and they'll treat you as such. They will assign material which they assume that you'll comprehend. If you fail to ask questions and don't indicate that you're having difficulty, they'll assume otherwise and move ahead with the material. Professors usually aren't monsters, and will help you if you need it, but if you wait until after you fail the mid-term exam to tell the professor you need help, you'll have no one to blame but yourself.

Prepare yourself to work harder, to work alone, and to budget your time more efficiently. You'll only be attending classes between twelve and fifteen hours every week. At first you'll have a lot of spare time, especially when you discover that class attendance is usually optional. Some of your professors won't be the least concerned about your presence in class, and no one will notice your empty seat in the lecture hall. You'll easily be able to cut a lot of classes. But when the grades come out — again, you'll have only yourself to blame.

The S.A.T.'s cannot test your ability to adapt to a college environment. Students with desire and self-discipline will usually outshine more intelligent students who are less motivated and less mature. Obviously, parties and clubs are more fun than studying; there is some truth to the saying, "Don't let college interfere with your education." Most lifetime learning comes not from books, but from experience. At college, you'll meet students from many different backgrounds, with whom you'll probably spend some long evenings discussing the fate of the world over a bottle of wine. The diversity of students and social offerings will enhance your academic education, but use your best judgment and self-discipline. Some freshmen become overinvolved with extracurricular activities, and their classwork suffers. Remember – tuition pays for classes, for grades, and for a degree. It's the quality of your academic performance that will determine your future. Studies come first.

The book you are now holding will aid you in the preparation for your S.A.T.'s. The colleges to which you apply will use your S.A.T. scores and your high school grades as indicators of your academic potential. Use this book, learn the strategies for taking objective examinations, do the sample exercises, discover your strengths and weaknesses, and learn the techniques for achieving the highest possible scores on the S.A.T.'s. The higher your scores, the wider your choice of colleges will be; the more opportunities you have, the richer and more fulfilling your life will be.

2.

Pretest

There are certain skills with which you must be familiar in order to achieve a high score on the Scholastic Aptitude Test. This pretest is a simulated test designed to evaluate your test-taking skills and pinpoint those areas which may require further study. We have omitted Section Three, the Standard Test of Written English, since the results do not count toward your S.A.T. score.

To take this exam, go through each of the sections of this test, answering all the questions. Work slowly, but steadily. Blacken the space that corresponds to the number of the answers you have selected. Answer all the questions and then check your answer in the answer section that follows. Read the explanations thoroughly in order to understand what you might not know. Learn the types of questions that cause you the most difficulty. Once you have found your weaknesses, use this book to review those sections that will help you improve your future test score.

SECTION ONE: MATHEMATICS

In this section solve each problem, using any available space on the page for scratchwork. Then indicate the *best* answer by blackening the corresponding space on the answer grid.

Note: Figures that accompany problems in this test are drawn as accurately as possible *except* when it is stated in a specific problem that its figure is not drawn to scale. All figures lie in a plane unless otherwise indicated. All numbers used are real numbers.

1. At a meeting, five friends decide to buy a plaque for the club that will cost D dollars. One person decides not to participate in the plan. What will the increase in dollars amount to for each of the four people remaining?

   1. Ⓐ Ⓑ Ⓒ Ⓓ Ⓔ

(A) $\frac{D}{3}$ (B) $\frac{D}{20}$ (C) $2D$ (D) $\frac{D-5}{2}$ (E) $\frac{D}{5}$

2. If $A > B$ and C is a positive number, which of the following relationships is not true? 2. Ⓐ Ⓑ Ⓒ Ⓓ Ⓔ
(A) $AC > BC$ (B) $C - A > C - B$ (C) $A + C > B + C$
(D) $A - C > B - C$ (E) $A \div C > B \div C$

3. Determine the area of the curve. 3. Ⓐ Ⓑ Ⓒ Ⓓ Ⓔ

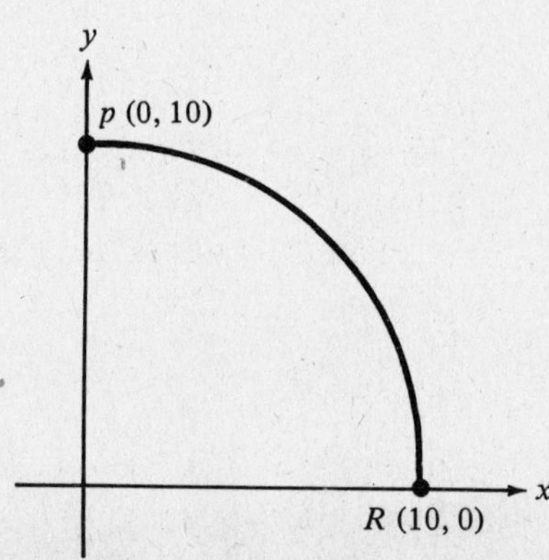

(A) 100π (B) 25π (C) 20π (D) 400π (E) 250π

4. (RB is parallel to TD.) 4. 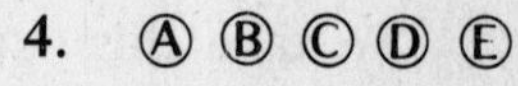
If $\measuredangle BAC = (a + 30)^\circ$, then $\measuredangle ACD$ expressed in terms of a is:

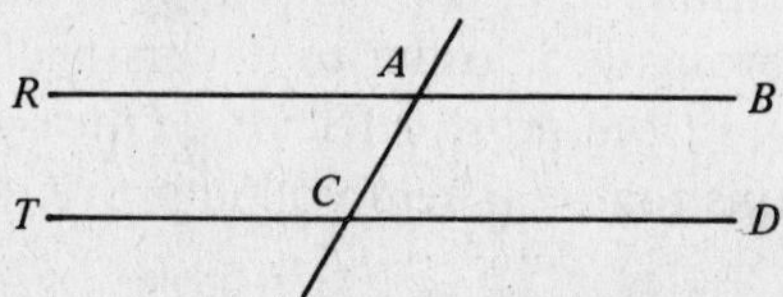

(A) $a + 30$ (B) $a + 120$ (C) $150 - a$ (D) $60 - a$ (E) $60 + a$

5. In the diagram, $QR = QS$ and R, S, and P are on a straight line. It is always true that: 5. 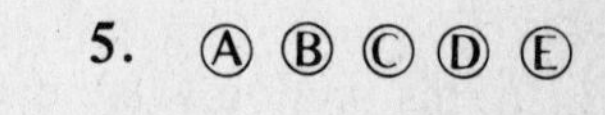

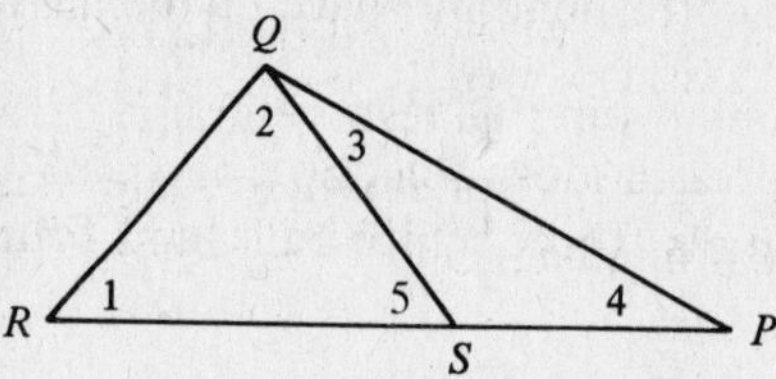

(A) $\measuredangle 1 > \measuredangle 2$ (B) $\measuredangle 1 > \measuredangle 4$ (C) $\measuredangle 3 > \measuredangle 4$ (D) $\measuredangle 4 > \measuredangle 2$
(E) $\measuredangle 1 = \measuredangle 4$

6. A dealer sold 200 pairs of ski poles. Some were sold at \$6 per pair, and the remainder were sold at \$11 per pair. The total receipts from this sale were \$1600. How many pairs of poles did he sell at \$6 each? 6. Ⓐ Ⓑ Ⓒ Ⓓ Ⓔ
(A) 120 (B) 150 (C) 60 (D) 80 (E) 140

7. If the length and the width of a rectangle are both tripled, the ratio of the area of the original rectangle to the area of the enlarged rectangle is:
(A) 1:3 (B) 1:6 (C) 1:9 (D) 1:18 (E) 2:9

7. Ⓐ Ⓑ Ⓒ Ⓓ Ⓔ

8. If the hypotenuse of a right triangle is 6 and one of the legs is 5, the length of the other leg is:
(A) 1 (B) 11 (C) $\sqrt{11}$ (D) 30 (E) $\sqrt{61}$

8. Ⓐ Ⓑ Ⓒ Ⓓ Ⓔ

9. If two fractions, each of which has a value between 0 and 1, are multiplied together, the product will be:
(A) Always greater than either of the original fractions
(B) Always less than either of the original fractions
(C) Sometimes greater and sometimes less than either of the original fractions
(D) Remains the same
(E) Never less than either of the original fractions

9. Ⓐ Ⓑ Ⓒ Ⓓ Ⓔ

10. What percent of the entire figure is shaded?

10. Ⓐ Ⓑ Ⓒ Ⓓ Ⓔ

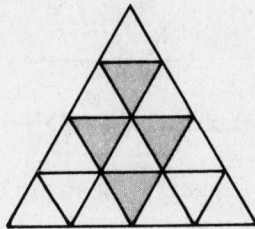

(A) $\frac{1}{4}$ (B) 40 (C) 25 (D) 50 (E) 60

11. One wheel rotates once every 3 minutes and another wheel rotates once every 7 minutes. When will both wheels begin to rotate at the same time?
(A) 3 (B) 7 (C) 14 (D) 10 (E) 21

11. Ⓐ Ⓑ Ⓒ Ⓓ Ⓔ

12. From a work force of 500,000 employed last year, 8% of the total employees had to be fired. How many were dismissed at that time?
(A) 100,000 (B) 200,000 (C) 30,000 (D) 40,000 (E) 8000

12. Ⓐ Ⓑ Ⓒ Ⓓ Ⓔ

13. What is the probability that a random selection of a ball drawn from a box containing two red balls, three white balls, and four blue balls, will be white?
(A) $\frac{2}{9}$ (B) $\frac{4}{9}$ (C) $\frac{7}{9}$ (D) $\frac{2}{7}$ (E) $\frac{1}{3}$

13. Ⓐ Ⓑ Ⓒ Ⓓ Ⓔ

14. On a map, a line segment 3 inches long represents a distance of 15 miles. Using the same scale, how many miles is a road that is $4\frac{3}{8}$ inches on a map?
(A) $21\frac{3}{4}$ (B) $12\frac{3}{8}$ (C) $21\frac{7}{8}$ (D) 33 (E) $62\frac{3}{8}$

14. Ⓐ Ⓑ Ⓒ Ⓓ Ⓔ

15. A certain dress requires $2\frac{2}{3}$ yards of material. How many dresses of this type can a manufacturer make from 120 yards of material? **15.** Ⓐ Ⓑ Ⓒ Ⓓ Ⓔ
(A) 60 (B) 55 (C) 65 (D) 40 (E) 45

16. A department store advertised a summer sale on fur coats, quoting the following prices: **16.** Ⓐ Ⓑ Ⓒ Ⓓ Ⓔ
(A) $1350 coats reduced to $1200
(B) $800 coats reduced to $650
(C) $2250 coats reduced to $2000
(D) $1000 coats reduced to $900
(E) $3000 coats reduced to $2500

Which group of coats had the greatest rate of discount?
(A) A (B) B (C) C (D) D (E) E

17. Line AB is parallel to CD. Line EG bisects $\measuredangle BEF$. How many degrees in angle GFD? **17.**

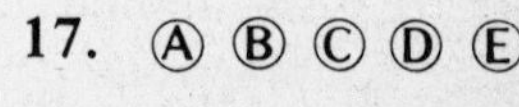

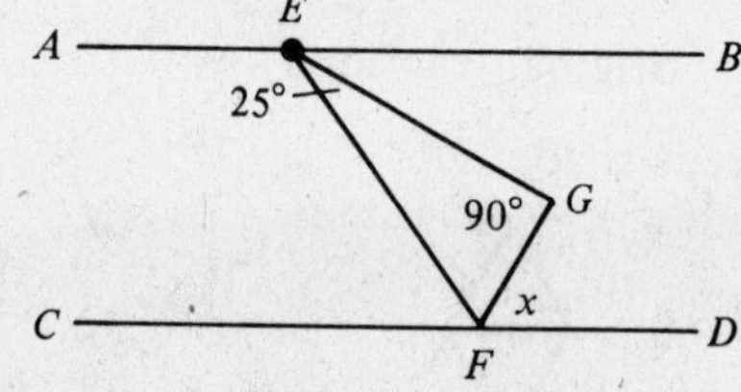

(A) 65 (B) 105 (C) 45 (D) 90 (E) 25

18. The recipe for a cake called for $\frac{2}{3}$ cup of sugar. How many cakes did Jane bake for a baked goods sale if she used 4 cups of sugar? **18.** Ⓐ Ⓑ Ⓒ Ⓓ Ⓔ
(A) 2 (B) 3 (C) 4 (D) 5 (E) 6

19. In a class election, 190 votes were cast for three candidates. Jack received 6 votes more than twice as many as Sam received, while Arthur received 8 votes less than three times as many as Sam. How many votes did Jack receive? **19.**

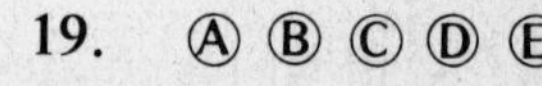

(A) 32 (B) 88 (C) 70 (D) 80 (E) 90

20. Three congruent squares are arranged in a row. If the perimeter of $ABCD$ is 80, the area of $ABCD$ is: **20.** Ⓐ Ⓑ Ⓒ Ⓓ Ⓔ

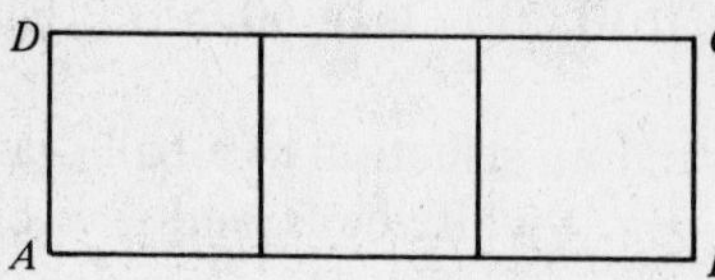

(A) 64 (B) 100 (C) 193 (D) 300 (E) 260

21. The number of points at a given distance from a given line and also equally distant from two points on the given line is: **21.**

(A) 1 (B) 2 (C) 3 (D) 10 (E) 6

22. Multiply $(4+\sqrt{5})(4-\sqrt{5})$. **22.** Ⓐ Ⓑ Ⓒ Ⓓ Ⓔ
(A) 11 (B) $10-\sqrt{5}$ (C) $11-8\sqrt{5}$ (D) $16-2\sqrt{5}$ (E) $8-\sqrt{5}$

23. A formula for finding volume of a cylinder is $V = \pi r^2 h$, where r is the radius of the base and h is the altitude of the cylinder. Find the volume of a cylinder in which the radius of the base is 7 and the altitude is 10. (Use $\pi = \frac{22}{7}$). 23. Ⓐ Ⓑ Ⓒ Ⓓ Ⓔ

(A) 220 (B) 170 (C) 154 (D) 2200 (E) 1540

24. *ROS* is a diameter of circle *O*. Radius *OT* and chords *RT* and *TS* are drawn. If ∡*TRO* = 50°, find the measure of ∡1. 24. Ⓐ Ⓑ Ⓒ Ⓓ Ⓔ

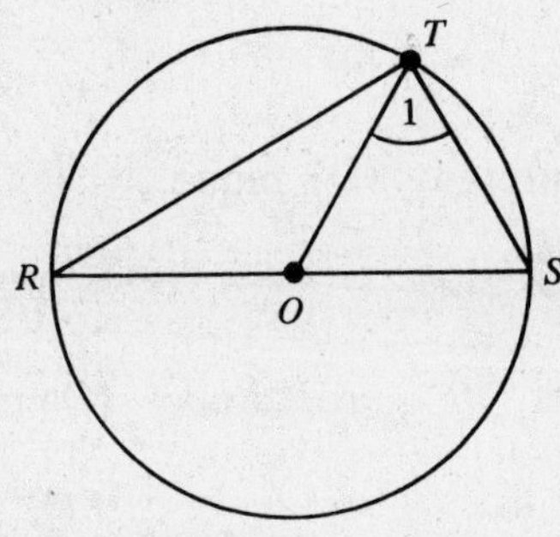

(A) 40° (B) 50° (C) 60° (D) 80° (E) 90°

25. A building contractor estimates that he will need 19,850 bricks at $40.83 per thousand. The approximate cost of this number of bricks will be: 25. Ⓐ Ⓑ Ⓒ Ⓓ Ⓔ

(A) $81 (B) $810,000 (C) $810 (D) $8100 (E) $81,000

SECTION TWO: VERBAL

Antonyms

Each question that follows consists of a word printed in capital letters, followed by five words or phrases lettered A through E. Choose the lettered word or phrase that is most nearly *opposite* in meaning to the word in capital letters. Since some of the questions require you to distinguish fine shades of meaning, be sure to consider all the choices before deciding which one is best.

1. UNCOUTH 1. Ⓐ Ⓑ Ⓒ Ⓓ Ⓔ
(A) urbane (B) travail (C) sentient (D) prevaricate
(E) maladroit

2. ZEAL 2. Ⓐ Ⓑ Ⓒ Ⓓ Ⓔ
(A) flail (B) impute (C) ignoble (D) affable
(E) indifference

3. EMPYREAN 3. Ⓐ Ⓑ Ⓒ Ⓓ Ⓔ
(A) amenity (B) corpulent (C) exonerate (D) hellish
(E) indolent

4. INEXORABLE 4. Ⓐ Ⓑ Ⓒ Ⓓ Ⓔ
(A) surreptitious (B) tractable (C) jaded (D) iconoclast
(E) garish

5. PEREMPTORY 5. Ⓐ Ⓑ Ⓒ Ⓓ Ⓔ
(A) glaucous (B) docile (C) extricate (D) panegyric
(E) mnemonics

6. SAGACIOUS 6. Ⓐ Ⓑ Ⓒ Ⓓ Ⓔ
(A) trepidation (B) perspicuity (C) frugal (D) garish
(E) ignorant

7. TRUNCATE 7. Ⓐ Ⓑ Ⓒ Ⓓ Ⓔ
(A) enlarge (B) extrude (C) intrepid (D) pique
(E) vacillate

8. INTREPID 8. Ⓐ Ⓑ Ⓒ Ⓓ Ⓔ
(A) scurrilous (B) pusillanimous (C) propitious (D) mellifluent
(E) militate

9. EFFRONTERY 9. Ⓐ Ⓑ Ⓒ Ⓓ Ⓔ
(A) timidity (B) palpable (C) raillery (D) libel (E) forensic

10. TURBULENT 10. Ⓐ Ⓑ Ⓒ Ⓓ Ⓔ
(A) quiescent (B) cursory (C) extol (D) gyrate (E) imbibe

Sentence Completions

Each of the sentences that follow has one or more blank spaces, each blank indicating that a word has been omitted. Following the sentence are five lettered words or sets of words. You are to choose the one word or set of words that, when inserted in the sentence, *best* fits in with the meaning of the sentence as a whole.

11. He rambled on in an .... and .... manner. 11. Ⓐ Ⓑ Ⓒ Ⓓ Ⓔ
(A) inane .... incoherent
(B) agnostic.................. petrified
(C) ossified .... frugal
(D) expeditious .... dour
(E) incestuous .... wanton

12. She often had temper tantrums and behaved in a thoroughly....... manner. 12. Ⓐ Ⓑ Ⓒ Ⓓ Ⓔ
(A) decorous
(B) atheist
(C) verbose
(D) puerile
(E) cynical

13. His .... beliefs led him to .... behavior. 13. Ⓐ Ⓑ Ⓒ Ⓓ Ⓔ
(A) dissonant................ obsolete
(B) incoherent............... prodigal
(C) atheistic................ iconoclastic
(D) vindictive............... thespian
(E) recalcitrant .... prenatal

14. He had an extensive library. One could readily see that he was a .... 14. Ⓐ Ⓑ Ⓒ Ⓓ Ⓔ

(A) balletomane
(B) bibliophile
(C) philatelist
(D) charlatan
(E) masochist

15. The two women .... the charge of .... 15. Ⓐ Ⓑ Ⓒ Ⓓ Ⓔ

(A) amplified................ larceny
(B) corroborated............ bigamy
(C) mollified .... parole
(D) facilitated .... felony
(E) ameliorated............. misdemeanor

16. His.................. size was a source of.................. 16. Ⓐ Ⓑ Ⓒ Ⓓ Ⓔ

(A) auspicious.............. embezzlement
(B) sacrilegious............. incest
(C) licentious............... premonition
(D) precarious .... celibacy
(E) prodigious .... stupefaction

17. He was very............ and............ in doing his assignment. 17. Ⓐ Ⓑ Ⓒ Ⓓ Ⓔ

(A) debilitated.............. precipitated
(B) resonant................ captivated
(C) dogmatic .... impeded
(D) indolent .... procrastinated
(E) innate................... nullified

18. His vow of............... did not make him a .... 18. Ⓐ Ⓑ Ⓒ Ⓓ Ⓔ

(A) contrition............... naiad
(B) indolence............... proletarian
(C) celibacy................. recluse
(D) renascence .... bigamist
(E) dissonance.............. cynic

19. She had a/an .... of danger and uttered a severe .... 19. Ⓐ Ⓑ Ⓒ Ⓓ Ⓔ

(A) premonition............. admonition
(B) forgery................... culmination
(C) covenant .... fortitude
(D) innuendo .... castigation
(E) fathom................... blasphemy

20. His.................. made him suspect her .... 20. Ⓐ Ⓑ Ⓒ Ⓓ Ⓔ

(A) autonomy .... unison
(B) cynicism .... veracity
(C) embezzlement........... diffidence
(D) conglomerate .... mayhem
(E) dexterity .... perjury

Reading Comprehension

Each passage in this group is followed by questions based on its content. After reading a passage, choose the best answer to each question and blacken the corresponding space on the answer grid. Answer all questions following a passage on the basis of what is *stated* or *implied* in that passage.

Passage One

Science for self-reliance has, in recent years, become a matter of great concern for Third World and developing nations. These nations increasingly realize that science is the key to material development in their society and that without it, industrial and social and technological progress would be impossible.

Many leaders of formerly colonized nations have cried out for the development of the scientific and technological skills among their peoples. With such skills, these nations will be better able to utilize the resources which their own lands supply. There exists an acute need for scientists, engineers, technicians, economists, physicians, lawyers skilled in domestic and international law, and most importantly, perhaps, teachers and administrators with a commitment to sharing their skills with the underdeveloped nations. These nations would then be able to devise educational strategies and techniques needed to teach their students essential skills.

Science for self-reliance: Perhaps this might be a good slogan for Third World nations looking to improve their positions among other nations, as well as the lives of their citizens.

21. The purpose of this selection is to
    (A) describe the superiority of the developed nations
    (B) indicate the need for scientific and educational development for economic and political independence
    (C) describe cultural and social conditions in Africa
    (D) prove that underdeveloped nations are backward
    (E) show the poverty and ignorance in Third World countries

21. Ⓐ Ⓑ Ⓒ Ⓓ Ⓔ

22. The most appropriate title for this selection would be
    (A) The Development of a Materialistic Society
    (B) The Colonizers
    (C) Science for Self-Reliance
    (D) Exploitation and Its Consequences
    (E) Natural Resources

22. Ⓐ Ⓑ Ⓒ Ⓓ Ⓔ

23. One of the solutions suggested to correct the conditions of underdevelopment is
    (A) building more factories
    (B) obtaining technical advisors from the Western world
    (C) upgrading the educational and science programs for indigenous Third World peoples
    (D) increasing production and profit sharing in underdeveloped nations
    (E) supplying greater amounts of natural resources to developed countries

23. Ⓐ Ⓑ Ⓒ Ⓓ Ⓔ

24. The major complaint expressed by underdeveloped nations regarding current economic conditions is that
(A) they produce an overabundance of unsalable goods
(B) their preoccupation with profits overlooks the need for more humanistic values
(C) their lawyers are ignorant of international trade laws
(D) they have an acute need for physicians
(E) they do not always make the best use of their own resources

24. Ⓐ Ⓑ Ⓒ Ⓓ Ⓔ

25. According to the selection, the keys to social development and material progress are
(A) more profits and power
(B) land and natural resources
(C) science and education
(D) industry and technology
(E) skilled domestic and international lawyers

25. Ⓐ Ⓑ Ⓒ Ⓓ Ⓔ

Passage Two

There is an accelerating trend toward greater realism in media communications. This trend can be attributed to technological innovations.

Years ago the radio sounded brassy and full of static. Now, since the development of frequency modulation (FM), radio sound is of a much higher fidelity. Stereophonic sound (stereo), another technological innovation, was a further step toward an improvement in the method of retaining realistic sound.

Perhaps a greater advance in the trend toward realism in communications was the invention of television, in which images—first in black and white and now in color—were added to sound. Wall-to-wall television with carved panels for a cineramic effect may indeed be what tomorrow holds in store for us. Only three-dimensional and true-size projection remain to be developed in the continuing search for realism in visual communications.

It was not until 1960 that the first major breakthrough in the capability for the production of a practical stereoscopic system took place. At the time, the invention of the laser ray, which incorporated the principles of light and radio radiation, was utilized by communications media technicians. With the laser ray, which created an energy form known as electromagnetic radiation, it became possible to record the actual distance from each object to the photographic plate. This finished plate, called a hologram (whole picture), permits three-dimensional viewing.

The only areas not yet near perfection in the technological communication search for realism are the sensations of touch, taste, and smell. Who knows what sensations of realism we may yet experience in the communications world of tomorrow?

26. The best title for this selection would be
(A) The Search for Stereophonic Sound
(B) Technological Trends in the Communications Search for Realism
(C) The Laser Ray and Improved Visual Quality
(D) Synchronizing the Sensations of Sight and Sound
(E) none of the above

26. Ⓐ Ⓑ Ⓒ Ⓓ Ⓔ

27. The words which might accurately describe tonal and visual naturalness are: 27. Ⓐ Ⓑ Ⓒ Ⓓ Ⓔ
(A) third-dimensional cineramic viewing
(B) electromagnetic radiation and laser light
(C) synchronized sound and projected images
(D) hi-fidelity and television
(E) stereophonic and stereoscopic quality

28. The most recent technological advance in the production of realistic media projection is 28. Ⓐ Ⓑ Ⓒ Ⓓ Ⓔ
(A) improved frequency modulation
(B) stereophonic sound
(C) stereopticon viewing
(D) the laser ray
(E) cineramic projection

29. It would be most accurate to say that scientists have 29. Ⓐ Ⓑ Ⓒ Ⓓ Ⓔ
(A) successfully completed their search for realism in communications media
(B) yet to discover techniques of visual realism
(C) failed to produce sensational realism
(D) to probe ways for the reproduction of sound naturalness
(E) none of the above

30. The area not yet perfected in the search for technological realism is 30. Ⓐ Ⓑ Ⓒ Ⓓ Ⓔ
(A) three-dimensional viewing
(B) sound reproduction
(C) touch, taste, and smell reproduction
(D) laser viewing
(E) holography

Analogies

In each of the following questions, a related pair of words, phrases, or numbers is followed by five lettered pairs of words, phrases, or numbers. Select the lettered pair that best expresses a relationship similar to that expressed in the original pair.

31. **POLITICS:BRIBE::** 31. Ⓐ Ⓑ Ⓒ Ⓓ Ⓔ
(A) parking : meter
(B) business : contract
(C) examinations : cheat
(D) nesting : leaving
(E) painting : commission

32. **PROFESSOR : LEARN : :**
(A) cook : ladle
(B) paper : signed
(C) musician : practice
(D) child : games
(E) artist : canvas

32. Ⓐ Ⓑ Ⓒ Ⓓ Ⓔ

33. **RELIGION : VOW : :**
(A) promise : seal
(B) tank : gas
(C) business : contract
(D) school : report
(E) celibacy : priest

33. Ⓐ Ⓑ Ⓒ Ⓓ Ⓔ

34. **COMPUTER : ABACUS : :**
(A) drink : swallow
(B) charcoal : brush
(C) paper : glass
(D) addition : counting
(E) chronometer : sundial

34. Ⓐ Ⓑ Ⓒ Ⓓ Ⓔ

35. **NOVEL : AUTHOR : :**
(A) rain : flood
(B) form : shape
(C) switch : light
(D) opera : composer
(E) song : tape

35. Ⓐ Ⓑ Ⓒ Ⓓ Ⓔ

36. **MISER : GOLD : :**
(A) engine : caboose
(B) toastmaster : dinner
(C) general : victories
(D) prison : criminal
(E) button : zipper

36. Ⓐ Ⓑ Ⓒ Ⓓ Ⓔ

37. **TOUCH:PUSH::**
(A) water : milk
(B) angry : choleric
(C) glass : water
(D) translucent : opaque
(E) sip : gulp

37. Ⓐ Ⓑ Ⓒ Ⓓ Ⓔ

38. **BANANAS:BUNCH::**
(A) capon : rooster
(B) ram : ewe
(C) chicken : duck
(D) lettuce : head
(E) surgeon : operation

38. Ⓐ Ⓑ Ⓒ Ⓓ Ⓔ

39. **FRAUD : CHARLATAN ::** — 39. Ⓐ Ⓑ Ⓒ Ⓓ Ⓔ
    (A) infatuation : love
    (B) obsession : interest
    (C) impostor : poseur
    (D) ignominy : disloyalty
    (E) castigation : praise

40. **CURSORY : SUPERFICIAL ::** — 40. Ⓐ Ⓑ Ⓒ Ⓓ Ⓔ
    (A) dismal : cheerful
    (B) approbation : consecration
    (C) death : victory
    (D) desultory : aimless
    (E) heroism : reward

SECTION FOUR: VERBAL

Antonyms

Each question that follows consists of a word printed in capital letters, followed by five words or phrases lettered A through E. Choose the lettered word or phrase that is most nearly *opposite* in meaning to the word in capital letters. Since some of the questions require you to distinguish fine shades of meaning, be sure to consider all the choices before deciding which one is best.

1. **JUDICIOUS** — 1. Ⓐ Ⓑ Ⓒ Ⓓ Ⓔ
   (A) incongruous (B) poignant (C) imprudent (D) volition
   (E) syncope

2. **VOCIFERATE** — 2. Ⓐ Ⓑ Ⓒ Ⓓ Ⓔ
   (A) turgid (B) listen (C) resurgent (D) rapacity (E) vilify

3. **ABJURE** — 3. Ⓐ Ⓑ Ⓒ Ⓓ Ⓔ
   (A) venerate (B) maintain (C) transpire (D) obdurate
   (E) lacerate

4. **RECALCITRANT** — 4. Ⓐ Ⓑ Ⓒ Ⓓ Ⓔ
   (A) submissive (B) paroxysm (C) cryptic (D) exhort
   (E) divert

5. **OBJURGATION** — 5. Ⓐ Ⓑ Ⓒ Ⓓ Ⓔ
   (A) exogenous (B) approbation (C) decry (D) covetous
   (E) deference

6. **ENCOMIUM** — 6. Ⓐ Ⓑ Ⓒ Ⓓ Ⓔ
   (A) censure (B) invoke (C) sequence (D) coherence
   (E) paradox

7. **FLUCTUATE** — 7. Ⓐ Ⓑ Ⓒ Ⓓ Ⓔ
   (A) magnate (B) canter (C) inflate (D) spin (E) stabilize

8. **ANOMALOUS** 8. Ⓐ Ⓑ Ⓒ Ⓓ Ⓔ
(A) audacious (B) timely (C) obsolete (D) ominous
(E) chronicle

9. **TIMOROUS** 9. Ⓐ Ⓑ Ⓒ Ⓓ Ⓔ
(A) daring (B) rigorous (C) perceptive (D) frugal
(E) unctuous

10. **LACERATE** 10. Ⓐ Ⓑ Ⓒ Ⓓ Ⓔ
(A) mend (B) tolerate (C) profligate (D) accept
(E) masticate

11. **CIRCUMSPECT** 11. Ⓐ Ⓑ Ⓒ Ⓓ Ⓔ
(A) negligent (B) fortuitous (C) delude (D) repressive
(E) extrinsic

12. **IMPERTURBABLE** 12. Ⓐ Ⓑ Ⓒ Ⓓ Ⓔ
(A) interim (B) total (C) intermediate (D) turbulent (E) fearsome

13. **COERCE** 13. Ⓐ Ⓑ Ⓒ Ⓓ Ⓔ
(A) anathema (B) deter (C) evolve (D) intransigent
(E) invidious

14. **DISCOMFIT** 14. Ⓐ Ⓑ Ⓒ Ⓓ Ⓔ
(A) comfort (B) gain (C) capitulate (D) ease (E) mandate

15. **MITIGATE** 15. Ⓐ Ⓑ Ⓒ Ⓓ Ⓔ
(A) lie (B) correct (C) increase (D) remark (E) integrate

Sentence Completions

Each of the sentences that follow has one or more blank spaces, each blank indicating that a word has been omitted. Following the sentence are five lettered words or sets of words. You are to choose the one word or set of words that, when inserted in the sentence, *best* fits in with the meaning of the sentence as a whole.

16. A good night's sleep has a.................................effect. 16. ⒶⒷⒸⒹⒺ
(A) baleful
(B) phlegmatic
(C) recalcitrant
(D) decrepit
(E) rejuvenating

17. His..................led him into..................situations. 17. ⒶⒷⒸⒹⒺ
(A) celibacy.................zany
(B) concupiscence ....illicit
(C) egotism ....whimsical
(D) quiescence...............resplendent
(E) vertigo ....pristine

18. She plotted .... with great .... 18. Ⓐ Ⓑ Ⓒ Ⓓ Ⓔ
(A) ossification .... probity
(B) mayhem................. vindictiveness
(C) agoraphobia .... spuriousness
(D) obliteration .... succulence
(E) progeny .... impunity

19. His coin collection indicated a thorough knowledge of .... 19. Ⓐ Ⓑ Ⓒ Ⓓ Ⓔ
(A) ichthyology
(B) holography
(C) divination
(D) numismatics
(E) philately

20. You cannot.............. and.............. an event at the same time. 20. Ⓐ Ⓑ Ⓒ Ⓓ Ⓔ
(A) impede.................. expedite
(B) incite .... divest
(C) castigate .... fulminate
(D) berate.................... arbitrate
(E) collate .... flout

21. He loves to hear himself argue; he is a/an .... bore. 21. Ⓐ Ⓑ Ⓒ Ⓓ Ⓔ
(A) germane
(B) humorous
(C) insolvent
(D) lucid
(E) contentious

22. After he hit his son he felt so................ that he bought him a present. 22. Ⓐ Ⓑ Ⓒ Ⓓ Ⓔ
(A) ominous
(B) contrite
(C) penurious
(D) replete
(E) vapid

23. The.................................. the contract. 23. Ⓐ Ⓑ Ⓒ Ⓓ Ⓔ
(A) kith...................... jettisoned
(B) nimrod................... obfuscated
(C) forgery................... invalidated
(D) sybarite .... twitted
(E) vanguard .... tithed

24. If you are .... by nature you would not be .... 24. Ⓐ Ⓑ Ⓒ Ⓓ Ⓔ
(A) vindictive................ illicit
(B) iconoclastic.............. precarious
(C) obsolete.................. voluptuary
(D) licentious................ wanton
(E) prodigal .... frugal

25. His .... behavior seemed almost .... 25. Ⓐ Ⓑ Ⓒ Ⓓ Ⓔ
(A) wanton.................. sadistic
(B) auspicious .... prodigal
(C) inherent .... fractious
(D) masochistic .... prenatal
(E) extant................... heinous

Reading Comprehension

Each passage in this group is followed by questions based on its content. After reading a passage, choose the best answer to each question and blacken the corresponding space on the answer grid. Answer all questions following a passage on the basis of what is *stated* or *implied* in that passage.

Passage One

A father's relationship to his child's current and future academic success, the level of his potential academic development and scholastic achievement are factors with interesting implications that educators are beginning to study and appraise. As a matter of fact, "life with father" has been discovered to be very important in determining a child's progress or lack of progress in school.

A recent survey of over 16,000 children made by the National Child Development Study in London, England, revealed that children whose fathers came to school conferences and accompanied their children on outings did measurably better in school than did those children whose fathers were not involved in these activities. The study, which monitored children born during a week in March, 1958, from the time of their birth through their early school years, further revealed that the children of actively involved fathers scored as much as seven months higher in reading and math than those children whose only involved parent was the mother. The purpose of the study was to evaluate the role played by fathers in the raising of a child. It indicated a much higher level of parental involvement by the father than had been anticipated. Over 66% of the fathers were said to have played a major role in parental responsibility.

The study also suggested that the greatest level of paternal parenting took place in the families of only children. As the number of children and financial obligations increased, the father's apparent interest and involvement with the children decreased. However, no matter what the size or financial condition of the family, a father's active participation in the child's development made a definite difference in the child's progress.

The study further revealed that while the frequency of a father's overnight absences reflected a corresponding deficiency of the child's level in math and reading, a father's employment on late shifts appeared to have little effect on the child's academic progress. The data from the study was obtained primarily from interviews with parents, teachers, and physicians. The information evaluating the level of the father's parenting performance was elicited primarily from the admittedly subjective observations of their wives.

26. The most unusual discovery implied in the study was that 26. Ⓐ Ⓑ Ⓒ Ⓓ Ⓔ
(A) children in large families tend to do poorly in school
(B) a father's influence was a significant factor in the level of the child's academic progress

(C) mothers were subjective in evaluating the roles played by fathers
(D) fathers are parents, too
(E) there is a correlation between socioeconomic status and scholastic achievement.

27. The data accumulated was most probably obtained from
(A) observation by social psychologists
(B) conversations with mothers of the children
(C) interviews, school records, and physicians' reports
(D) observation of fathers with their children
(E) intensive objective testing

27. Ⓐ Ⓑ Ⓒ Ⓓ Ⓔ

28. All of the children that were studied
(A) attended the same school
(B) lived in the same neighborhood
(C) were in the same socioeconomic class
(D) were the same age
(E) knew each other

28. Ⓐ Ⓑ Ⓒ Ⓓ Ⓔ

29. In general, children who tended to progress academically were
(A) those whose mothers gave them the most affection
(B) children who had been given a balanced diet
(C) from one-parent families
(D) those whose fathers worked the night shift
(E) those who had no brothers or sisters

29. Ⓐ Ⓑ Ⓒ Ⓓ Ⓔ

30. Evidence indicated that what percentage of fathers was involved in the parenting process?
(A) about two-thirds of the fathers involved in the study
(B) a little less than 100% of all fathers
(C) slightly less than half of the fathers studied
(D) more than three-quarters of all the fathers
(E) slightly more than one-third of the fathers

30. Ⓐ Ⓑ Ⓒ Ⓓ Ⓔ

Passage Two

The United States Supreme Court decision on the Bakke case promises to be one of the landmark decisions relating to education and human (or civil) rights in American history. It is, perhaps, the most important case relating to the rights of black Americans since the days of the Reconstruction Era.

Emotions ran high and tempers even higher during private and public discussions of this extremely sensitive issue.

"Bakke (Wins): We Lose!!!" spelled out the headlines of a local black weekly after the announcement of the court decision was made public on June 27, 1978. On the same day, several news channels programmed special events segments for provocative and candid discussions of the decision and the related issue of "reverse discrimination."

Who is Bakke and why was so much public attention given to his particular case? In 1973 and 1974, Allen Bakke, a 34-year-old white engineer, applied for admission to the Davis Medical School at the University of California. He was rejected both times.

The medical school, as part of its Affirmative Action admissions program, in the effort to balance the scale of educational and economic inequities against "minority" students from "disadvantaged" backgrounds, reserved 16 minority admissions seats out of the 100 openings in its medical school. Bakke contended that his eligibility was discounted specifically because of the university's policy of reserving an exclusive number of guaranteed admissions for minorities. This, he felt, constituted discrimination in reverse, and he sued for consideration of admission to the medical school, which he purported was denied him in violation of his civil rights.

Those in opposition to Bakke's allegations felt that the reverse discrimination charge was a serious attack on the rights of minorities for quality educational and employment opportunities, and stated that a decision concurring with Bakke's charges would threaten to abort all Affirmative Action programs for minorities.

The decision of the Court is said by some to have been tempered with the judicious wisdom of a contemporary Solomon. Others complained that the decision was a compromising cop-out and a strategy to sabotage existing opportunities for minority educational and occupational advancement. Finally, some observers felt that in the Bakke case, no one had lost and all involved had won. These observers felt that the decision stated that while there was merit in the efforts to equalize economic and educational opportunities with the provision of Affirmative Action programs, Allen Bakke had been a victim of reverse discrimination. Therefore, they reasoned, the Davis Medical School had to admit him.

31. The Bakke case was a Supreme Court decision which took place in — 31. Ⓐ Ⓑ Ⓒ Ⓓ Ⓔ
   (A) the period after Reconstruction
   (B) the Civil War
   (C) 1954
   (D) 1963
   (E) none of the above

32. According to the facts of the case, Allen Bakke was — 32. Ⓐ Ⓑ Ⓒ Ⓓ Ⓔ
   (A) a medical student
   (B) a black student
   (C) an attorney
   (D) a white engineer
   (E) a frustrated dentist

33. Affirmative Action is a policy of — 33. Ⓐ Ⓑ Ⓒ Ⓓ Ⓔ
   (A) compensatory opportunities for "disadvantaged" minorities
   (B) supplementary assistance for highly qualified minorities
   (C) discrimination against the majority
   (D) recruitment of poverty-stricken ethnics
   (E) regulatory programs disqualifying engineers

34. Those in opposition to the Supreme Court decision said that 34. Ⓐ Ⓑ Ⓒ Ⓓ Ⓔ
(A) Affirmative Action would accelerate abortions
(B) minorities always seemed to be losers
(C) the decision was a strategy to sabotage opportunities for minorities
(D) Bakke was a victim of reverse discrimination
(E) none of the above

35. Those who supported the decision felt 35. Ⓐ Ⓑ Ⓒ Ⓓ Ⓔ
(A) the Davis Medical School would have to admit Bakke
(B) it was a judicious decision in which all parties gained something
(C) Bakke had suffered too long
(D) Affirmative Action programs should be stopped
(E) it was a landmark decision which discriminated against blacks and Hispanics

Analogies

In each of the following questions, a related pair of words or phrases is followed by five lettered pairs of words or phrases. Select the lettered pair that best expresses a relationship similar to that expressed in the original pair.

36. **NEEDLE : SEW : :** 36. Ⓐ Ⓑ Ⓒ Ⓓ Ⓔ
(A) pencil : paper
(B) radio : electricity
(C) picture : color
(D) towel : dry
(E) book : cover

37. **FAST : HUNGER : :** 37. Ⓐ Ⓑ Ⓒ Ⓓ Ⓔ
(A) camp : fire
(B) jog : fatigue
(C) sing : voice
(D) tight : choke
(E) play : win

38. **STONE : RING : :** 38. Ⓐ Ⓑ Ⓒ Ⓓ Ⓔ
(A) catch : bracelet
(B) earring : hang
(C) face : watch
(D) mask : hat
(E) cane : stick

39. **APPETIZER : DESSERT : :** 39. Ⓐ Ⓑ Ⓒ Ⓓ Ⓔ
(A) hat : shoes
(B) right : left
(C) rug : carpet
(D) introduction : epilogue
(E) step : stair

40. **PRESS : BUTTON : :**
(A) oak : acorn
(B) eat : plate
(C) perish : starve
(D) plunge : knife
(E) hammock : swing

40. Ⓐ Ⓑ Ⓒ Ⓓ Ⓔ

41. **CANDLE : WICK : :**
(A) hammer : nail
(B) light : bulb
(C) over : fire
(D) bicycle : ride
(E) drill : bit

41. Ⓐ Ⓑ Ⓒ Ⓓ Ⓔ

42. **HORSE : CENTAUR : :**
(A) Pegasus : fly
(B) cat : lion
(C) unicorn : tapestry
(D) worm : snake
(E) fish : mermaid

42. Ⓐ Ⓑ Ⓒ Ⓓ Ⓔ

43. **BAT : BALL : :**
(A) stove : pan
(B) foot : pedal
(C) theatre : seats
(D) glove : hand
(E) fist : mitt

43. Ⓐ Ⓑ Ⓒ Ⓓ Ⓔ

44. **POVERTY : IGNORANCE : :**
(A) disease : illness
(B) wound : blood
(C) river : stream
(D) cough : cold
(E) hold : drop

44. Ⓐ Ⓑ Ⓒ Ⓓ Ⓔ

45. **GUN : DEER : :**
(A) knife : elephant
(B) room : chair
(C) binocular : bird
(D) rope : noose
(E) table : food

45. Ⓐ Ⓑ Ⓒ Ⓓ Ⓔ

SECTION FIVE: MATHEMATICS

Part A

In this section solve each problem, using any available space on the page for scratchwork. Then indicate the *best* answer in the appropriate space on the answer grid.
Note: Figures that accompany problems in this test are intended to provide information useful in solving the problems. They are drawn as accurately as possible *except* when it is stated in a specific problem that its figure is not drawn to scale. All figures lie in a plane unless otherwise indicated. All numbers used are real numbers.

1. A student's marks are 75, 92, 68, and 95. What must his next mark be in order for him to have an average of 85? — 1. Ⓐ Ⓑ Ⓒ Ⓓ Ⓔ
   (A) 100 (B) 95 (C) 85 (D) 80 (E) 90

2. Which of the following fractions is larger than $\frac{3}{5}$? — 2. Ⓐ Ⓑ Ⓒ Ⓓ Ⓔ
   (A) $\frac{1}{2}$ (B) $\frac{39}{50}$ (C) $\frac{7}{25}$ (D) $\frac{3}{10}$ (E) $\frac{59}{100}$

3. Find the perimeter of the figure below if the area of each square is 25. — 3. Ⓐ Ⓑ Ⓒ Ⓓ Ⓔ
   (A) 36 (B) 40 (C) 48 (D) 60 (E) 80

4. If $\frac{px - r}{x - 1} = s$, solve for x. — 4. Ⓐ Ⓑ Ⓒ Ⓓ Ⓔ
   (A) $\frac{s-p}{r-s}$ (B) $\frac{p}{r}$ (C) $\frac{p-s}{r-1}$ (D) $\frac{r-s}{p-s}$ (E) $\frac{1-p}{s-r}$

5. Write in descending order: .009, .010, .504, .194. — 5. Ⓐ Ⓑ Ⓒ Ⓓ Ⓔ
   (A) .009, .194, .504, .010
   (B) .194, .504, .009, .010
   (C) .504, .194, .009, .010
   (D) .504, .194, .010, .009
   (E) none of the above

Use the diagram to answer questions 6 and 7.

A boy usually spends his day (24 hours) as represented in the circle.

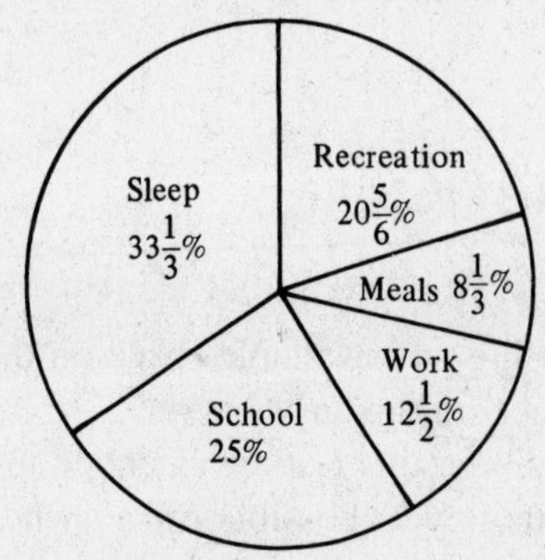

6. How many degrees in the circle represent the amount of time spent at work? 6. Ⓐ Ⓑ Ⓒ Ⓓ Ⓔ
(A) 60 (B) 90 (C) 120 (D) 45 (E) 100

7. How many hours daily does he spend eating? 7. Ⓐ Ⓑ Ⓒ Ⓓ Ⓔ
(A) 8 (B) 6 (C) 4 (D) 10 (E) 2

8. If the three angles of a triangle are represented by $(x + 30)$, $(4x + 30)$, and $(10x - 30)$, the triangle must be: 8. Ⓐ Ⓑ Ⓒ Ⓓ Ⓔ
(A) Obtuse (B) Isosceles (C) Right (D) Scalene (E) Equilateral

9. *PA* and *PB* are tangents drawn to circle *O* from external point *P*. What is the number of degrees in angle *X*? 9. Ⓐ Ⓑ Ⓒ Ⓓ Ⓔ

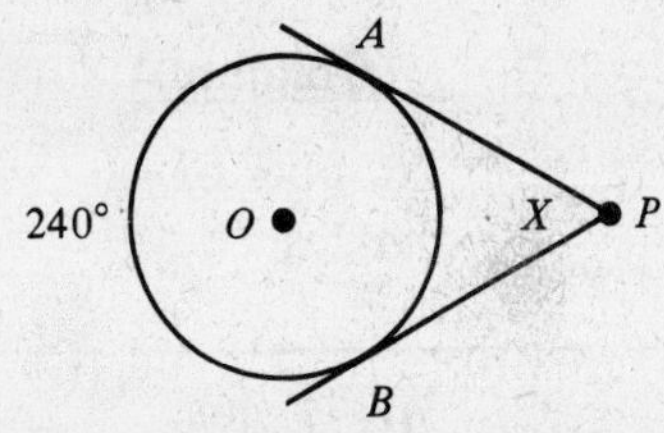

(A) 120 (B) 60 (C) 360 (D) 240 (E) 180

10. If 63 questions answered correctly represented $\frac{7}{9}$ of the total questions submitted, indicate the total number of submitted questions. 10. Ⓐ Ⓑ Ⓒ Ⓓ Ⓔ
(A) 72 (B) 81 (C) 54 (D) 85 (E) 88

Part B

Each question in this section consists of two quantities, one in column A and one in column B. You are to compare the two quantities and on the answer grid blacken space

(A) if the quantity in Column A is the greater;
(B) if the quantity in Column B is the greater;
(C) if the two quantities are equal;
(D) if the relationships cannot be determined from the information given.

Common Information: In a question, information concerning one or both of the quantities to be compared is centered above or to the left of the two columns. A symbol that appears in both columns represents the same thing in Column A as it does in Column B.

Numbers: All numbers used are real numbers.

Figures: Position of points, angles, regions, etc., can be assumed to be in the order shown.

Lines shown as straight can be assumed to be straight.

Figures are assumed to lie in the plane unless otherwise indicated.

Figures that accompany questions are intended to provide information useful in answering the questions. However, unless a note states that a figure is drawn to scale, you should solve these problems NOT by estimating the sizes by sight or by measurement, but by using your knowledge of mathematics.

Use this graph for questions 11 and 12.

1956 Baseball Record of Hits and Walks for John Perkins

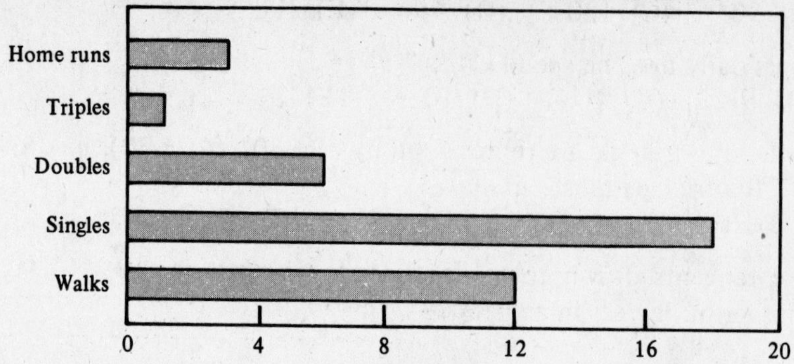

	Column A	Column B	
11.	Number of singles	Three times the number of doubles	11. Ⓐ Ⓑ Ⓒ Ⓓ
12.	Walks plus doubles	Singles	12. Ⓐ Ⓑ Ⓒ Ⓓ
13.	$\frac{1}{4} \div \frac{3}{8}$	$66\frac{2}{3}\%$	13. Ⓐ Ⓑ Ⓒ Ⓓ
14. 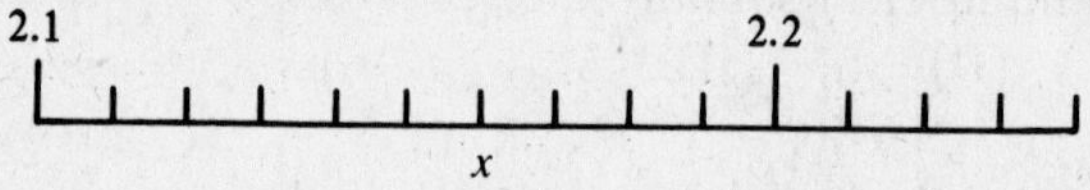		$2\frac{4}{25}$	14. Ⓐ Ⓑ Ⓒ Ⓓ
15.	8^2	2^8	15. Ⓐ Ⓑ Ⓒ Ⓓ
16.	7^3	3^7	16. Ⓐ Ⓑ Ⓒ Ⓓ
17. If $\frac{3}{4} = \frac{81}{108}$	$3 \times 108 \div 3$	$81 \times 4 \div 4$	17. Ⓐ Ⓑ Ⓒ Ⓓ
18.	$\frac{1}{2}\%$	$\frac{1}{200}$	18. Ⓐ Ⓑ Ⓒ Ⓓ
19.	3:4	$\frac{1}{4}:\frac{1}{3}$	19. Ⓐ Ⓑ Ⓒ Ⓓ
20.	$\left(\frac{1}{10}\right)^2$	$\left(\frac{1}{10}\right)^3 \times 10$	20. Ⓐ Ⓑ Ⓒ Ⓓ
21. Let $x = 2, y = 3$	$\frac{-35x^2y^3}{45x^3y^2}$	$\frac{3x - 2y}{4} - \frac{x}{2}$	21. Ⓐ Ⓑ Ⓒ Ⓓ
22.	Average of +0.3, −0.8, −0.2, +0.2, 0.0	.1	22. Ⓐ Ⓑ Ⓒ Ⓓ
23. $2x - y = 3, x + y = -6$	x	y	23. Ⓐ Ⓑ Ⓒ Ⓓ
24. $r < 0$	$\frac{1}{r}$	r^2	24. Ⓐ Ⓑ Ⓒ Ⓓ

	Column A	Column B	
25. $p < 0, q > 0$	pq	0	25. Ⓐ Ⓑ Ⓒ Ⓓ
26.	$36x^2 - 12x + 1 = 0$ x	$16y^2 - 8y + 1 = 0$ y	26. Ⓐ Ⓑ Ⓒ Ⓓ
27.	$\frac{\sqrt{4}}{2}$	$\frac{4}{\sqrt{2}}$	27. Ⓐ Ⓑ Ⓒ Ⓓ
28.	$\sqrt{106}$	11	28. Ⓐ Ⓑ Ⓒ Ⓓ
29.	$\sqrt{2^6}$	$\sqrt{4^3}$	29. Ⓐ Ⓑ Ⓒ Ⓓ
30.	$32 - 49 - 21 + 10$	$-51 - (-84) - 27$	30. Ⓐ Ⓑ Ⓒ Ⓓ

SECTION SIX: VERBAL

Antonyms

Each question that follows consists of a word printed in capital letters, followed by five words or phrases lettered A through E. Choose the lettered word or phrase that is most nearly *opposite* in meaning to the word in capital letters. Because some of the choices require you to distinguish fine shades of meaning, be sure to consider all the choices before deciding which one is best.

1. **FRIVOLOUS** 1. Ⓐ Ⓑ Ⓒ Ⓓ Ⓔ
(A) bright (B) wicked (C) momentous (D) humble
(E) prolific

2. **SECULAR** 2. Ⓐ Ⓑ Ⓒ Ⓓ Ⓔ
(A) spiritual (B) convex (C) satanic (D) academic
(E) aching

3. **GIST** 3. Ⓐ Ⓑ Ⓒ Ⓓ Ⓔ
(A) bland (B) solitude (C) convex (D) entirety (E) cure

4. **PROSELYTE** 4. Ⓐ Ⓑ Ⓒ Ⓓ Ⓔ
(A) caress (B) fasten (C) agitate (D) saturnine
(E) renegade

5. **LUGUBRIOUS** 5. Ⓐ Ⓑ Ⓒ Ⓓ Ⓔ
(A) vigorous (B) happy (C) oily (D) curious
(E) unpretentious

6. **DROLL** 6. Ⓐ Ⓑ Ⓒ Ⓓ Ⓔ
(A) humorous (B) foreign (C) ordinary (D) polite
(E) willing

7. **GRATUITY** 7. Ⓐ Ⓑ Ⓒ Ⓓ Ⓔ
(A) tyranny (B) grant (C) remuneration (D) beginning
(E) silence

8. **BANEFUL** 8. Ⓐ Ⓑ Ⓒ Ⓓ Ⓔ
(A) esculent (B) permeable (C) tumid (D) benevolent
(E) poisonous

9. **HOMUNCULUS** 9. Ⓐ Ⓑ Ⓒ Ⓓ Ⓔ
(A) rudiment (B) proclivity (C) giant (D) chthonian
(E) turgid

10. **CALUMNIATE** 10. Ⓐ Ⓑ Ⓒ Ⓓ Ⓔ
(A) charitable (B) extol (C) lacking (D) surrogate
(E) terminate

Sentence Completions

Each of the sentences that follow has one or more blank spaces, each blank indicating that a word has been omitted. Following the sentence are five lettered words or sets of words. You are to choose the one word or set of words that, when inserted in the sentence, *best* fits in with the meaning of the sentence as a whole.

11. As he neared his .... he became a/an .... ruler. 11. Ⓐ Ⓑ Ⓒ Ⓓ Ⓔ
(A) pinnacle.................. blatant
(B) dotage .... effete
(C) prime .... voluble
(D) euphony.................. dissident
(E) prerogative .... covert

12. When definite moral issues are involved, I am.................... 12. Ⓐ Ⓑ Ⓒ Ⓓ Ⓔ
(A) pejorative
(B) intermittent
(C) vituperative
(D) undulating
(E) intransigent

13. .... is a phase of the study of.................... 13. Ⓐ Ⓑ Ⓒ Ⓓ Ⓔ
(A) nihilism .... gynecology
(B) hypertension.............. etymology
(C) recidivism .... criminology
(D) altruism.................. paleontology
(E) hallucination.............. chivalry

14. A refugee may be forced to................ allegiance to his former country and................ all his former friends. 14. Ⓐ Ⓑ Ⓒ Ⓓ Ⓔ
(A) fabricate.................. garble
(B) forswear.................. extradite
(C) fluctuate.................. expurgate
(D) abjure.................... abnegate
(E) lacerate .... occlude

15. Some experts think schizophrenia is ....; others believe it is.................. 15. Ⓐ Ⓑ Ⓒ Ⓓ Ⓔ

(A) contiguous............... environmental
(B) congenital .... environmental
(C) congenital .... deleterious
(D) hereditary .... pathological
(E) exogenous .... celestial

Reading Comprehension

Each passage in this group is followed by questions based on its content. After reading a passage, choose the best answer to each question and blacken the corresponding space on the answer grid. Answer all questions following a passage on the basis of what is *stated* or *implied* in that passage.

Passage One

In recent years it has been pointed out that the widespread growth of the population is perhaps the most serious problem facing the world today. Demographers estimate that by the year 2000 the world's population will increase to six billion. Students of geography recognize that there is no more basic relationship than that which exists between man and land. The ratio between man and the land is an important consideration in all societies.

During the nineteenth century, Thomas Malthus (1766-1834), in his famous *Essay on Population,* pointed out that the population tends to grow geometrically (2, 4, 8, 16, 32, 64 . . .) while the food supply increases only at an arithmetic rate (1, 2, 3, 4 . . .). Malthus therefore concluded that the majority of the world's population would exist at a subsistence level unless measures were taken to curb its growth. Famine, pestilence, and war might serve to bring the ratio of man to land into better balance. For the most part, stated Malthus, people would have to practice moral restraint if they expected to survive.

All of Malthus's dire predictions did not come true. He could not have foreseen the miracles of technology, which have greatly improved living standards for many more people. Let there be no mistake about it, there is a kernel of truth in what Malthus wrote. Problems of overpopulation in relation to the land still exist in India, China, and in many areas of Africa.

It is highly conceivable that it would be technically possible to feed a much greater population than the world now has. However, scientists continue to warn us that it is likely that increases in food production might be much smaller than those which are technically possible. It has been estimated that three-fifths of the world's population is growing faster than subsistence, and prevailing economic conditions in many areas on the globe may prevent any hope of increasing subsistence, even with modern technological means.

16. From the passage, it can be inferred that a demographer is one who 16. Ⓐ Ⓑ Ⓒ Ⓓ Ⓔ

(A) analyzes soil conditions in the world
(B) analyzes the areas in which land is good for crop growing
(C) analyzes population trends
(D) analyzes movements of continents
(E) analyzes changes in climate

17. According to the passage, it is likely that
(A) food production will outpace the rate of population growth
(B) technology will increase food production in proportion to population growth
(C) technology will not increase food production in proportion to population growth
(D) the rate of population growth will be checked by future wars
(E) the problem of population growth will become less important as technology improves

17. Ⓐ Ⓑ Ⓒ Ⓓ Ⓔ

18. The check on the rate of population growth ultimately depends on
(A) soil and climate conditions
(B) finding new sources of food from the sea
(C) the attitude of mankind towards rates of population growth
(D) the area and size of available land
(E) the ratio of man to land

18. Ⓐ Ⓑ Ⓒ Ⓓ Ⓔ

19. Which of the following statements is true regarding Malthus's *Essay on Population*?
(A) Malthus's assumptions may have been valid for the nineteenth century but are clearly invalid in our time.
(B) Malthus implies that resources are unlimited relative to man's limited wants or needs
(C) technology provides an antidote to the problem of overpopulation
(D) the food supply tends to increase at an arithmetic rate while the population expands at a geometric rate
(E) in spite of the advances in medicine, technology can provide the world with more than enough food to guarantee survival

19. Ⓐ Ⓑ Ⓒ Ⓓ Ⓔ

20. A good title for this passage would be
(A) The Annual Rate of Population Growth and the Food Supply
(B) The Annual Rate of Population Growth and Its Significance to the Survival of Mankind
(C) The Annual Rate of Population Growth and Its Significance to Warlike Tendencies of People
(D) The Annual Rate of Population in the Year 2000
(E) The Annual Rate of Population Growth and Technology

20. Ⓐ Ⓑ Ⓒ Ⓓ Ⓔ

Passage Two

A cell is a unit of structure and function. This means that bodies of plants and animals are in units called cells. Any function performed by an organ like a root or a liver is performed by the cells of that organ.

Cells have boundaries called plasma membranes. They are about 7.5 millimicrons thick, which is less than a millionth of an inch. Yet this film regulates entry and exit of materials into and out of the cell. Thirty years ago Davson and Danielli predicted the structure of the membrane by observing behavior of chemicals passing through the membrane. The electron microscope proved that they were essentially correct.

The membrane is a sort of sandwich. There are two layers of protein, with a double layer of fat molecules between them. The membrane appears under the electron microscope as two dark lines with a lightly shaded space between them.

Inside the cell is a mass of cytoplasm, in which the electron microscope has found many discrete particles. But the general microscopic view does not show as many particles. Cytoplasm has been known to contain colloids. These are substances that can change readily from a "solid" like Jello, to a liquid like melted Jello, and back to solid. The cytoplasm, with its invisible, intricate structure, performs many activities of the cell.

But the control of the activities in each cell seems to reside in the nucleus. Its genes are used as templates or patterns for the manufacture of messenger RNA molecules. They proceed out of the nucleus to tiny factories called ribosomes. The ribosomes then manufacture needed proteins.

The plasma membrane, the cytoplasm, and the nucleus are involved in interrelationships called "feedback." The rate of entrance of material through the membrane will be affected by how much is already in the cell. The cytoplasm also "turns off" the nucleus when a certain manufactured product is in sufficient supply.

21. It can be inferred that the author thinks that 21. Ⓐ Ⓑ Ⓒ Ⓓ Ⓔ

I. the nucleus directs the activities of the cell
II. the cytoplasm carries out orders and has no control
III. the membrane is an active structure

(A) I only
(B) II only
(C) III only
(D) I and II only
(E) I and III only

22. According to the passage, the plasma membrane is made up of 22. Ⓐ Ⓑ Ⓒ Ⓓ Ⓔ
(A) a very thin layer of carbohydrate
(B) a very thin layer of protein
(C) alternating layers of fat, proteins, and fat
(D) a double layer of fat between two layers of protein
(E) a mosaic of protein and lipid

23. According to the passage, the electron microscope corroborated predictions of Davson and Danielli by the appearance of 23. Ⓐ Ⓑ Ⓒ Ⓓ Ⓔ
(A) two dark lines with a space between them
(B) carbohydrates associated with a layer of protein
(C) a double row of particles
(D) cytoplasmic attachments
(E) nuclear chemicals acting as messengers

24. According to the passage, the cytoplasm functions by
    (A) changing liquids to solids and back to liquids
    (B) interaction of parts not seen with the light microscope
    (C) sending stimuli to the nucleus
    (D) receiving materials from the outside of the cell
    (E) all of these

24. Ⓐ Ⓑ Ⓒ Ⓓ Ⓔ

25. Which of the following would be the best title for this selection?
    (A) Davson and Danielli
    (B) The Nature of the Cell
    (C) The Changing Cell
    (D) Using the Electronic Microscope
    (E) The Cell's Membrane

25. Ⓐ Ⓑ Ⓒ Ⓓ Ⓔ

Passage Three

In the South American rain forest abide the greatest acrobats on earth. The monkeys of the Old World, agile as they are, cannot hang by their tails. It is only the monkeys of America that possess this skill. They are called ceboids, and their unique group includes marmosets, owl monkeys, sakis, spider monkeys, squirrel monkeys, and howlers. Among these the star gymnast is the skinny, intelligent spider monkey. Hanging head down like a trapeze artist from the loop of a liana, he may suddenly give a short swing, launch himself into space and, soaring outward and downward across a fifty-foot void, lightly catch a bough on which he spied a shining berry. No owl monkey can match his leap, for their arms are shorter, their tails untalented. The marmosets, smallest of the tribe, tough, noisy hoodlums that travel in gangs, are also capable of leaps into space, but their landings are rough: smack against a tree trunk with arms and legs spread wide.

26. Which of the following statements is clearly stated by the author?
    (A) the monkeys of South America are an exceedingly gregarious group and exhibit great affection for each other
    (B) the monkeys of the Old World reveal an unusually high order of intelligence
    (C) the monkeys of South America have the ability to hang by their tails
    (D) monkeys in general are very hostile toward other species of animals
    (E) South American monkeys reveal an amazing ability to adapt to captivity and therefore they make splendid house pets

26. Ⓐ Ⓑ Ⓒ Ⓓ Ⓔ

27. It may be inferred from the passage that monkeys which have the ability to hang by their tails
    (A) are of considerable intelligence as compared with others
    (B) are grouped together under the technical name *ceboids*
    (C) are natural rivals of the monkeys of the Old World
    (D) are either marmosets, owl monkeys, or howlers
    (E) are among those species that are being protected by international law

27. Ⓐ Ⓑ Ⓒ Ⓓ Ⓔ

28. The author implies that the marmosets, smallest of the tribe, are
(A) tough, noisy hoodlums
(B) wilder than the other monkeys mentioned
(C) somewhat less intelligent than the spider monkeys
(D) capable of great leaps into space
(E) the clowns of the jungle

28. Ⓐ Ⓑ Ⓒ Ⓓ Ⓔ

29. Which of the following statements is *not* justified by the contents of the selection?
(A) the monkeys of the Old World are not particularly agile
(B) these monkeys and skilled trapeze artists have something in common
(C) the arms of the owl monkey are shorter than those of the spider monkey
(D) the spider monkey has what the author refers to as a "talented tail"
(E) the group of monkeys that includes those mentioned in the selection is unique

29. Ⓐ Ⓑ Ⓒ Ⓓ Ⓔ

30. The best title for this selection would probably be
(A) Old World Monkeys
(B) The Greatest Acrobats on Earth
(C) Talented Marmosets
(D) Noisy Hoodlums
(E) South American Wildlife

30. Ⓐ Ⓑ Ⓒ Ⓓ Ⓔ

ANALOGIES

In each of the following questions, a related pair of words or phrases is followed by five lettered pairs of words or phrases. Select the lettered pair that best expresses a relationship similar to that expressed in the original pair.

31. **MAN : MOON : :**
(A) elf : shoes
(B) fairy : wand
(C) leprechaun : mushroom
(D) gnome : bridge
(E) witch : apple

31. Ⓐ Ⓑ Ⓒ Ⓓ Ⓔ

32. **IGNITION : START : :**
(A) radio : antenna
(B) shut : door
(C) brake : stop
(D) air : tire
(E) gas : tank

32. Ⓐ Ⓑ Ⓒ Ⓓ Ⓔ

33. **BRAID : HAIR : :**
(A) stocking : run
(B) watch : movie
(C) laugh : joke
(D) ribbon : bow
(E) wind : clock

33. Ⓐ Ⓑ Ⓒ Ⓓ Ⓔ

34. **BRITTLE : BREAK : :**
(A) glass : crack
(B) sharp : scratches
(C) tree : wind
(D) flexible : bend
(E) ice : melt

34. Ⓐ Ⓑ Ⓒ Ⓓ Ⓔ

35. **SATELLITE : ORBIT : :**
(A) projectile : trajectory
(B) protuberance : swell
(C) arrow : range
(D) bullet : barrel
(E) elevator : shaft

35. Ⓐ Ⓑ Ⓒ Ⓓ Ⓔ

36. **ALUMNI : ALUMNAE : :**
(A) girl : boy
(B) school : schools
(C) roosters : hens
(D) boredom : ennui
(E) mothers : fathers

36. Ⓐ Ⓑ Ⓒ Ⓓ Ⓔ

37. **SHEEP : FLOCK : :**
(A) deer : horses
(B) flowers : bunch
(C) group : crowd
(D) cows : herd
(E) eggs : dozen

37. Ⓐ Ⓑ Ⓒ Ⓓ Ⓔ

38. **BORROW : LEND : :**
(A) lengthen : abridge
(B) pretty : ugly
(C) in : out
(D) people : animal
(E) cat : dog

38. Ⓐ Ⓑ Ⓒ Ⓓ Ⓔ

39. **2 : 4 : :**
(A) 12 : 20
(B) 5 : 25
(C) 3 : 12
(D) 4 : 2
(E) 6 : 8

39. Ⓐ Ⓑ Ⓒ Ⓓ Ⓔ

40. **HIS : HE : :**
(A) theirs : them
(B) hers : his
(C) mine : I
(D) ours : us
(E) she : her

40. Ⓐ Ⓑ Ⓒ Ⓓ Ⓔ

Answers and Analysis

SECTION ONE: MATHEMATICS

1. **(B)** $\dfrac{\text{Total amount}}{\text{Number of people}} = \dfrac{D}{4}$

Subtract:

$$\frac{\text{Total amount}}{\text{Original number of people}} = \frac{D}{5}$$

Find equivalent fractions.

$$\frac{D}{4} = \frac{5D}{20}$$

$$-\frac{D}{5} = \frac{4D}{20}$$

$$\text{Difference} = \frac{D}{20}$$

2. **(B)** If unequals are subtracted from equals, the differences are unequal in opposite order.

Let $C = C$. Since $A > B$, subtract $C - A < C - B$, which is false for **(B)**.

If $A > B$ and C is positive:

(A) $AC > BC$ True
(C) $A + C > B + C$ True
(D) $A - C > B - C$ True
(E) $A - C > B - C$ True

3. **(B)** A circle has a radius of 10 units. The area of the curve is $\frac{1}{4}$ that of the entire circle.

$$A = \pi r^2$$

$$A \text{ of } \frac{1}{4} \text{ circle} = \frac{1}{4}(\pi)(10)^2$$

$$A = \frac{1}{4}(\pi)(100)$$

$$= 25\pi$$

4. **(C)** $\measuredangle BAC$ and $\measuredangle ACD$ are supplementary angles; hence $m\measuredangle BAC + m\measuredangle ACD = 180$.

Substitute $a + 30 + m\measuredangle ACD = 180$.

$$m\measuredangle ACD = 180 - (a + 30)$$

$$= 180 - a - 30$$

$$= 150 - a$$

5. **(B)** In the diagram, $\measuredangle 1 = \measuredangle 5$ because ΔRQS is isosceles since $QR = QS$. Angle 5 is an exterior angle of triangle II and is equal to the sum of $\measuredangle 3$ and $\measuredangle 4$. Hence $\measuredangle 5 >$ either $\measuredangle 3$ or $\measuredangle 4$, $\measuredangle 5 > \measuredangle 4$. Substitute: $\measuredangle 1 > \measuredangle 4$

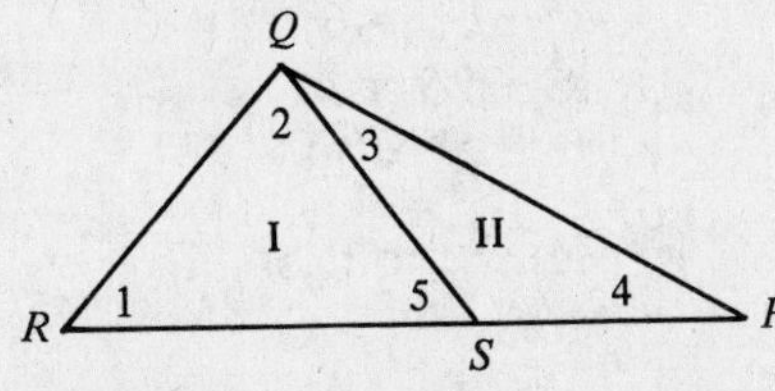

6. **(A)** Let

x = number of poles at \$6 per pair
y = number of poles at \$11 per pair

(1) $x + \quad y = 200$
(2) $6y + 11y = 1600 \rightarrow$ number of poles, x times price per pole, \$6, plus number of poles, y times price per pole, \$11 = total receipts

Substitute from equation (1) (that $x = 200 - y$) into equation (2):

$$6(200 - y) + 11y = 1600$$
$$1200 - 6y + 11y = 1600$$
$$1200 + 5y = 1600$$
$$5y = 400$$
$$y = 80 \text{ pairs of skis sold at \$11}$$

$$x = 200 - y = 120 \text{ pairs of skis sold at \$6}$$

7. **(C)** Let the original rectangle be expressed as:

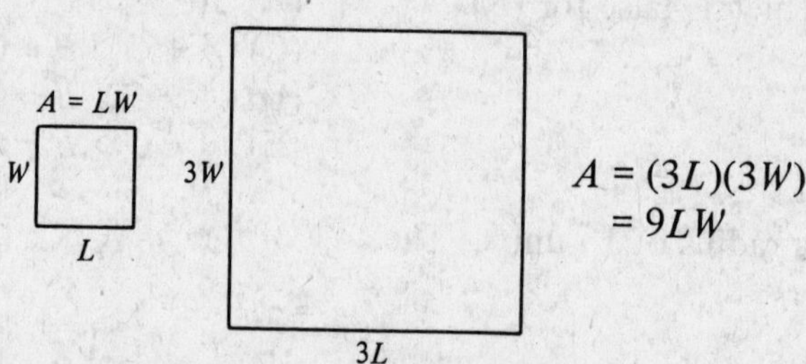

$$\text{Ratio} = \frac{\text{original rectangle}}{\text{enlarged rectangle}} = \frac{1LW}{9LW} = \frac{1}{9} = 1:9$$

8. **(C)** In a right triangle the sum of the squares of the legs equals the square of the hypotenuse:

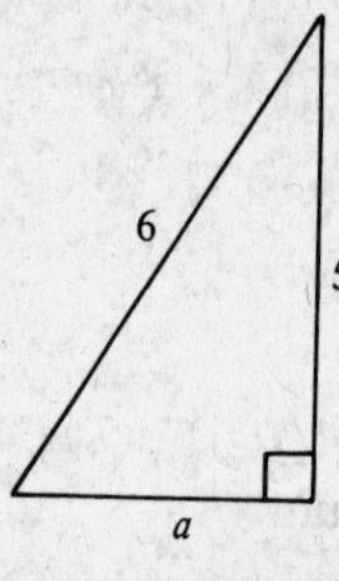

$$a^2 + 5^2 = 6^2$$
$$a^2 + 25 = 36$$
$$a^2 = 11$$

Take the square root of $a^2 \rightarrow a = 11 \leftarrow$ square root of 11

9. **(B)** The product of two fractions between 0 and 1 is *always* less than either of the original fractions: *Example:* $\frac{1}{2}$ and $\frac{3}{4}$.

$$\frac{1}{2} \times \frac{3}{4} = \frac{3}{8}$$

$$\frac{1}{2} = .50$$

$$\frac{3}{4} = .75$$

$$\frac{3}{8} = .37\tfrac{1}{2}$$

Hence only **(B)** can be true.

10. **(C)** The total number of triangles is 16; the total number of shaded triangles is 4.

$$\text{Ratio of } \frac{\text{shaded triangles}}{\text{total number of triangles}} = \frac{4}{16} = \frac{1}{4} = 25\%$$

11. **(E)** Find multiples of 3: 3, 6, 9, 12, 15, 18, 21, 24, etc. Find multiples of 7: 7, 14, 21, 28, etc. Since the least common multiple is 21, they will start a rotation together after 21 minutes.

12. **(D)** *Of* means to multiply. 8% = .08

$$\begin{array}{r} 500{,}000 \\ \times \qquad .08 \\ \hline 40{,}000.00 \end{array} = 40{,}000 \text{ dismissed}$$

13. **(E)** There are a total of nine balls, and since there are three white balls, this represents 3 chances out of 9 of selecting one white ball; $\frac{3}{9} = \frac{1}{3}$.

14. **(C)** Let x = number of miles

Set up proportion: $\frac{x}{15} = \frac{4\frac{3}{8}}{3}$

Cross-multiply:

$$3x = (15)\left(4\tfrac{3}{8}\right)$$

$$= (15)\left(\tfrac{35}{8}\right)$$

$$\left(\tfrac{1}{3}\right)3x = (15)\left(\tfrac{35}{8}\right)\left(\tfrac{1}{3}\right) \quad \text{cancel out 3's}$$

$$x = (5)\left(\tfrac{35}{8}\right)$$

$$= 21\tfrac{7}{8} \text{ miles}$$

15. **(E)** Divide 120 by $2\frac{2}{3} = \frac{120}{2\frac{2}{3}} = \frac{120}{\frac{8}{3}} = 120 \times \frac{3}{8} = 45$ dresses

16. **(B)** Find the ratio

$$\frac{\text{Amount of decrease}}{\text{Original price}} = \text{percent}$$

(A) $\frac{150}{1350} = \frac{1}{9} = 11\%$

(B) $\frac{150}{800} = \frac{3}{16} = 18\%$ greatest rate of discount

(C) $\frac{250}{2000} = \frac{1}{8} = 12\frac{1}{2}\%$

(D) $\frac{100}{1000} = \frac{1}{10} = 10\%$

(E) $\frac{500}{3000} = \frac{1}{6} = 16\frac{2}{3}\%$

17. **(A)** Since acute angles of right △ are supplementary, $\measuredangle GFE = 90 - 25 = 65$. If $\measuredangle FEG = 25$, $\measuredangle FEB = 2(25) = 50$ because $\measuredangle BEF$ was bisected. $\measuredangle EFC = \measuredangle FEB$ because the measure of alternate interior angles is equal. Since the measure of a straight angle equals 180 degrees,

$$\measuredangle EFC + \measuredangle GFE + \measuredangle GFD = 180$$

Substitute: $50 + 65 + x = 180$

$115 + x = 180$

$x = 65$

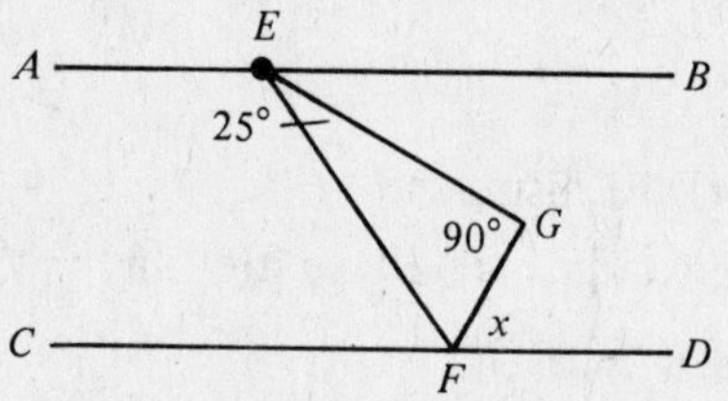

18. **(E)** Since 1 cake uses $\frac{2}{3}$ cup of sugar, let x = number of cakes that use 4 cups of sugar. In the proportion:

$$\frac{1}{x} = \frac{\frac{2}{3}}{4}$$

$$(4)(1) = \frac{2}{3}x$$

$$4\left(\frac{3}{2}\right) = \left(\frac{3}{2}\right)\frac{2}{3}x \quad \text{cross-multiply; solve for } x$$

$$6 = x$$

19. **(C)** Let x = number of votes Sam received.

$2x + 6$ = number of votes Jack received

$3x - 8$ = number of votes Arthur received

$$x + 2x + 6 + 3x - 8 = 190$$

Collect like terms and solve for x.

$6x - 2 = 190$

$6x = 192$

$x = 32$ votes (Sam)

$2x + 6 = 70$ votes (Jack)

$3x - 8 = 88$ votes (Arthur)

20. **(D)** If the perimeter is 80, count all the exterior sides of $ABCD$; hence 8 sides = 80, 1 side = 10.

Area of rectangle = (length) × (width)
Length (DC) = 30
Width (AD) = 10

$$A = (30)(10)$$
$$= 300$$

21. **(B)** Draw a line with two points on it. The set of points equally distant from A and B is a line GH perpendicular to both A and B. Note that $GA = GB = HA = HB = \frac{1}{2}GH$.

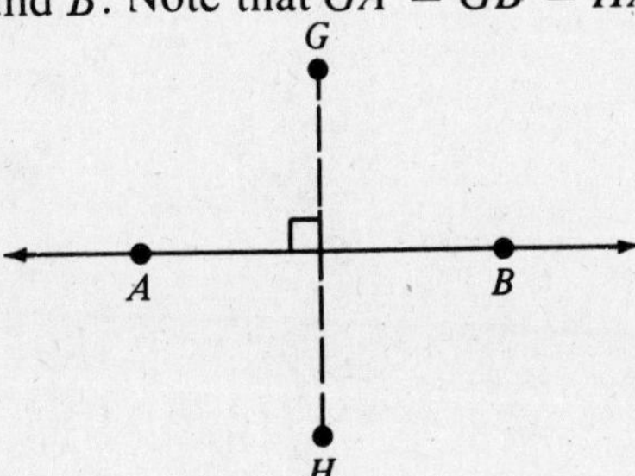

22. **(A)** Multiply $(4+\sqrt{5})(4-\sqrt{5})$ in the following manner:

(1) Multiply first terms: $(4)(4) = 16$

(2) Add inner and outer products:

$(-4\sqrt{5})$

$(4+\sqrt{5})$ $(4-\sqrt{5})$ → $(-4\sqrt{5}) + (4\sqrt{5}) = 0$

$(+4\sqrt{5})$

(3) Multiply last terms:

$$(+\sqrt{5})(-\sqrt{5}) = -\sqrt{25} = -5$$

(4) Combine results: $16 - 5 = 11$

23. **(E)** Find $V = \pi r^2 h$ by substituting $r = 7$, $h = 10$, $\pi = \frac{22}{7}$.

$$V = \frac{22}{7}(7)^2(10)$$
$$= \frac{22}{7}(49)(10)$$
$$= (22)(7)(10)$$
$$= 1540$$

24. **(A)** Diameter ROS divides circle O into two semicircles. Hence $\measuredangle RTS$ is a right angle because an angle inscribed in a semicircle equals a right angle, or 90°. Also, $OT = OR$: equal radii in same circle. Since ΔRTO is an isosceles triangle, $\measuredangle TRO = \measuredangle RTO$.

$$\measuredangle RTS = \measuredangle RTO + \measuredangle 1$$

Substitute:

$$90° = 50° + \measuredangle 1$$
$$40° = \measuredangle 1$$

25. (C) Divide 19,850 by 1000 to obtain the price per thousand.

```
             19.85
1000 ) 19850.00            Multiply:     $40.83
       1000                            × 19.85
        9850                           $810.4755, which is approximately $810.
        9000
         8500
         8000
          5000
          5000
```

SECTION TWO: VERBAL

1. **(A) UNCOUTH:** barbarous, crude
2. **(E) ZEAL:** enthusiasm, keenness
3. **(D) EMPYREAN:** heavenly, celestial
4. **(B) INEXORABLE:** uncompromising, rigid
5. **(B) PEREMPTORY:** authoritative, positive
6. **(E) SAGACIOUS:** rational, knowledgeable
7. **(A) TRUNCATE:** amputate, shorten
8. **(B) INTREPID:** valorous, heroic
9. **(A) EFFRONTERY:** audacity, boldness
10. **(A) TURBULENT:** disorderly, unruly
11. **(A)** This pair is the only one related to rambling.
12. **(D)** Temper tantrums are childish.
13. **(C)** Since he didn't believe in God, he broke many traditions.
14. **(B)** A bibliophile would collect books.
15. **(B)** Both women backed up the charge of bigamy or marriage to more than one spouse.
16. **(E)** His enormous size astonished everyone.
17. **(D)** Since he was lazy, he delayed doing his assignment.
18. **(C)** Although he vowed not to become attached to any woman, he did not leave all human contact.
19. **(A)** She had a feeling of danger and uttered a warning.
20. **(B)** Since he suspected most human behavior, he didn't trust her honesty.

21. (B) is the correct answer. It describes the theme and main idea of the entire selection. (A) is incorrect.because it is too general. (C), (D) and (E) list details that are stated or implied in support of the main idea.

22. (C) is the best answer and is specifically stated in the introduction and restated throughout the selection. (A), (B), (D) and (E) are generally discussed in support of the general theme.

23. (C) is the correct answer and is specifically referred to in the statement "science for self-reliance." (A), (B) and (D) are implied remedies. (E) is obviously incorrect.

24. (E) is the best answer and is referred to in paragraphs 1 and 2.

25. (C) is the correct answer and specifically described in detail in support of the idea of science for self-reliance. (A), (B), (D) and (E) are suggested benefits but not the keys to obtaining such benefits.

26. (B) is the correct answer. It describes the main idea. (A), (C) and (D) are supporting details. (E) is obviously incorrect.

27. (E) is the correct answer, inferred by the definition of stereophonic as the method of retaining realistic sound. Therefore, stereoscopic would indicate visual naturalness.

28. (D) is the best answer and is specifically referred to in paragraph 4 with the description of the laser ray as a major breakthrough in stereoscopic production. It is the final technique described and would therefore most logically be the most recent technological advance.

29. (E) is obviously the best answer since the ideas described in the selection would indicate that (A), (B), (C) and (D) all are incorrect.

30. (C) is the only correct selection. Sound is the only other sensation given, and paragraph 2 indicates that sound production has improved.

31. (C) is correct. A wrongdoing connected with politics is bribery, as cheating is wrongdoing connected with examinations.

32. (C) is the correct answer. A professor must always learn, and a musician must practice, for each to become proficient.

33. (C) is the best answer. A religious promise is a vow; a business promise is a contract.

34. (E) is correct. A computer is a technologically advanced abacus. A chronometer is a technologically advanced sundial.

35. (D) is correct. A novel is written by an author. An opera is written by a composer.

36. (C) is correct. A miser desires gold as a general desires victories.

37. (E) To push is an extreme touch; to gulp is an extreme sip. All four words are verbs.

38. (D) Bananas are collected by the bunch; lettuce is collected by the head.

39. (C) A fraud, a charlatan, an impostor, and a poseur refer to people who are fakes.

40. (D) Synonyms and adjectives are needed as answers.

SECTION FOUR: VERBAL

1. **(C) JUDICIOUS: discreet, sensible**
2. **(B) VOCIFERATE: bellow, shout**
3. **(B) ABJURE: forswear, repudiate**
4. **(A) RECALCITRANT: obstinate, rebellious**
5. **(B) OBJURGATION: condemnation, reproof**
6. **(A) ENCOMIUM: adulation, praise**
7. **(E) FLUCTUATE: undulate, move**
8. **(B) ANOMALOUS: anachronous, abnormal**
9. **(A) TIMOROUS: afraid, faint-hearted**
10. **(A) LACERATE: rend, sever**
11. **(A) CIRCUMSPECT: careful, watchful**
12. **(D) IMPERTURBABLE: tranquil, serene**
13. **(B) COERCE: force, oblige**
14. **(C) DISCOMFIT: defeat, conquer**
15. **(C) MITIGATE: lessen, ameliorate**
16. (E) is correct. A good night's sleep makes one feel young.
17. (B) is correct. His overwhelming lust resulted in illegal actions.
18. (B) is the correct answer. She plotted physical disfigurement as an act of revenge.
19. (D) is the best answer. Coin collectors are numismatists.
20. (A) is the only pair of opposites.
21. (E) is correct. *Contentious* means *argumentative*.
22. (B) is correct. He was sorry he hit his son.
23. (C) is correct. Since the signature was forged, the contract was null and void.
24. (E) is correct. The two words are antonyms.
25. (A) is the correct answer. He had such contempt for the feelings of others that he seemed cruel.
26. (B) is the correct answer and states the main idea of the entire selection. While (A) is generally assumed to be true, the study did not validate this conclusively. (C), (D) and (E), while true, were not unusual discoveries borne out by the study.
27. (C) is the answer. (A), (B) and (D) may have been true on a limited level not described in the passage. (E) is incorrect.

28. **(D)** is the correct answer. It is stated in paragraph 2. **(A), (B)** and **(E)** are most unlikely, since over 16,000 children were studied. As implied in paragraph 2, **(C)** is not true.

29. **(E)** is the correct answer, as specifically stated in paragraph 2. While there may be truth in **(A)** and **(B)**, no information regarding these factors is given. **(C)** and **(D)** are incorrect.

30. **(A)** is the correct answer. As stated in paragraph 1, "over 66%" of fathers played a major parental role.

31. **(E)** is the correct answer, since paragraph 2 indicates the announcement was made public in June, 1978.

32. **(D)** is the correct answer. It is given specifically in paragraph 2, which describes Bakke.

33. **(A)** is the right answer. It is found in paragraph 3.

34. **(C)** is the best answer. It is described in the last paragraph.

35. **(B)** is the correct answer. It is described in the last paragraph.

36. **(D)** is the correct answer. A needle is used by a person to sew; a towel is used to dry.

37. **(B)** is the correct answer. Fasting causes hunger. Jogging causes fatigue.

38. **(C)** is the correct answer. A stone is the prominent part of a ring and is worn to be seen. The same is true of the face of a watch.

39. **(D)** Both sets list the beginning of something; in the first case a dinner, in **(D)**, a book.

40. **(D)** is the correct answer. *To press* and *to plunge* are both verbs. It is common to press a button and to plunge a knife. Note in (B), a plate does not receive the direct action of *eat*.

41. **(E)** is the correct answer. A candle cannot serve its purpose without a wick. Similarly, a drill cannot serve its purpose without a bit.

42. **(E)** is the correct answer. A centaur is a mythological creature, half man and half horse; a mermaid is half woman and half fish.

43. **(B)** is the correct answer. A foot moves against a pedal as a bat hits against a ball.

44. **(B)** is the correct answer. Poverty brings forth ignorance as a wound brings forth blood.

45. **(C)** is the correct answer. Gun is to a deer in hunting as binoculars are to a bird in birdwatching.

SECTION FIVE: MATHEMATICS

1. **(B)** Let x be the fifth mark:

$$\frac{75 + 92 + 68 + 95 + x}{5} = 85$$

Cross-multiply and solve for x

$$\begin{aligned} 75 + 92 + 68 + 95 + x &= 85(5) \\ 330 + x &= 425 \\ x &= 95 \end{aligned}$$

2. **(B)** Find the least common denominator for all the fractions, which is 100. Convert each fraction to equivalent fractions.

$$\frac{3}{5} \times \frac{20}{20} = \frac{60}{100}$$

(A) $\frac{1}{2} \times \frac{50}{50} = \frac{50}{100}$ **(B)** $\frac{39}{50} \times \frac{2}{2} = \frac{78}{100}$ **(C)** $\frac{7}{25} \times \frac{4}{4} = \frac{28}{100}$ **(D)** $\frac{3}{10} \times \frac{10}{10} = \frac{30}{100}$

(E) $\frac{59}{100} \times \frac{1}{1} = \frac{59}{100}$ Hence $\frac{39}{50} > \frac{3}{5}$

3. **(D)** The area of the square = s^2.

$$25 = s$$
$$5 = s$$

Each side is 5 units and there are 12 exterior sides. Hence (5)(12) = 60.

4. **(D)** $\frac{px - r}{x - 1} = s$

Cross-multiply: $px - r = s(x - 1)$

$px - r = sx - s$

Collect like terms: $px - sx = r - s$

Factor out x: $x(p - s) = r - s$

Divide by $p - s$: $\frac{x(p-s)}{p-s} = \frac{r-s}{p-s}$

$$x = \frac{r-s}{p-s}$$

5. **(D)** Compare each decimal to its fractional equivalent:

$$.009 = \frac{9}{1000}$$
$$.010 = \frac{10}{1000}$$
$$.504 = \frac{504}{1000}$$
$$.194 = \frac{194}{1000}$$

$$.504 > .194 > .010 > .009$$

6. **(D)** $12\frac{1}{2}\%$ written as a fraction:

$$12\tfrac{1}{2}\% = \frac{12\frac{1}{2}}{100} = \frac{\frac{25}{2}}{100} = \frac{25}{2} \times \frac{1}{100} = \frac{1}{8}$$

There are 360 degrees in a circle:

$$\frac{1}{8} \times 360° = 45°$$

7. **(E)** $8\frac{1}{3}\%$ written as a fraction:

$$8\frac{1}{3}\% = \frac{8\frac{1}{3}}{100} = \frac{\frac{25}{3}}{100} = \frac{25}{3} \times \frac{1}{100} = \frac{1}{12}$$

There are 24 hours in a day:

$$\frac{1}{12} \times 24 = 2 \text{ hours}$$

8. **(B)** The sum of the angles of a triangle equals 180°. Hence

$$\begin{aligned} x + 30 + 4x + 30 + 10x - 30 &= 180 \\ 15x + 30 &= 180 \\ 15x &= 150 \\ x &= 10 \end{aligned}$$

Substitute:

$$\begin{aligned} (x + 30)^\circ &= 10 + 30 = 40^\circ \\ (4x + 30)^\circ &= 40 + 30 = 70^\circ \\ (10x - 30)^\circ &= 100 - 30 = 70^\circ \end{aligned}$$

The triangle is an isosceles triangle if two angles in the triangle are equal in measurement.

9. **(B)** An external angle formed by two tangents is equal to $\frac{1}{2}$ the difference of the intercepted arcs. Hence

$$\begin{aligned} \measuredangle X &= \frac{1}{2}(240 - \overset{\frown}{AB}) \\ &= \frac{1}{2}(240 - 120) \\ &= \frac{1}{2}(120) \\ &= 60 \end{aligned}$$

$$\text{Arc } AB = 360 - 240$$
$$\overset{\frown}{AB} = 120$$

10. **(B)** Divide 63 by $\frac{7}{9}$ to get the total number.

$$\begin{aligned} 63 \div \frac{7}{9} &= 64 \times \frac{9}{7} \\ &= 9 \times 9 \\ &= 81 \end{aligned}$$

11. **(C)** The number of singles is

$16 + \frac{1}{2}$ (4 units)

$16 + 2 = 18$

The number of doubles is

$4 + \frac{1}{2}$ (4 units)

$(3)(6) = 18$

12. **(C)** Walks = 12; singles = 18; doubles = $\frac{6}{18}$.

13. (C) $\frac{1}{4} \div \frac{3}{8}$ simplified as

$\frac{1}{4} \times \frac{8}{3}$ invert divisor and multiply

$\frac{1}{\not{4}_1} \times \frac{\not{8}^2}{3} = \frac{2}{3}$ cancel out 4's

Change $\frac{2}{3}$ into a decimal. Add a decimal point after the 2 and affix zeros.

$$3\overline{)2.00} = .66\tfrac{2}{3} = 66\tfrac{2}{3}\%$$

18
20
18
2

from decimal to percent, move decimal point left to right two places

14. (C) Affix zeros to 2.1 and 2.2. Count 2.10, 2.11, 2.12, 2.13, 2.14, 2.15, 2.16, 2.17, 2.18, 2.19, 2.20. $x = 2.16$.

$$2\frac{4}{25} = 2\frac{4}{25} \times \frac{4}{4} = 2\frac{16}{100} = 2.16$$

15. (B) $8^2 = 8 \times 8$
$= 64$

$2^8 = 2 \times 2 \times 2 \times 2 \times 2 \times 2 \times 2 \times 2$
$= 256$

16. (B) $7^3 = 7 \times 7 \times 7$
$= 289$

$3^7 = 3 \times 3 \times 3 \times 3 \times 3 \times 3 \times 3$
$= 2187$

17. (A) $3 \times 108 \div 3 = \frac{3 \times 108}{3}$
$= \frac{3}{3} \times 108$
$= 1 \times 108$
$= 108$

$81 \times 4 \div 4 = 81 \times \frac{4}{4}$
$= 81 \times 1$
$= 81$

18. (B) Change the percents to decimals. Move the decimal point from the right to the left two places and affix zeros if necessary.

$$\tfrac{1}{2}\% = .00\tfrac{1}{2} = \frac{1}{2} \times \frac{1}{1000} = \frac{1}{2000}$$

19. (C) The ratio 3:4 is

$\frac{3}{4}$

The ratio $\frac{1}{4}:\frac{1}{3}$ is

$\frac{\frac{1}{4}}{\frac{1}{3}} = \frac{1}{4} \times \frac{3}{1}$ invert divisor and multiply

$= \frac{3}{4}$

20. (C) $\left(\frac{1}{10}\right)^2 = \left(\frac{1}{10}\right)\left(\frac{1}{10}\right) = \frac{1}{100} = .01$

$$\left(\frac{1}{10}\right)^3 \times 10 = \left(\frac{1}{10}\right)\left(\frac{1}{10}\right)\left(\frac{1}{10}\right)\left(\frac{10}{1}\right) = \frac{10}{1000} = \frac{1}{100} = .01$$

21. (B) Reduce:

$$\frac{-35x^2y^3}{45x^3y^2}$$

Cancel out 5's, x's, y's:

$$\frac{-7y}{9x}$$

Evaluate for $x = 2, y = 3$:

$$\frac{-7(3)}{9(2)}$$

Cancel out 3's:

$$\frac{-7}{(3)(2)} = \frac{-7}{6}$$

Combine two fractions by multiplying:

$$\frac{x}{2} \text{ by } \frac{2}{2} = \frac{2x}{4}$$

$$\frac{3x-2y}{4} - \frac{2x}{4} =$$

$$\frac{3x-2y-2x}{4} = \frac{x-2y}{4}$$

Evaluate for $x = 2, y = 3$:

$$\frac{2-2(3)}{4} = \frac{2-6}{4}$$

$$= \frac{-4}{4}$$

$$= -1$$

$$\frac{-7}{6} < -1$$

22. (B) To find the average, add all positive numbers and all negative numbers. Take their difference and divide by the number of items (five in this case).

+0.3	−0.8
+0.2	−0.2
+0.5	−1.0

$$-1.0 + 0.5 = -0.5$$

$$\frac{-0.5}{5} = -.1$$

$$-.1 < .1$$

23. (A) Add:

$$\begin{aligned} 2x - y &= 3 \\ x + y &= -6 \\ \hline 3x \quad &= -3 \end{aligned}$$

Divide by 3: $x = -1$

Substitute in the first equation:

$$\begin{aligned} 2(-1) - y &= 3 \\ -2 \quad - y &= 3 \\ +2 \qquad &+2 \quad \text{(additive inverse)} \\ \hline -y &= 5 \end{aligned}$$

Divide by −1: $y = -5$

$$-1 > -5$$

24. (B) If $r < 0$, then r is a negative number. But r^2 is a positive number since negative times negative is positive.

25. (B) If $p < 0$ and $q > 0$, the product is a negative number that is less than zero.

26. (B) Factor:

$$36x^2 - 12x + 1 = 0$$
$$(6x - 1)(6x - 1) = 0$$
Let: $6x - 1 = 0$ and
$$6x - 1 = 0$$
$$6x = 1$$

Divide by 6:

$$x = \frac{1}{6}$$

Factor:

$$16y^2 - 8y + 1 = 0$$
$$(4y - 1)(4y - 1) = 0$$
Let: $4y - 1 = 0$ and
$$4y - 1 = 0$$
$$4y = 1$$

Divide by 4:

$$y = \frac{1}{4}$$

$$\frac{1}{6} < \frac{1}{4}$$

The same numerator, the smaller denominator—the larger the number.

27. (B) $\frac{\sqrt{4}}{2} = \frac{2}{2} = 1$

Multiply: $\frac{4}{\sqrt{2}}$ by $\frac{\sqrt{2}}{\sqrt{2}}$.

$$\frac{4\sqrt{2}}{\sqrt{2}\sqrt{2}} = \frac{4\sqrt{2}}{\sqrt{4}} = \frac{4\sqrt{2}}{2}$$
$$= 2\sqrt{2}$$

$2 \times 1.414 = 2.828$

$$\frac{\sqrt{4}}{2} < \frac{4}{\sqrt{2}}$$

28. (B) $\sqrt{106}$ is between the integers 10 and 11.

$$10 < \sqrt{106} < 11$$
$$\sqrt{100} < \sqrt{106} \quad \sqrt{121}$$

29. (C) $\sqrt{2^6} = \sqrt{2 \cdot 2 \cdot 2 \cdot 2 \cdot 2 \cdot 2}$

$$= \sqrt{64}$$
$$= 8$$

$\sqrt{4^3} = \sqrt{4 \cdot 4 \cdot 4}$

$$= \sqrt{64}$$
$$= 8$$

30. (B) Add the positive numbers together and add the negative numbers. Take their difference.

$$\begin{array}{r} +32 \\ \underline{+10} \\ +42 \end{array} \qquad \begin{array}{r} -49 \\ \underline{-21} \\ -70 \end{array}$$

$$\begin{array}{r} -70 \\ \underline{+42} \\ -32 \end{array}$$

$-51 - (-84) - 27$

$-51 + 84 - 27$

Add the negative numbers together and take their difference.

$$\begin{array}{r} -51 \\ \underline{-27} \\ -78 \end{array} \qquad \begin{array}{r} +84 \\ \underline{-78} \\ +6 \end{array}$$

$$-32 < +6$$

SECTION SIX: VERBAL

1. **(C) FRIVOLOUS: insignificant, unimportant**
2. **(A) SECULAR: unconsecrated, worldly**
3. **(D) GIST: essence, distillation**
4. **(E) PROSELYTE: convert, neophyte**
5. **(B) LUGUBRIOUS: melancholy, mournful**
6. **(C) DROLL: quaint, whimsical**
7. **(C) GRATUITY: tip, donation**
8. **(D) BANEFUL: malign, malevolent**
9. **(C) HOMUNCULUS: dwarf, pygmy**
10. **(B) CALUMNIATE: libel, slander**
11. **(B) As he became old and senile his ability to rule was weakened.**
12. (E) *Intransigent* means *stubborn.*
13. **(C) Only this pair is related.**
14. **(D) Two synonyms are needed for the blanks.**
15. (B) Only (B) contains two opposites.

16. (C) is the correct answer. The second sentence in the paragraph describes the functions performed by demographers.

17. (C) is the correct answer. Although science and technology have tended to double food production, some scientists do not believe that technology will be able to supply enough food to meet the expanding rate of population. See paragraph 4.

18. (E) is the correct answer. Paragraph 1 tells us that the ratio between man and land is an important consideration of life in all societies. Therefore it can be inferred that population growth is ultimately limited by what the land can support.

19. (D) is the correct answer. Reread paragraph 2 to verify the answer.

20. (B) is the correct answer. The passage discusses the problem of the relationship between the food supply and the expanding rate of population growth.

21. (E) is the correct answer. **I**, the nucleus controls the cell by means of the RNA messengers it sends to the ribosomes. **III**, the fact that the membrane responds to the cytoplasm allows us to infer that it will also actively stop or speed up passage of material. **II**, cytoplasm can "turn off" the nucleus; therefore, it controls its own activities in some measure.

22. (D) The sandwich effect was predicted by Davson and Danielli. There are two layers of protein, with a double layer of fat molecules between them.

23. (A) The sandwich conditions appeared under the electron microscope; two dark lines and a lighter space between them. (E) is wrong. It is a correct statement but not related to the question.

24. **(E)** (A) and (B) describe the colloid cycles and the invisible intricate structures of the cytoplasm. (C) and (D) describe the "turn off" effect that cytoplasm has on the nucleus and on the traffic into and out of the cell.

25. **(B)** The first line of a selection will often indicate the theme of the passage, and may suggest an appropriate title.

26. **(C)** This correct answer is drawn from *sentences 2 and 3,* in which the author says *specifically* that the monkeys of the Old World *cannot* hang by their tails; only the monkeys of America can. Thus, while the statement was not made in one sentence, you find the direct facts stated in the two sentences mentioned. **(A)** There is nothing in the paragraph to bear out this conclusion. **(B)** The only mention of *intelligence* is with regard to the *spider monkey,* one of the South American breed. **(D)** While this statement may or may not be true in general, there is no indication of this fact in the paragraph. **(E)** Again, there is nothing stated to substantiate this inference.

27. **(B)** *Sentences 3 and 4* supply the facts which support this inference: only the monkeys of America possess the skill to hang by their tails, and they belong to the group called *ceboids.* **(A)** There is no overall correlation established between the ability to hang by the tail and intelligence. **(C)** This is, of course, an impossibility, since there can be no contact between the two groups. **(D)** This grouping omits several of the other ceboids—the sakis, spider monkeys, and squirrel monkeys. **(E)** There is no statement or implication that this is true.

28. **(C)** First, it is only the spider monkey to whom the attribute of intelligence is applied at all. Therefore, it would seem that the spider monkey is the most intelligent of all the monkeys. Secondly, the application of the term *hoodlums* to the marmosets would *imply* that they are lesser in intelligence. **(A)** This is not implied but directly stated. Therefore, it is not what the question seeks. **(B)** There is no comparison of the degree of wildness of the various types of monkeys. **(D)** Again, this is a statement specifically made in the paragraph. **(E)** There is no such statement made nor any such implication.

29. **(A)** *Sentence 2* states clearly that the monkeys of the Old World *are* agile. The difference is that they cannot hang by their tails. **(B)** The first sentence establishes the comparison of the monkeys and acrobats—thus the relationship to trapeze artists. **(C)** This is specifically stated in the paragraph. **(D)** By implication, when the author says of the owl monkeys that their tails are *untalented,* he indicates that the spider monkey's tail *is talented.* **(E)** This is substantiated by the phrase "their unique group."

30. **(B)** The first sentence indicates the theme of this passage. Selections (C) and (D) are too limited. The second sentence says this is not about the talented monkeys. (E) is too general. The passage is more specific, and is about monkeys only.

31. **(C)** We speak of a man in the moon and a leprechaun under a mushroom.

32. **(C)** We start a car with the ignition; we stop a car with the brake.

33. **(E)** We braid hair as we wind a clock. To braid and to wind are actions applied to nouns.

34. **(D)** When something is brittle it breaks; when it is flexible it bends. In **(B),** a sharp object scratches something else.

35. **(A)** A satellite travels along an orbit, whereas any projectile travels along a trajectory.

36. **(C)** Alumni are male graduates and alumnae are female graduates. "Roosters" is also male and plural; "hens" is female and plural.

37. **(D)** Sheep travel in a flock, as cows travel in a herd. Both cows and sheep are animals.

38. **(A)** The opposite of borrow is lend; the opposite of lengthen is abridge. All these words are verbs.

39. **(B)** Four is the square of 2; 25 is the square of 5.

40. **(C)** "His" is a possessive pronoun and "he" is the nominative form of "his." "I" is the nominative form of the possessive "mine."

3.

Mathematics Review

The Mathematics section of the Scholastic Aptitude Test measures both quantitative and analytical abilities and requires background in the basics of arithmetic, algebra, plane geometry, analytic geometry, and charts and graphs. There are essentially two types of test questions–straight quantitative problems and quantitative comparisons.

Quantitative Ability

This section assumes familiarity with the arithmetic, algebra, and geometry that would probably have been learned by most high school students. The questions require reasoning based on an understanding of these areas. Some of the questions may involve the interpretation of data presented in maps, charts, graphs, or tables. The questions that follow are representative of the types of questions that can be found in these sections of the S.A.T.

Directions: In this section solve each problem, using any available space on the page for scratchwork. Then indicate the *best* answer by blackening the corresponding space on the answer grid. *Note:* Figures that accompany problems in this section are intended to provide information useful in solving the problems. They are drawn as accurately as possible *except* when it is stated in a specific problem that its figure is not drawn to scale. All figures lie in a plane unless otherwise indicated.

Sample Graph Questions

Use this grouped bar graph for questions 1 through 3.

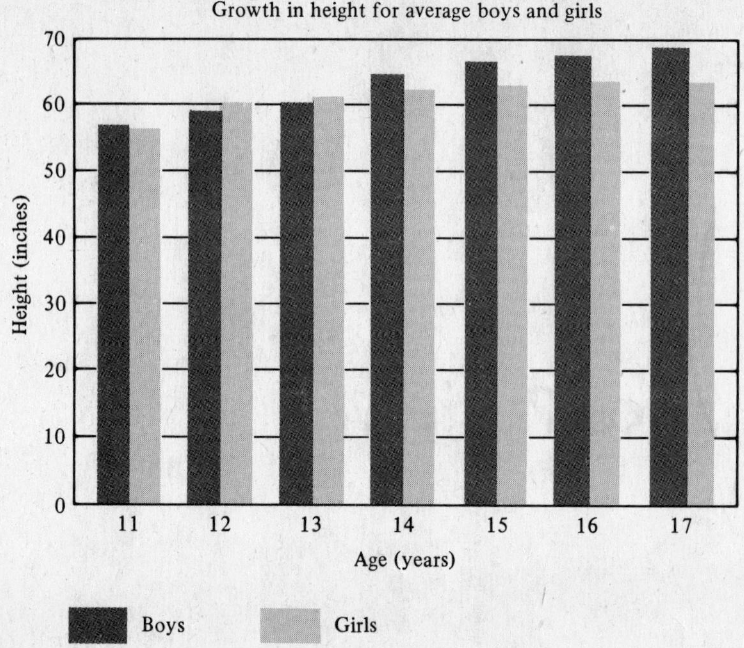

1. At what age is the average girl 57 inches tall? 1. Ⓐ Ⓑ Ⓒ Ⓓ Ⓔ
   (A) 11 (B) 12 (C) 14 (D) 16 (E) 13

Analysis: At 11 years old, the vertical bar graph reaches 57 inches.

2. By how many inches does the boys' height exceed the girls' at age 17? 2. Ⓐ Ⓑ Ⓒ Ⓓ Ⓔ
   (A) 1 in. (B) 2 in. (C) 3 in. (D) 4 in. (E) 5 in.

Analysis: Boys' height at 17 years equals 68 in.; girls' height at 17 years equals 64 in.; difference = 4 in.

3. At what age is there the greatest increase in the girls' height over the previous year? 3. Ⓐ Ⓑ Ⓒ Ⓓ Ⓔ
   (A) 11 (B) 12 (C) 13 (D) 14 (E) 15

Analysis: From 11 years to 12 years increase of 3 in. (57 to 60).
From 12 years to 13 years increase of 2 in. (60 to 62).
From 13 years to 14 years increase of 1 in. (62 to 63).
From 14 years to 15 years increase of 1 in. (63 to 64).
From 15 years to 16 years increase of ½ in. (64 to 64½).
From 16 years to 17 years no increase.

The greatest increase is at 12 years.

Sample Word Problems

1. A number of dimes and quarters are worth \$2.55. If the number of dimes and quarters were interchanged, the resulting new amount would be \$2.70. How many of each kind of coin were there before the interchange? 1. Ⓐ Ⓑ Ⓒ Ⓓ Ⓔ
   (A) 6 dimes, 9 quarters (B) 9 dimes, 6 quarters (C) 7 dimes, 7 quarters (D) 8 dimes, 7 quarters (E) 7 dimes, 8 quarters

Analysis: Let d = number of dimes
Let q = number of quarters

total value in cents for dimes $= 10d$
total value in cents for quarters $= 25q$

(a) $10d + 25q = 255$ (cents)
(b) $10q + 25d = 270$ (cents)

Multiply (a) by 2: $2(10d + 25q = 255)$ $\quad 20d + 50q = 510$

Multiply (b) by 5: $5(10q + 25d = 270)$ $\quad 125d + 50q = 1350$

Subtract (b) from (a): $\quad -105d = -840$

Divide by −105: $\quad \frac{-105d}{-105} = \frac{-840}{-105}$

Substitute value in (a) $\quad d = 8$

$$10(8) + 25q = 255$$
$$80 + 25q = 255$$
$$25q = 175$$
$$q = 7$$

Check in (b):
$$10(7) + 25(8) = 270$$
$$70 + 200 = 270$$
$$270 = 270$$

2. A father can do a certain job in x hours. His son takes twice as long to do the job. Working together, they can do the job in 6 hours. How many hours does it take the father to do the job alone?
(A) 9 **(B)** 18 **(C)** 12 **(D)** 20 **(E)** 16

2. Ⓐ Ⓑ Ⓒ Ⓓ Ⓔ

Analysis: Let
x = number of hours to complete a job (father)
$\frac{1}{x}$ = rate of work so that a job can be completed in 1 hour (father)
Let
$2x$ = number of hours to complete a job (son)
$\frac{1}{2x}$ = rate of work so that a job can be completed in 1 hour (son)

(rate of work) × (time of work) = part of job done

$$\frac{1}{x}(6) + \frac{1}{2x}(6) = 1 \text{ job (completed)}$$

$$\frac{6}{x} + \frac{6}{2x} = 1$$

Multiply by $2x$: $$2x\left(\frac{6}{x} + \frac{6}{2x} = 1\right)$$

$$\frac{12x}{x} + \frac{12x}{2x} = 2x$$

Reduce: $$12 + 6 = 2x$$
$$18 = 2x$$
$$2x = 18$$

Divide by 2: $x = 9$ (hours for father to complete the job alone)

$2x = 18$ (hours for son to complete the job alone)

3. Six years ago in a state park the deer outnumbered the foxes by 80. Since then, the number of deer has doubled and the number of foxes has increased by 20. If there are now a total of 240 deer and foxes in the park, how many foxes were there 6 years ago? 3. Ⓐ Ⓑ Ⓒ Ⓓ Ⓔ

(A) 10 **(B)** 20 **(C)** 30 **(D)** 40 **(E)** 100

Analysis: Let f = number of foxes 6 years ago

(a) $d = f + 80$ = number of deer 6 years ago

(b) $2d + f + 20 = 240$ (present time)

Substitute (a) for d in (b): $d = f + 80$

$$2(f + 80) + f + 20 = 240$$
$$2f + 160 + f + 20 = 240$$
$$3f + 180 = 240$$
$$3f = 60$$

Divide by 3: $f = 20$ foxes 6 years ago.

Samples: Equation Solving

1. Solve for x and y: 1. Ⓐ Ⓑ Ⓒ Ⓓ Ⓔ

$$x + 4y = 6$$
$$9x - 4y = 14$$

(A) (1, 2) **(B)** (2, 1) **(C)** (−1, 2) **(D)** (−2, 1) **(E)** (−2, −1)

Analysis: Add the two equations:

$$\begin{array}{r} x + 4y = 6 \\ \underline{9x - 4y = 14} \\ 10x = 20 \end{array}$$

Divide by 10: $x = 2$

Substitute in the first equation to find y:

$$2 + 4y = 6$$
$$4y = 4$$

Divide by 4: $y = 1$

$\{2, 1\}$

2. If $ab + c = 2$ is solved for a, then a is equal to: 2. Ⓐ Ⓑ Ⓒ Ⓓ Ⓔ

(A) $bc - 2$ **(B)** $2 - c - b$ **(C)** $\frac{c+2}{b}$ **(D)** $\frac{2-c}{b}$ **(E)** $b + c + 2$

Analysis: $ab + c = 2$

Subtract c:

$$\begin{array}{r} ab + c = 2 \\ \underline{-c \quad -c} \\ ab = 2 - c \end{array}$$

Divide by b: $\frac{ab}{b} = \frac{2-c}{b}$

$$a = \frac{2-c}{b}$$

3. Solve for y: 3. Ⓐ Ⓑ Ⓒ Ⓓ Ⓔ

$$\frac{y}{8} - \frac{y}{10} = 3$$

(A) 50 **(B)** 40 **(C)** 6 **(D)** 120 **(E)** 5

Analysis: Solve for y:

$$\frac{y}{8} - \frac{y}{10} = 3$$

Multiply by L.C.M.:

$$40\left(\frac{y}{8} - \frac{y}{10} = 3\right)$$
$$5y - 4y = 120$$
$$y = 120$$

4. The solution set for $x^2 + 7x + 12 = 0$ is 4. Ⓐ Ⓑ Ⓒ Ⓓ Ⓔ
(A) $\{1, 6\}$ **(B)** $\{-1, -6\}$ **(C)** $\{3, 4\}$ **(D)** $\{-3, -4\}$ **(E)** $\{0, -2\}$

Analysis: Set $x^2 + 7x + 12 = 0$.

Factor: $(x + 4)(x + 3) = 0$

Set each binomial equal to zero: $x + 4 = 0$ and $x + 3 = 0$
$x = -4$ and $x = -3$

$$\{-3, -4\}$$

Samples: Coordinate Geometry and Locus

Use the following information to answer questions **1** through **3**:

Triangle ABC has vertices $A\ (-6, -4)$, $B\ (4, 2)$, and $C\ (0, 4)$.

1. Find the area of triangle ABC. 1. Ⓐ Ⓑ Ⓒ Ⓓ Ⓔ
(A) 24 **(B)** 22 **(C)** 8 **(D)** 30 **(E)** 4

Analysis: Draw a triangle on the coordinate axes.

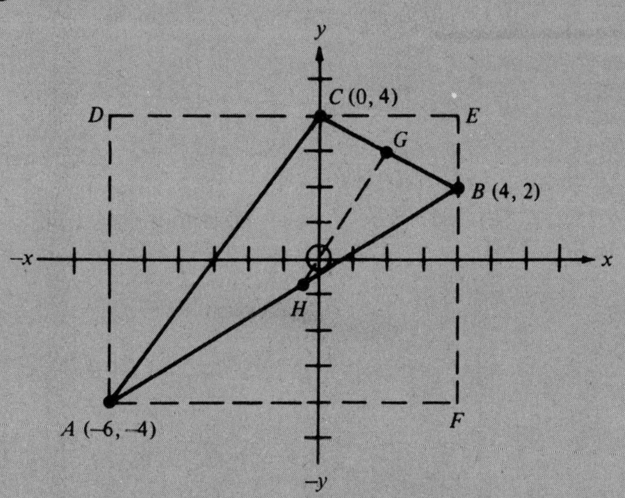

Draw the rectangle *DEFA*.
$DE = AF = 10$
$DA = EF = 8$
area of $DEFA = (10)(8)$
$= 80$

To find the area of $\triangle ABC$:
(1) Find the area of $\triangle ADC$, $\triangle CEB$, $\triangle BFA$.
(2) Subtract the result from the area of rectangle *DEFA*.

area of $\triangle ADC = \frac{1}{2}(8 \times 6) = \frac{1}{2}(48) = 24$

area of $\triangle CEB = \frac{1}{2}(4 \times 2) = \frac{1}{2}(8) = 4$

area of $\triangle BFA = \frac{1}{2}(10 \times 6) = \frac{1}{2}(60) = 30$

area of $\triangle ABC = 80 - (24 + 4 + 30)$
$= 80 - 58$
$= 22$

2. Find the length of $\overline{AC}$. — 2. Ⓐ Ⓑ Ⓒ ● Ⓔ
(A) 24 (B) 22 (C) 15 (D) 10 (E) 8

Analysis: $AC = \sqrt{(x_1 - x_2)^2 + (y_1 - y_2)^2}$
$= \sqrt{(-6-0)^2 + (-4-4)^2}$
$= \sqrt{(-6)^2 + (-8)^2}$
$= \sqrt{36 + 64}$
$= \sqrt{100}$
$= 10$

3. Find the length of the line segment joining the midpoint of *BA* and *BC*. — 3. Ⓐ Ⓑ Ⓒ Ⓓ ●
(A) 24 (B) 22 (C) 15 (D) 10 (E) 5

Analysis: The line segment joining the midpoint of two sides of the triangle is half the length of the third side of the triangle. *GH* is the line segment joining the midpoints of the other two sides. Hence
$AC = 10$
$GH = \frac{1}{2}(AC)$
$= \frac{1}{2}(10)$
$= 5$

Samples: Similar Triangles and Inequalities

1. In the accompanying figure, triangle *ABC* is a right triangle and $\overline{DE}$ is perpendicular to leg $\overline{BC}$. If $AB = 12$, $DE = 4$, and $EC = 6$, find *BE*. — 1. ● Ⓑ Ⓒ Ⓓ Ⓔ

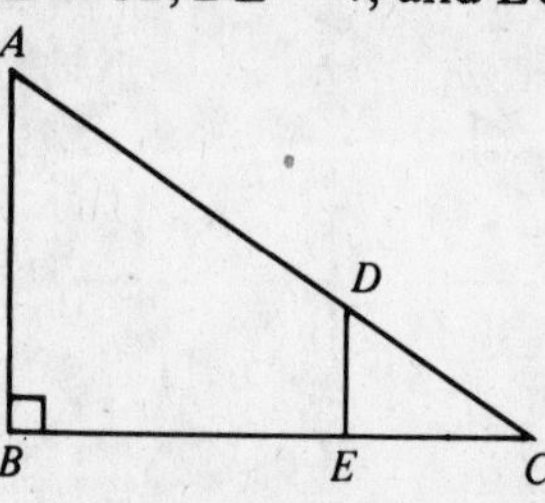

(A) 12 (B) 18 (C) 9 (D) 14 (E) 24

Analysis: Two right triangles are similar if two angles of one triangle are equal to two angles of the other triangle.

$\Delta ABC \sim \Delta DEC$

$\frac{EC}{BC} = \frac{DE}{AB}$ $\qquad BC = BE + EC = x + 6$

$\frac{6}{x+6} = \frac{4}{12}$

$4(x + 6) = (6)(12)$

$4x + 24 = 72$

$4x = 48$

$x = 12 = BE$

Samples: Angle Sum in Triangles

Use the figure below to answer questions **1** through **4**.

$AB \parallel CD$.

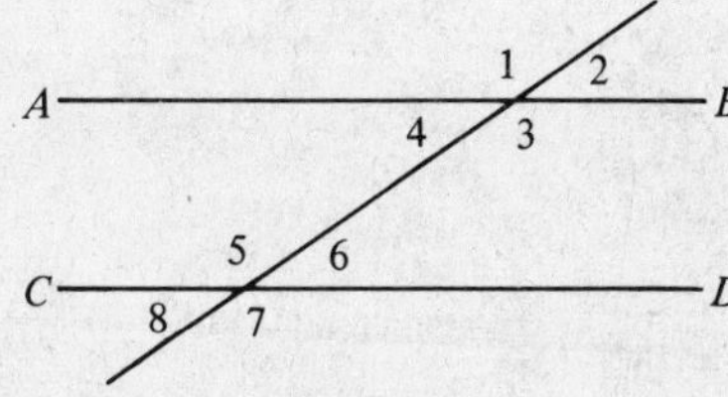

1. List one pair of corresponding angles. **1.** Ⓐ Ⓑ Ⓒ Ⓓ Ⓔ
   (A) ∡5 + ∡8 **(B)** ∡1 + ∡2 **(C)** ∡2 + ∡6 **(D)** ∡4 + ∡6 **(E)** ∡4 + ∡5

Analysis: Corresponding angles are on the same side of the transversal and in the same position in regard to the parallel lines.

2. Find the measure of ∡ 5 if the measure of ∡3 is 110°. **2.** Ⓐ Ⓑ Ⓒ Ⓓ Ⓔ
   (A) 70° **(B)** 80° **(C)** 90° **(D)** 100° **(E)** 110°

Analysis: ∡5 and ∡3 are alternate interior angles. Hence ∡5 = ∡3.

3. If the measure of ∡1 = 105°, find the measure of ∡7. **3.** Ⓐ Ⓑ Ⓒ Ⓓ Ⓔ
   (A) 75° **(B)** 85° **(C)** 95° **(D)** 105° **(E)** 115°

Analysis: ∡1 and ∡7 are alternate exterior angles. Hence ∡1 = ∡7.

4. ∡6 and ∡8 are: **4.** Ⓐ Ⓑ Ⓒ Ⓓ Ⓔ
   (A) Alternate exterior angles
   (B) Alternate interior angles
   (C) Supplementary angles
   (D) Corresponding angles
   (E) Vertical angles

Analysis: ∡6 and ∡8 are vertical angles.

Samples: Area and Perimeter of Triangles and Quadrilaterals and the Pythagorean Theorem

1. The hypotenuse of a right triangle is 10 and one leg is 6. Find the length of the other leg of the triangle. **1.** Ⓐ Ⓑ Ⓒ Ⓓ Ⓔ
   (A) 16 **(B)** 10 **(C)** 8 **(D)** 12 **(E)** 4

Analysis: By the Pythagorean theorem:

$$a^2 + b^2 = c^2$$
$$a^2 + b^2 = 10^2$$
$$a^2 + 36 = 100$$
$$a^2 = 64$$
$$\sqrt{a^2} = \sqrt{64}$$
$$a = 8$$

2. The length of a side of a square is represented by $x + 2$ and the length of a side of an equilateral triangle by $2x$. If the square and the equilateral triangle have equal perimeters, find x. 2. Ⓐ Ⓑ Ⓒ Ⓓ Ⓔ
(A) 24 **(B)** 16 **(C)** 12 **(D)** 8 **(E)** 4

Analysis: The perimeter of the square = $4s$.

$$P = 4s$$
$$= 4(x+2)$$
$$= 4x + 8$$

The perimeter of the equilateral triangle = $3s$.

$$P = 3s$$
$$= 3(2x)$$
$$= 6x$$

$$4x + 8 = 6x$$
$$8 = 2x$$
$$4 = x$$

Arithmetic

Decimals

1. What is .03 expressed as a percent? 1. Ⓐ Ⓑ Ⓒ Ⓓ Ⓔ
(A) .0003% **(B)** 3% **(C)** .3% **(D)** .03% **(E)** .003%

2. What is .1% expressed as a decimal? 2. Ⓐ Ⓑ Ⓒ Ⓓ Ⓔ
(A) .001 **(B)** .01 **(C)** .1 **(D)** 1 **(E)** 10.0

3. Find the sum of 1.98 + 6.42 + .02 + 3. 3. Ⓐ Ⓑ Ⓒ Ⓓ Ⓔ
(A) 7.45 **(B)** 10.40 **(C)** 11.42 **(D)** 8.98 **(E)** 8.42

4. From .05 subtract .0045. 4. Ⓐ Ⓑ Ⓒ Ⓓ Ⓔ
(A) .0045 **(B)** .0455 **(C)** .004 **(D)** .0005 **(E)** .005

5. 12.5 × .75 = ? 5. Ⓐ Ⓑ Ⓒ Ⓓ Ⓔ
(A) 86.25 **(B)** 13.27 **(C)** 9.375 **(D)** 17.45 **(E)** 93.75

Fractions

6. If $\frac{2}{c} = \frac{6}{9}$, find the value of c: 6. Ⓐ Ⓑ Ⓒ Ⓓ Ⓔ
(A) 3 **(B)** 2 **(C)** c **(D)** 9 **(E)** 18

7. If numerator and denominator of a fraction are multiplied by the same number, the value of the fraction:
(A) Increases (B) Decreases (C) Remains the same (D) Doubles (E) Triples

7. Ⓐ Ⓑ Ⓒ Ⓓ Ⓔ

8. Which fraction lies between $\frac{2}{3}$ and $\frac{4}{5}$?
(A) $\frac{5}{6}$ (B) $\frac{17}{20}$ (C) $\frac{7}{10}$ (D) $\frac{13}{15}$ (E) $\frac{9}{10}$

8. Ⓐ Ⓑ Ⓒ Ⓓ Ⓔ

9. Which fraction has the greatest value?
(A) $\frac{4}{13}$ (B) $\frac{5}{12}$ (C) $\frac{3}{11}$ (D) $\frac{4}{11}$ (E) $\frac{5}{13}$

9. Ⓐ Ⓑ Ⓒ Ⓓ Ⓔ

10. $\frac{8}{15} \times 5 = ?$
(A) $\frac{3}{8}$ (B) $2\frac{2}{3}$ (C) $\frac{8}{75}$ (D) $3\frac{2}{3}$ (E) $2\frac{1}{3}$

10. Ⓐ Ⓑ Ⓒ Ⓓ Ⓔ

Probability and Combinations

11. An urn contains five red and three black marbles. If one marble is drawn, what is the probability that it will be red?
(A) $\frac{5}{3}$ (B) $\frac{3}{5}$ (C) $\frac{5}{8}$ (D) $\frac{3}{8}$ (E) $\frac{8}{3}$

11. Ⓐ Ⓑ Ⓒ Ⓓ Ⓔ

12. Sally has three skirts and four blouses ready for wear on a particular day. How many different outfits can Sally choose?
(A) 12 (B) 7 (C) 9 (D) 16 (E) 20

12. Ⓐ Ⓑ Ⓒ Ⓓ Ⓔ

13. Suppose there are seven roads between Troy and Utica. In how many different ways can Mr. Smythe travel from Troy to Utica and return by a different route?
(A) 36 (B) 49 (C) 35 (D) 42 (E) 54

13. Ⓐ Ⓑ Ⓒ Ⓓ Ⓔ

Measurement

14. Which fraction most accurately represents the part of the year remaining after August 31?
(A) $\frac{1}{2}$ (B) $\frac{2}{3}$ (C) $\frac{1}{3}$ (D) $\frac{1}{4}$ (E) $\frac{5}{6}$

14. Ⓐ Ⓑ Ⓒ Ⓓ Ⓔ

15. A girl worked one Saturday from 7:30 A.M. until 3:00 P.M. at the rate of $2.65 per hour. How much did she receive?
(A) $19.88 (B) $22.53 (C) $19.00 (D) $22.00 (E) $18.55

15. Ⓐ Ⓑ Ⓒ Ⓓ Ⓔ

16. Subtract 10 yards, 2 feet from 13 yards, 1 foot.
(A) 2 yd (B) 2 yd, 2 ft (C) 3 yd, 1 ft (D) 2 yd, 9 ft (E) 2.9 yd

16. Ⓐ Ⓑ Ⓒ Ⓓ Ⓔ

17. Express in simplest form the following ratio: 15 hours to 2 days. 17. Ⓐ Ⓑ Ⓒ Ⓓ Ⓔ
(A) $7\frac{1}{2}$ (B) $\frac{16}{5}$ (C) $\frac{5}{8}$ (D) $\frac{15}{2}$ (E) $\frac{5}{16}$

18. The second-grade teacher bought 4 pounds of candy for all her students. How many students were in the class if she planned to put 2 ounces exactly in individual bags for each student? 18. Ⓐ Ⓑ Ⓒ Ⓓ Ⓔ
(A) 24 (B) 40 (C) 32 (D) 36 (E) 30

Percent

19. If 35% of a number is 70, find the number. 19. Ⓐ Ⓑ Ⓒ Ⓓ Ⓔ
(A) 24.5 (B) 200 (C) 50 (D) 65 (E) 140

20. The price of a 3-pound can of vegetables increased from 80 cents to 93 cents. What percent of increase was this? 20. Ⓐ Ⓑ Ⓒ Ⓓ Ⓔ
(A) 1.6 (B) 14.0 (C) 16.25 (D) 86 (E) 20

21. The marked price of a coat was $36.75, which represented 75% of the original selling price. What was the original selling price? 21. Ⓐ Ⓑ Ⓒ Ⓓ Ⓔ
(A) $27.56 (B) $42.35 (C) $45.94 (D) $49.00 (E) $45.35

Number Theory

22. Rounded to the nearest tenth, 46.97 would equal: 22. Ⓐ Ⓑ Ⓒ Ⓓ Ⓔ
(A) 46.0 (B) 46.9 (C) 46.10 (D) 47.0 (E) 50

23. What is 72 expressed as the product of prime factors? 23. Ⓐ Ⓑ Ⓒ Ⓓ Ⓔ
(A) (2)(3) (B) (2)(3)(12) (C) (2)(2)(2)(3)(3) (D) (8)(9)
(E) (6)(6)(2)

24. Which of the following numbers would make this a true statement? If x is divisible by 3, then x is divisible by 2. 24. Ⓐ Ⓑ Ⓒ Ⓓ Ⓔ
(A) 9 (B) 6 (C) 201 (D) 27 (E) 15

Graphs

25. The drawing shown here is part of a bar graph showing population trends in a village. How many people lived in the village in 1920? 25. Ⓐ Ⓑ Ⓒ Ⓓ Ⓔ

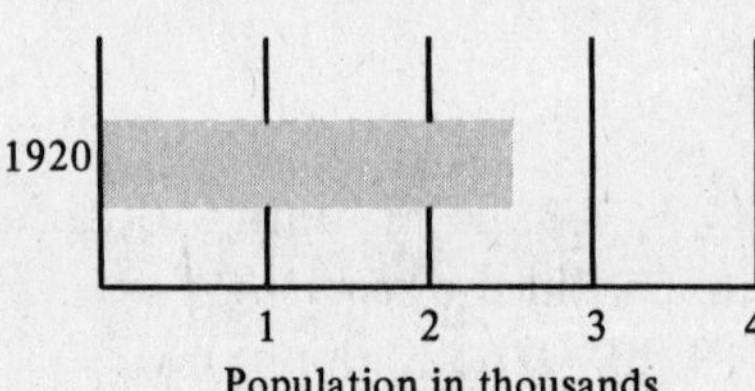

(A) 2.5 (B) 25 (C) 250 (D) 2500 (E) 25,000

26. What percent of pennies show heads at the 10,000th toss? 26. Ⓐ Ⓑ Ⓒ Ⓓ Ⓔ

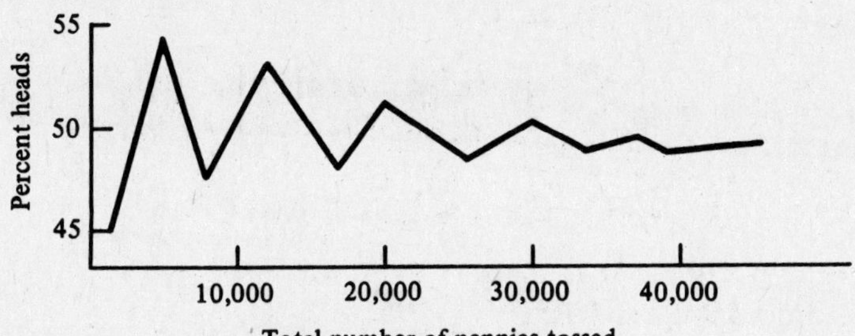

(A) 46 **(B)** 47 **(C)** 48 **(D)** 49 **(E)** 50

Algebra

Ratio and Proportion

27. Solve for d: 27. Ⓐ Ⓑ Ⓒ Ⓓ Ⓔ

$$\frac{d-4}{d} = \frac{5}{6}$$

(A) 24 **(B)** 20 **(C)** −20 **(D)** 5 **(E)** 4

28. A boy takes 3 minutes to read a story of 315 words. How many minutes will it take him to read a story of 945 words at the same rate? 28. Ⓐ Ⓑ Ⓒ Ⓓ Ⓔ

(A) 2 **(B)** 8 **(C)** 6 **(D)** 3 **(E)** 9

29. On level ground, a man 6 feet tall casts a shadow 8 feet long at the same time that a tree casts a shadow 20 feet long. Find the number of feet in the height of the tree. 29. Ⓐ Ⓑ Ⓒ Ⓓ Ⓔ

(A) $46\frac{2}{3}$ **(B)** $2\frac{4}{5}$ **(C)** 15 **(D)** 8 **(E)** 120

30. Find the value of y in the proportion: 30. Ⓐ Ⓑ Ⓒ Ⓓ Ⓔ

$$\frac{20}{12} = \frac{5}{y}$$

(A) $8\frac{1}{3}$ **(B)** 3 **(C)** 15 **(D)** 8 **(E)** $8\frac{1}{3}$

Inequalities

31. If the replacement set for x is $\{7, 8, 9, 10\}$, find the solution set of $x - 1 < 8$. 31. Ⓐ Ⓑ Ⓒ Ⓓ Ⓔ

(A) $\{10\}$ **(B)** $\{7, 8\}$ **(C)** $\{7, 8, 9\}$ **(D)** $\{9\}$ **(E)** $\{9, 10\}$

32. If $x < y$ and $y < z$, which statement about the integers x, y, and z must be true? 32. Ⓐ Ⓑ Ⓒ Ⓓ Ⓔ

(A) $x < z$ **(B)** $x = z$ **(C)** $x > z$ **(D)** $y - x = z$ **(E)** $y > z$

33. The graph shown is the graph of which inequality? 33. 

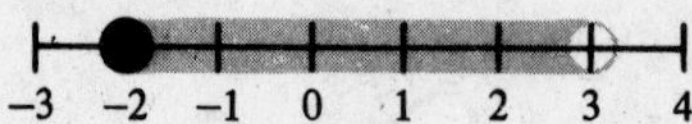

(A) $-2 < x < 3$ (B) $-2 \leqslant x < 3$ (C) $-2 \leqslant x \leqslant 3$ (D) $-2 < x \leqslant 3$
(E) $-2 < x$

34. The solution set of $3x - 3 > 2x + 1$ is: 34. Ⓐ Ⓑ Ⓒ Ⓓ Ⓔ
(A) $\{x \mid x < 4\}$ (B) $\{x \mid x > -2\}$ (C) $\{x \mid x > 4\}$ (D) $\{x \mid x > -4\}$
(E) $\{x \mid x < -2\}$

Factoring

35. When $12x^4 - 3x^3 + 6x^2 \div 3x^2$, the quotient is: 35. Ⓐ Ⓑ Ⓒ Ⓓ Ⓔ
(A) $9x^2 - 3$ (B) $5x^2$ (C) $4x^2 - 3x + 2$ (D) $4x^2 - x + 2$ (E) $6x$

36. Express as a fraction in lowest terms: 36. Ⓐ Ⓑ Ⓒ Ⓓ Ⓔ
$$\frac{y^2 - 9}{2y + 6} \div \frac{y - 3}{y + 2}$$
(A) $\frac{y + 2}{2}$ (B) $\frac{y - 3}{2y + 6}$ (C) $\frac{9}{4}$ (D) $\frac{y}{-2}$ (E) $y + 2$

37. Factor completely: $3x^2 + 2x - 5$ 37. Ⓐ Ⓑ Ⓒ Ⓓ Ⓔ
(A) $(3x + 5)(x - 1)$ (B) $(3x - 5)(x + 1)$ (C) $(3x - 2)(x - 5)$
(D) $(x + 5)(3x - 1)$ (E) $(x - 5)(3x + 1)$

38. The result of multiplying 38. Ⓐ Ⓑ Ⓒ Ⓓ Ⓔ
$$\frac{x^2 - 1}{x} \cdot \frac{4x^2}{x + 1}$$
is:
(A) $\frac{x - 1}{4x^3}$ (B) $\frac{(x^2 - 1)(x + 1)}{4x^3}$ (C) $4x(x + 1)$ (D) $4x(x - 1)$ (E) $\frac{4x}{x + 1}$

Equation Solving

39. Solve for x: $.02x + .12 = .20$ 39. Ⓐ Ⓑ Ⓒ Ⓓ Ⓔ
(A) 3 (B) −1 (C) 4 (D) 2 (E) −4

40. Solve for x: $7x - 3 = 4x + 6$ 40. Ⓐ Ⓑ Ⓒ Ⓓ Ⓔ
(A) 3 (B) −1 (C) 4 (D) 2 (E) −4

41. Using the formula $A = p + prt$, find A when $p = 500$, $r = .04$, and $t = 2\frac{1}{2}$. 41. Ⓐ Ⓑ Ⓒ Ⓓ Ⓔ
(A) 700 (B) 600 (C) 550 (D) 500 (E) 450

Signed Numbers

42. Find the sum of $2b + 5$, $4b - 4$, and $3b - 6$. 42. Ⓐ Ⓑ Ⓒ Ⓓ Ⓔ
(A) $9b - 5$ (B) $7b - 10$ (C) $24b^2 + 120$ (D) $6b - 1$ (E) $7b - 10$

43. Which fraction is equivalent to $-2\frac{1}{4}$? 43. Ⓐ Ⓑ Ⓒ Ⓓ Ⓔ

(A) $\frac{-9}{4}$ (B) $\frac{-7}{4}$ (C) $\frac{-7}{-4}$ (D) $\frac{-9}{-4}$ (E) $\frac{-4}{9}$

44. If $\frac{3}{x}$ is subtracted from $\frac{4}{x}$, the result is: 44. Ⓐ Ⓑ Ⓒ Ⓓ Ⓔ

(A) 1 (B) $\frac{7}{x}$ (C) $\frac{-1}{x}$ (D) $\frac{1}{x}$ (E) $\frac{1}{x^2}$

Expressions

45. The expression $(3K^2)^3$ is equivalent to: 45. Ⓐ Ⓑ Ⓒ Ⓓ Ⓔ
(A) $9K^6$ (B) $27K^6$ (C) $27K^5$ (D) $9K^5$ (E) $3K^5$

46. Find the value of $-5ST^2$ when $S = -2$ and $T = 3$. 46. Ⓐ Ⓑ Ⓒ Ⓓ Ⓔ
(A) −90 (B) 90 (C) −60 (D) 60 (E) 30

47. The expression $2(a + 1) - (1 + 2a)$ is equivalent to: 47. Ⓐ Ⓑ Ⓒ Ⓓ Ⓔ
(A) 1 (B) −1 (C) 0 (D) $4a$ (E) 2

48. The expression $\frac{-40D^2E^5}{-5DE^2}$ is equivalent to: 48. Ⓐ Ⓑ Ⓒ Ⓓ Ⓔ

(A) $\frac{-8D}{E^3}$ (B) $\frac{-8}{DE^7}$ (C) $8DE^3$ (D) $\frac{8D}{E^3}$ (E) $\frac{-8D^3}{E^7}$

49. The product of $3X^5$ and $5X^3$ is: 49. Ⓐ Ⓑ Ⓒ Ⓓ Ⓔ
(A) $15X^8$ (B) $8X^{15}$ (C) $15X^{15}$ (D) $8X^8$ (E) $35X^8$

Word Problems

50. If the average of 2 and x is 7, find the value of x. 50. Ⓐ Ⓑ Ⓒ Ⓓ Ⓔ
(A) 9 (B) 18 (C) 12 (D) 14 (E) 16

51. An owner of a pizza stand sold small slices of pizza for 15 cents each and large slices for 25 cents each. One night, he sold 500 slices, for a total of $105. How many small slices were sold? 51. Ⓐ Ⓑ Ⓒ Ⓓ Ⓔ
(A) 300 (B) 200 (C) 400 (D) 250 (E) 350

52. There are 240 seats in the balcony of a theater. The number of seats in each row is 14 more than the number of rows. Find the number of rows. 52. Ⓐ Ⓑ Ⓒ Ⓓ Ⓔ
(A) 3 (B) 6 (C) 8 (D) 10 (E) 24

53. Jack has 3 more cards than Bill. Together they have 47 cards. If x represents the number of cards Bill has, then an equation that can be used to determine the number of cards each boy has is: 53. Ⓐ Ⓑ Ⓒ Ⓓ Ⓔ

(A) $x + 3 = 47$ **(B)** $x - 3 = 47$ **(C)** $x + 3x = 47$ **(D)** $2x + 3 = 47$ **(E)** $2x - 3 = 47$

Radicals

54. The expression $\frac{1}{2}\sqrt{28}$ is equivalent to: 54. Ⓐ Ⓑ Ⓒ Ⓓ Ⓔ

(A) $\sqrt{14}$ **(B)** $2\sqrt{7}$ **(C)** $\sqrt{7}$ **(D)** 7 **(E)** $4\sqrt{7}$

55. The expression $\sqrt{162}$ is equivalent to: 55. Ⓐ Ⓑ Ⓒ Ⓓ Ⓔ

(A) $4\sqrt{2}$ **(B)** $4 + \sqrt{2}$ **(C)** $9\sqrt{2}$ **(D)** $3\sqrt{2}$ **(E)** $9 + \sqrt{2}$

56. Which is a rational number? 56. Ⓐ Ⓑ Ⓒ Ⓓ Ⓔ

(A) $\sqrt{2}$ **(B)** $\sqrt{3}$ **(C)** $\sqrt{9}$ **(D)** $\sqrt{5}$ **(E)** $\sqrt{11}$

Geometry

Similar Triangles and Inequalities

57. In circle O, $\Delta ABC \sim \Delta ADE$. If $AE = 8$, $EB = 7$, and $AC = 12$, find AD. 57. Ⓐ Ⓑ Ⓒ Ⓓ Ⓔ

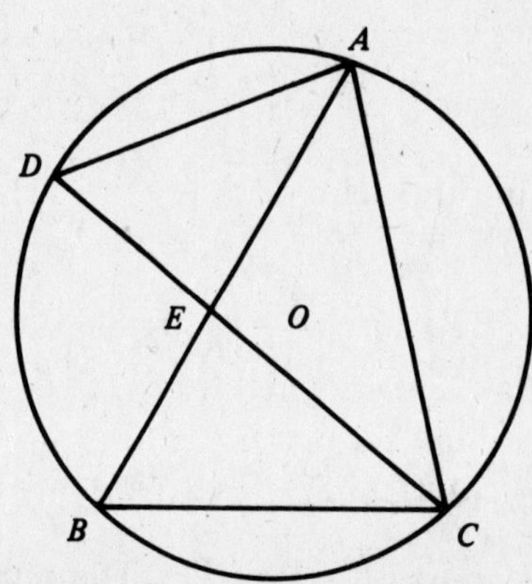

(A) 20 **(B)** 19 **(C)** 15 **(D)** 12 **(E)** 10

58. In the accompanying figure, the legs of a right triangle are 16 inches and 12 inches. Find the number of inches in the length of the line segment parallel to the 16-inch side and 3 inches from it.

58. Ⓐ Ⓑ Ⓒ Ⓓ Ⓔ

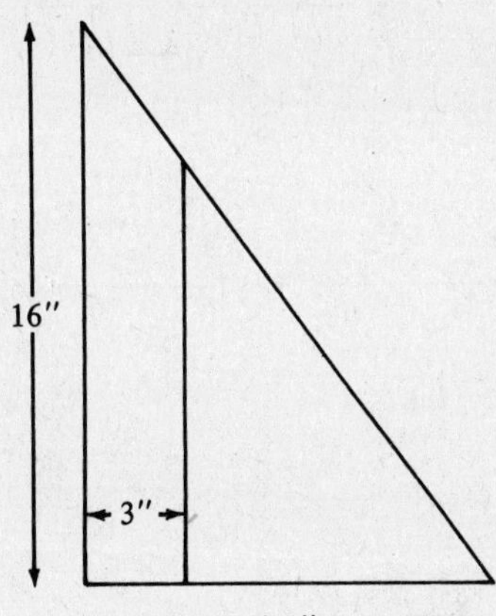

(A) 16 **(B)** 12 **(C)** 9 **(D)** 15 **(E)** 10

Coordinate Geometry and Locus

59. What are the coordinates of the origin in coordinate geometry?
(A) (x, y) **(B)** $(-1, -1)$ **(C)** $(0, 0)$ **(D)** $(0, 1)$ **(E)** $(1, 0)$

59. Ⓐ Ⓑ Ⓒ Ⓓ Ⓔ

60. At what point does the line cross the y-axis?

60. Ⓐ Ⓑ Ⓒ Ⓓ Ⓔ

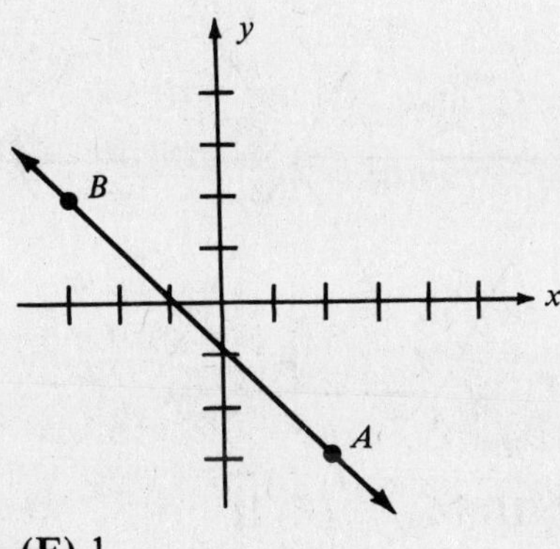

(A) -3 **(B)** -2 **(C)** -1 **(D)** 0 **(E)** 1

Area and Perimeter of Triangles and Quadrilaterals and the Pythagorean Theorem

61. The length of the side of an equilateral triangle is 10. Find the area of the triangle.
(A) 25 **(B)** 100 **(C)** $25\sqrt{3}$ **(D)** $\frac{5}{2}\sqrt{3}$ **(E)** $20\sqrt{3}$

61. Ⓐ Ⓑ Ⓒ Ⓓ Ⓔ

62. $AB \parallel CD$. What is the ratio of the area of ΔABD to the area of ΔACB? 62. 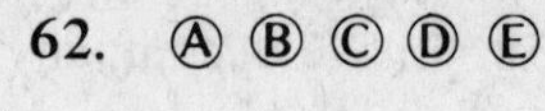

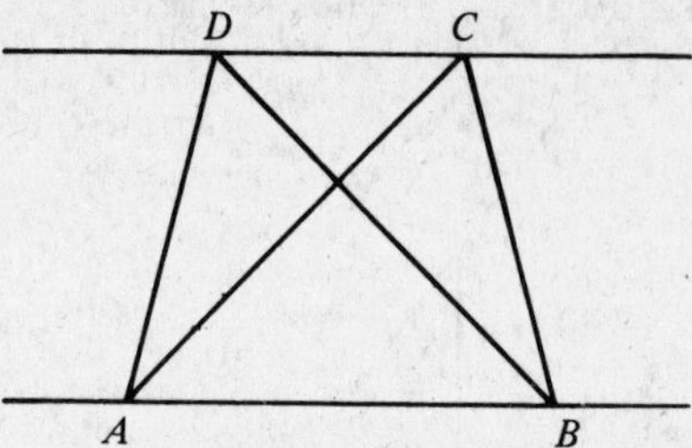

(A) 1:4 (B) 4:1 (C) 2:3 (D) 3:2 (E) 1:1

63. Find the area of trapezoid $RSTV$. 63. 

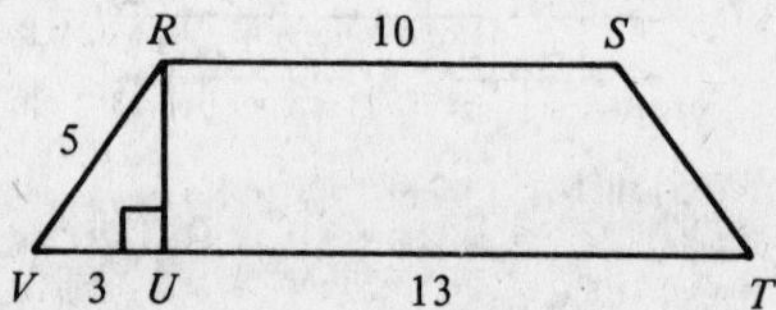

(A) 32 (B) 65 (C) 52 (D) 24 (E) 38

64. Calculate the area of the hexagon. $OP = 4\sqrt{3}$, $AB = 8$ 64. 

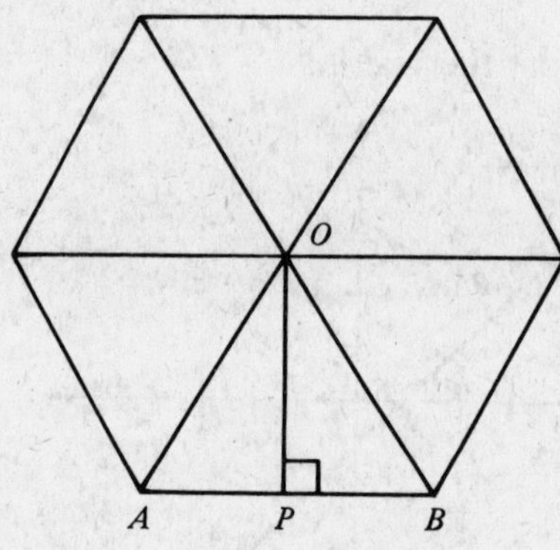

(A) $96\sqrt{3}$ (B) $32\sqrt{3}$ (C) 32 (D) $16\sqrt{3}$ (E) 16

Angle Measurement in Regular Polygons

65. Two consecutive angles of a parallelogram contain $x°$ and $(x + 20)°$. Find the value of x. 65. Ⓐ Ⓑ Ⓒ Ⓓ Ⓔ
(A) 100° (B) 180° (C) 360° (D) 80° (E) 40°

66. If each interior angle of a polygon contains 150°, how many sides does the polygon have? 66. Ⓐ Ⓑ Ⓒ Ⓓ Ⓔ
(A) 12 (B) 19 (C) 3 (D) 6 (E) 8

67. Figure $ABCD$ is a parallelogram. $\measuredangle A = 105°$, $\measuredangle B = 75°$. Find the measurement of $\measuredangle D$. 67. Ⓐ Ⓑ Ⓒ Ⓓ Ⓔ

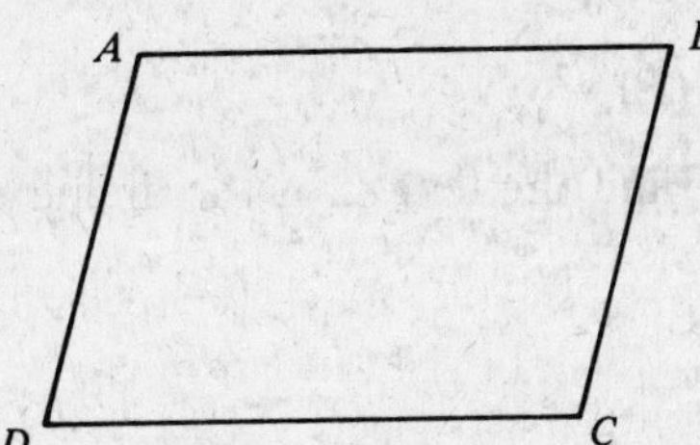

(A) 105° (B) 75° (C) 160° (D) 150° (E) 190°

Angle Sum in Triangles

68. The difference between the measures of two complementary angles is 50°. Find in degrees the measure of the smaller angle. 68. Ⓐ Ⓑ Ⓒ Ⓓ Ⓔ
(A) 40 (B) 50 (C) 70 (D) 20 (E) 10

69. Line AB is parallel to CD. 69. Ⓐ Ⓑ Ⓒ Ⓓ Ⓔ
$\measuredangle x = 40$
$\measuredangle y = 80$
Find the measurement of $\measuredangle z$.

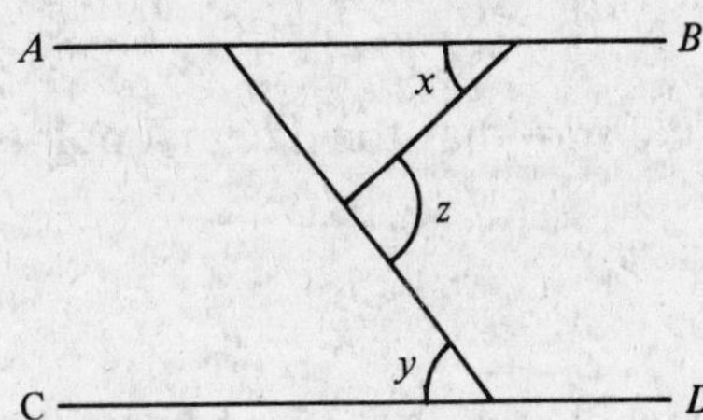

(A) 60 (B) 40 (C) 80 (D) 120 (E) 160

Circles: Angle Measurement, Area, and Circumference

70. AB, AC, and BC are tangents drawn to circle O. 70. Ⓐ Ⓑ Ⓒ Ⓓ Ⓔ
Find the length of AB.

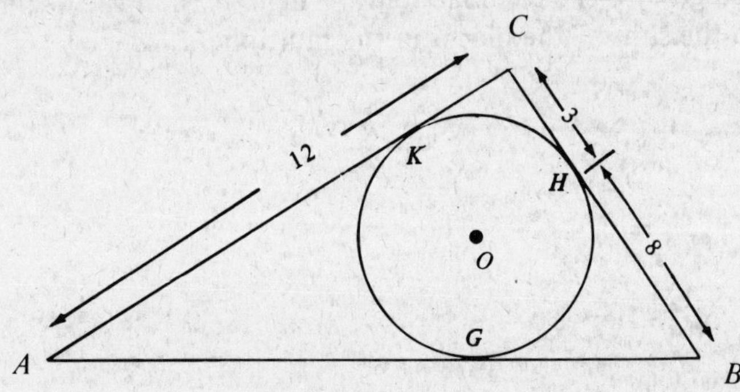

(A) 19 (B) 17 (C) 14 (D) 6 (E) 3

71. If x units are added to the length of the radius of a circle, what is the number of units by which the circumference of the circle is increased? 71. Ⓐ Ⓑ Ⓒ Ⓓ Ⓔ

(A) x (B) 2 (C) 2π (D) $2\pi x$ (E) x^2

72. The area of the circle is 16π. Find the length of the diameter of the circle. 72. Ⓐ Ⓑ Ⓒ Ⓓ Ⓔ

(A) 4 (B) 2 (C) 16 (D) 32 (E) 8

Answers and Analysis

1. (B) To convert decimals to percent, multiply the decimal by 100.

$.03 \times 100 = 3.00 = 3\%$

2. (A) To convert percents to decimals, multiply the percent by $\frac{1}{100}$.

$.1 \times \frac{1}{100} = \frac{.1}{100} = .001$

3. (C) To add decimals, make sure that the decimal points fall directly under each other:

$$\begin{array}{r} 1.98 \\ 6.42 \\ .02 \\ 3.00 \\ \hline 11.42 \end{array}$$

(whole number 3 has decimal point after the number)

4. (B) To subtract decimals, decimal points should fall directly under each other.

$$\begin{array}{r} .05 \\ -\ .0045 \\ \hline \end{array} \rightarrow \begin{array}{r} {}^{491} \\ .0500 \\ -\ .0045 \\ \hline .0455 \end{array}$$

↔ add extra zeros

5. (C) Multiply decimals without regard to the decimal point. Then position the decimal point in the product according to the sum of the places in the multipliers.

$$\begin{array}{r} 12.5 \\ \times\ .75 \\ \hline 625 \\ 875 \\ \hline 9.375 \end{array}$$

6. (A) Reduce $\frac{6}{9}$ to the equivalent of $\frac{2}{3}$. Hence $c = 3$.

7. (C) Multiplying the numerator and the denominator of a fraction by the same number, which is the "1" property, does not change the value of the fraction; it remains the same. The 1 property is ($a \times 1 = a$).

8. (C) Convert all fractions to decimal equivalents:

$\frac{2}{3} = .666\ldots \quad \frac{4}{5} = .800 \quad \frac{5}{6} = .8333\ldots \quad \frac{17}{20} = .85$

$\frac{7}{10} = .7 \quad \frac{13}{15} = .8666\ldots \quad \frac{9}{10} = .9$

$\frac{7}{10}$ is the only fraction between $\frac{2}{3}$ and $\frac{4}{5}$.

9. (B) Comparing fractions, use two rules: If fractions have the same numerator, the fraction with the smallest denominator is the larger number. If fractions have the same denominator, the fraction with the largest numerator is the larger number.

$\frac{3}{11} < \frac{4}{11} \quad \frac{4}{11} > \frac{4}{13} \quad \frac{5}{12} > \frac{5}{13}$

Now compare $\frac{4}{11}$ and $\frac{5}{12}$. Find the common denominator = 132.

$\frac{(4)(12)}{(11)(12)} \quad \frac{(5)(11)}{(12)(11)}$

$\frac{48}{132} < \frac{55}{132}$

Hence $\frac{5}{12}$ has the greatest value.

10. (B) To multiply two fractions, multiply the numerators together and multiply the denominators together.

$\frac{8}{15} \times \frac{5}{1}$

$\frac{8}{\cancel{15}_{3}} \times \frac{\cancel{5}^{1}}{1} = \frac{8}{3} = 2\frac{2}{3}$ cancel out 5's

11. (C) There are eight outcomes of which five are successes (red).

12. (A) There are 12 different outfits since for every skirt there is a choice of four different blouses.

$3 \times 4 = 12$

13. (D) Mr. Smythe can go in any of seven ways, but once a road is chosen there are only 6 roads to return by.

$6 \times 7 = 42$

14. (C) There are four remaining months; ratio = $\frac{4}{12} = \frac{1}{3}$.

15. (A) The number of hours from 7:30 A.M. to 3:00 P.M. totals $7\frac{1}{2}$ hours.

Multiply: $7\frac{1}{2}$ or $7.5 \times 2.65 = 19.875 = \$19.88$.

16. (B) 13 yd 1 ft − 10 yd 2 ft borrow 1 yd from 13 yd (= 3 ft)

$$\begin{array}{r} 12\text{ yd} + 4\text{ ft} \\ -\,10\text{ yd} + 2\text{ ft} \\ \hline 2\text{ yd} \quad 2\text{ ft} \end{array}$$

17. (E) Convert 2 days to 48 hours.

$\frac{15\text{ hours}}{48\text{ hours}}$ cancel out 3's $= \frac{5}{16}$

18. (C) Convert 4 pounds to ounces by multiplying by 16 ounces.

$4 \times 16 = 64$

$\frac{64}{2} = 32$

19. (B) 35% of $N = 70$. Divide the known part by the fractional equivalent of the percent.

$35\% = \frac{35}{100}$

$70 \div \frac{35}{100}$

$70 \times \frac{100}{35}$ invert divisor and multiply

$\overset{2}{\cancel{70}} \times \frac{100}{\underset{1}{\cancel{35}}} = 200$ cancel out 35's

20. (C) $\frac{\text{Increase}}{\text{Original number}}$ = fraction → converted into %

$\frac{93 - 80}{80} = \frac{13}{80}$ divide 80 into 13:

$$80\overline{)13.0000} = .1625$$

Decimals to percent → multiply by 100

$.1625 \times 100 = 16.25$

21. (D) 75% of $N = 36.75$. Divide the known part by the fractional equivalent of the percent.

$75\% = \frac{75}{100}$

$36.75 \div \frac{75}{100}$

$36.75 \times \frac{\overset{4}{\cancel{100}}}{\underset{3}{\cancel{75}}} =$ invert divisor and multiply; cancel out 25's

$36.75 \times \frac{4}{3} = \frac{36.75 \times 4}{3} = \frac{147}{3} = 49$

22. (D) 1. Write down as many digits of the given decimal as required and drop the other digits.
2. Starting from the left or going to the right, if the first digit dropped is 4 or less, the number obtained in the first step is correct. If the first digit dropped is 5 or more, increase by one the last digit in the number obtained in step one.

46.97
46.9 → to nearest tenth, 7 was dropped > 5; increase by 1

46.9 + .1

$$\begin{array}{r} 46.9 \\ +\ .1 \\ \hline 47.0 \end{array}$$

23. (C) Any prime number is a number that is divisible by itself and by 1. Hence

72 = 8.9 = 2.2.2.3.3 → 2 and 3 are prime numbers

24. (B)

(a) $9 \div 3$	but not divisible by 2
(b) $6 \div 3$	and also divisible by 2 → $6 \div 2 = 3$
(c) $201 \div 3$	but 201 is not divisible by 2
(d) $27 \div 3$	but 27 is not divisible by 2
(e) $15 \div 3$	but 15 is not divisible by 2

25. (D) Multiply 2.5 X 1000 = 2500.

26. (E) Draw a vertical line from 10,000; it intersects the horizontal line at 50%.

27. (A) The product of the means equals the product of the extremes.

$$\frac{d-4}{d} = \frac{5}{6}$$

$$6(d-4) = 5d$$

$$6d - 24 = 5d$$

$$-5d + 24 = -5d + 24 \quad \text{(additive inverse)}$$

$$d = 24$$

28. (E) Let x = number of minutes. The product of the means equals the product of the extremes.

$$\frac{3 \text{ minutes}}{x \text{ minutes}} = \frac{315 \text{ words}}{945 \text{ words}}$$

$$315x = (3)(945)$$

Divide by 315: $315x = 2835$

$$x = 9 \text{ minutes}$$

29. (C) Let x = height of the tree. The product of the means equals the product of the extremes.

$$\frac{6 \text{ ft}}{x \text{ ft}} = \frac{8 \text{ ft (shadow)}}{20 \text{ ft (shadow)}}$$

$$8x = (6)(20)$$

$$= 120$$

Divide by 8: $x = 15$ ft.

30. **(B)** The product of the means equals the product of the extremes.

$$\frac{20}{12} = \frac{5}{y}$$
$$20y = (5)(12)$$

Divide by 20: $$20y = 60$$
$$y = 3$$

31. **(B)** $x - 1 < 8$
$+1 \ +1$ (additive inverse)
$x < 9$

32. **(A)** If $x < y$ and $y < z$, then $x < z$. If one number is less than the second number and the second number is less than the third number, then the first number is less than the third number.

33. **(B)** The line graph with a dark circle on -2 includes -2 and all numbers greater than negative two. The open circle on 3 indicates all numbers less than 3. Put together: all numbers less than or equal to -2 and less than 3:

$$-2 \leqslant x < 3$$

34. **(C)** $3x - 3 > 2x + 1$
$-2x + 3 - 2x + 3$ (additive inverse)
$x > 4$

35. **(D)** $12x^4 - 3x^3 + 6x^2 \div 3x^2 = \frac{12x^4}{3x^2} - \frac{3x^3}{3x^2} + \frac{6x^2}{3x^2}$

Divide numbers and subtract exponents: $4x^2 - x + 2$

36. **(A)** $\frac{y^2 - 9}{2y + 6} \div \frac{y - 3}{y + 2}$

$y^2 - 9$ is the sum and difference of a perfect square
$y^2 - 9 = (y - 3)(y + 3)$
$2y + 6$ has the greatest common factor of $2(y + 3)$

$\frac{(y - 3)(y + 3)}{2(y + 3)} \cdot \frac{y + 2}{y - 3}$ invert divisor and multiply

$\frac{\cancel{(y - 3)}\cancel{(y + 3)}}{2\cancel{(y + 3)}} \cdot \frac{y + 2}{\cancel{y - 3}}$ cancel out common factors of $y + 3$ and $y - 3$

$\frac{y + 2}{2}$

37. **(A)** $3x^2 + 2x - 5$ is a trinomial: The first term is a product of $3x^2 = 3x(x)$. The last term is a product of $-5 = (-1)(+5)$. By trial and error, the trinomial is factored as two binomials.

$$(3x + 5)(x - 1)$$

38. **(D)** $\frac{x^2 - 1}{x} \cdot \frac{4x^2}{x + 1}$

$x^2 - 1$ is the sum and difference of a perfect square: $(x + 1)(x - 1)$

$$\frac{(x+1)(x-1)}{x} \cdot \frac{4x^2}{x+1}$$

$$\frac{\cancel{(x+1)}(x-1)}{\cancel{x}} \cdot \frac{4\cancel{x^2}^{x}}{\cancel{x+1}} = \frac{4x(x-1)}{1} = 4x(x-1)$$ cancel out common factors of $x + 1$ and x

39. (C) $.02x + .12 = .20$

Multiply by 100: $2x + 12 = 20$

$2x = 8$

Divide by 2: $x = 4$

40. (A) Combine like terms by additive inverse:

$$\begin{array}{r} 7x - 3 = 4x + 6 \\ -4x + 3 = -4x + 3 \\ \hline 3x = 9 \end{array}$$

Divide by 3: $x = 3$

41. (C) Substitute values for $p = 500$, $r = .04$, and $t = 2\frac{1}{2}$.

$A = 500 + (500)(.04)\ 2\frac{1}{2}$

$= 500 + 50$

$= 550$

42. (A) Add like monomials; add coefficients.

$$\begin{array}{r} 2b + 5 \\ 4b - 4 \\ 3b - 6 \\ \hline 9b - 5 \end{array}$$

43. (A) Change the mixed number to an improper fraction:

$$-2\frac{1}{4} = \frac{-9}{4}$$

44. (D) $\frac{4}{x} - \frac{3}{x} = \frac{1}{x}$. Common denominators; subtract the numerators.

45. (B) $(3K^2)^3 = (3K^2)(3K^2)(3K^2) = (3)(3)(3)(K^2)(K^2)(K^2)$

$= 27K^{2+2+2}$ (multiply numbers; add exponents)

$= 27K^6$

46. (B) $-5ST^2 = (-5)(-2)(3)^2 = (-5)(-2)(3)(3)$

$= 90$

47. (A) $2(a + 1) - (1 + 2a)$

$2(a + 1) = 2a + 2$ distribution property

$-(1 + 2a) = -1 - 2a$ subtraction property

Rewrite: $\begin{array}{r} 2a+2 \\ -2a-1 \\ \hline \end{array}$

Add: $+1$

48. (C) $\dfrac{-40D^2E^5}{-5DE^2} = \left(\dfrac{-40}{-5}\right)\left(\dfrac{D^2}{D}\right)\left(\dfrac{E^5}{E^2}\right)$

$= 8DE^3$ (*Note*) $D = D^1$ (subtract exponents in denominator from exponents in numerator)

49. (A) $(3X^5)(5X^3) = (3)(5)(X^5)(X^3)$

$= 15X^{5+3}$ (multiply numbers; add exponents)

$= 15X^8$

50. (C) To find the average of several numbers, find the sum and divide by the number of items.

$$\frac{2+x}{2} = 7$$

$$2+x = 14$$

$$x = 12$$

51. (B) Let

x = number of small pizzas for $.15 each

$500 - x$ = number of large pizzas for $.25 each

$.15(x) + .25(500 - x) = 105.00$

Multiply by 100 → $15(x) + 25(500 - x) = 10{,}500$

$15x + 12{,}500 - 25x = 10{,}500$

$-10x + 12{,}500 = 10{,}500$

$-12{,}500 \quad -12{,}500$ (additive inverse)

$\dfrac{-10x}{-10} = \dfrac{-2000}{-10}$

Divide by −10: $x = 200$ small pizzas

$500 - x = 300$ large pizzas

52. (D) Let

x = number of rows

$x + 14$ = number of seats

$x(x + 14) = 240$

$x^2 + 14x = 240$

$x^2 + 14x - 240 = 0$

Factor: $(x + 24)(x - 10) = 0$

Set each factor equal to 0: $x + 24 = 0 \qquad x - 10 = 0$

Solve for x: $x = -24 \qquad x = 10$

Discard negative number for objects: hence

$x = 10$ = rows

$x + 14 = 24$ = seats

53. **(D)** Let

x = number of cards Bill has

$x + 3$ = number of cards Jack has

Then:

$$x + x + 3 = 47$$
$$2x + 3 = 47$$

54. **(C)** Find two factors of 28, one of which is a perfect square.

$$\frac{1}{2}\sqrt{28} = \frac{1}{2}\sqrt{4}\sqrt{7} \quad \text{reduce perfect square } \sqrt{4} = 2$$
$$= \frac{1}{2}(2)\sqrt{7}$$
$$= 1\sqrt{7} = \sqrt{7}$$

55. **(C)** Find two factors of 162, one of which is a perfect square.

$$\sqrt{162} = \sqrt{81 \cdot 2}$$
$$= \sqrt{81}\sqrt{2} \quad \text{reduce perfect square } \sqrt{81} = 9$$
$$= 9\sqrt{2}$$

56. **(C)** A rational number is a quotient of two integers x and y; $y \neq 0$.

$\sqrt{2}, \sqrt{3}, \sqrt{5}, \sqrt{11}$ are all irrational numbers; not expressed as rationals

$\sqrt{9} = 3$ which can be expressed as $\frac{3}{1}$ (rational number)

Note: $\sim$ means similar; $\perp$ means perpendicular.

57. **(E)** $\Delta ABC \sim \Delta ADE$

$$\frac{AB}{AD} = \frac{AC}{AE} \qquad AB = AE + EB$$
$$\frac{15}{x} = \frac{12}{8} \qquad = 8 + 7$$
$$= 15$$
$$12x = (15)(8)$$
$$= 120$$
$$x = 10 = AD$$

58. **(B)** If a line is parallel to one side of a triangle and intersects the other two sides, the line divides those sides proportionately.

$$\frac{16}{12} = \frac{x}{9}$$
$$12x = (16)(9)$$
$$= 144$$
$$x = 12$$

59. (C) The origin is the point where the x-axis and the y-axis intersect, hence (0, 0).

60. (C) The line intersects one unit below zero on the y-axis, hence (−1).

61. (C) $A = \frac{1}{2}bh$

$h = \sqrt{10^2 - 5^2} = \sqrt{100-25} = \sqrt{75} = 5\sqrt{3}$

$\frac{1}{\not{2}} \times \overset{2}{\not{10}} \times 5\sqrt{3} = 25\sqrt{3}$

62. (E) Draw the altitudes. The area of $\Delta = \frac{1}{2}bh.$

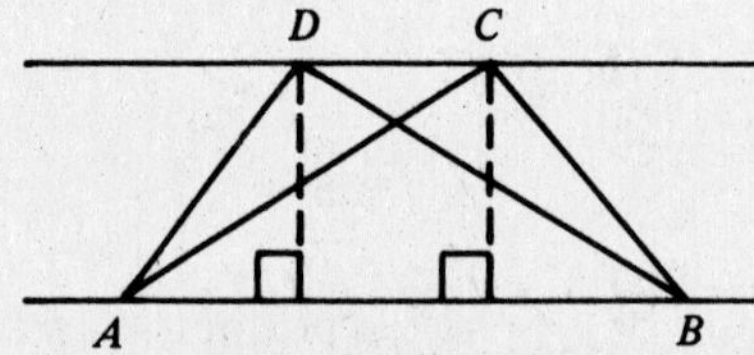

Each triangle has the same base, AB. If two lines are perpendicular to the parallel lines, the perpendicular segments are of equal measure. Hence the altitudes are equal. Therefore, the area of ΔADB = area of ΔACB. The ratio is 1:1.

63. (C) By the Pythagorean theorem, $a^2 + b^2 = c^2$.
To find $RU \rightarrow (RU)^2 + (3)^2 = 5^2$

$$a^2 + 9 = 25$$
$$a^2 = 16$$
$$a = 4$$
$$RU = 4$$

The area of the trapezoid is:

$$A = \frac{1}{2}h(b_1 + b_2)$$
$$= \frac{1}{2}(4)(10 + 16)$$
$$= \frac{1}{2}(4)(26)$$
$$= 52$$

64. (A) Area of $\Delta = \frac{1}{2}bh$

$$A = \frac{1}{2}(8)(4\sqrt{3})$$
$$= 16\sqrt{3}$$

There are six triangles in a hexagon.

$$6(16\sqrt{3}) = 96\sqrt{3}$$

65. (D) Consecutive angles of a parallelogram are supplementary. Hence

$$x + x + 20 = 180$$
$$2x + 20 = 180$$
$$2x = 160$$
$$x = 80$$

66. (A) The exterior angle of a regular polygon is the supplement of each interior angle, or the exterior angle = 180 − 150 = 30.

The formula for an exterior angle is

$\frac{360}{N}$ = exterior angle (N = number of sides)

$\frac{360}{N} = 30$ cross-multiply

$360 = 30N$

$12 = N$ (number of sides)

67. (B) In a parallelogram, opposite angles are equal; hence $\angle B = \angle D$, $\angle D = 75°$.

68. (D) Let

x = first angle

$90 - x$ = complement of first angle

Difference:

$$\begin{aligned} x - (90 - x) &= 50 \\ x - 90 + x &= 50 \\ 2x - 90 &= 50 \\ 2x &= 140 \\ x &= 70 \quad \text{first angle} \\ 90 - x &= 20 \quad \text{complement} \end{aligned}$$

69. (D) Extend the line to CD. $AB \parallel CD$, alternate interior angles $= \angle x = \angle 1$. Sum of angles in $\Delta = 180$.

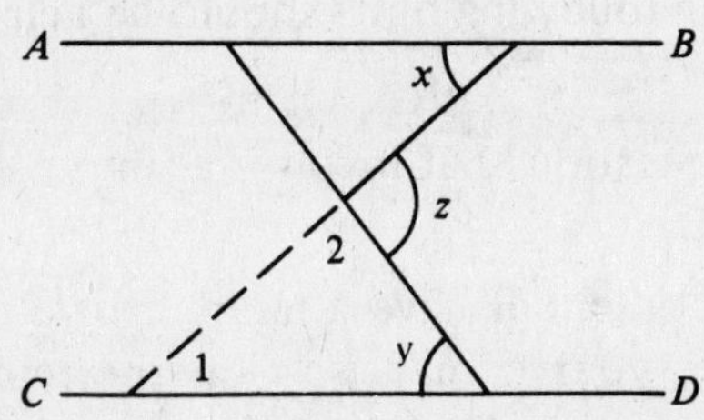

$$\begin{aligned} \angle 1 + \angle 2 + \angle y &= 180 \\ 40 + \angle 2 + 80 &= 180 \\ \angle 2 &= 60 \end{aligned}$$

$\angle 2 + \angle z$ are supplementary

$$\begin{aligned} \angle 2 + \angle z &= 180 \\ 60 + \angle z &= 180 \\ \angle z &= 120 \end{aligned}$$

70. (B) Tangents equal in length: $BG = BH = 8$; $CH = CK = 3$; $AG = AK$. Since

$AC = AK + CK$

$12 = AK + 3$

$9 = AK = AG$

then
$AB = BG + AG$
$= 8 + 9$
$= 17$

71. (D) Circumference of original circle: $c = 2\pi r$

Circumference of new circle: $c = 2\pi(r + x) = 2\pi r + 2\pi x$

Difference between new circle and original circle:

$$2\pi r + 2\pi x - 2\pi r = 2\pi x$$

72. (E) $A = \pi r^2$, $16\pi = \pi r^2$, $16 = r^2$, $4 = r$

$D = 2r = (2)(4) = 8$

Quantitative Comparisons

This section essentially alters the mathematics aptitude part of the SAT by combining mathematics with logical analysis. It consists of a new type of math question that is designed to measure the student's ability to compare relationships in arithmetic, geometry, and algebra. Each question requires you to choose from among four possible answers the best answer to a question based on a comparison of two quantities. The following hints should be helpful in becoming skilled in answering questions in this section.

1. The correct answer to a question that involves a simple mathematical computation cannot be **D**.
2. If both Column A and Column B have a number of elements in common, eliminate the common factors and base your comparison on the remaining factors. In other words, terms that are presented in both columns can be eliminated.
3. Negatives and zero should not be eliminated as answers. For example, if $x^2 = 64$, then $x = +8$ OR -8.

Read the directions for this section and then review the sample questions that follow. Analysis of each question is given immediately after each problem.

Directions: Each question in this part consists of two quantities, one in Column A and one in Column B. You are to compare the two quantities and on the answer grid blacken space

A if the quantity in Column A is the greater;
B if the quantity in Column B is the greater;
C if the two quantities are equal;
D if the relationship cannot be determined from the information given.

Common Information: In a question, information concerning one or both of the quantities to be compared is centered above or to the left of the two columns. A symbol that appears in both columns represents the same thing in Column A as it does in Column B.

Numbers: All numbers used are real numbers.

Figures: Position of points, angles, regions, etc., can be assumed to be in the order shown.

Lines shown as straight can be assumed to be straight.

Figures are assumed to lie in the plane unless otherwise indicated.

Figures that accompany questions are intended to provide information useful in answering the question. Unless a note states that a figure is drawn to scale, you should solve these problems *not* by estimating sizes by sight or by measurement, but by using your knowledge of mathematics.

	Column A	Column B	
1.	r	$180 - p$	1. Ⓐ Ⓑ Ⓒ Ⓓ

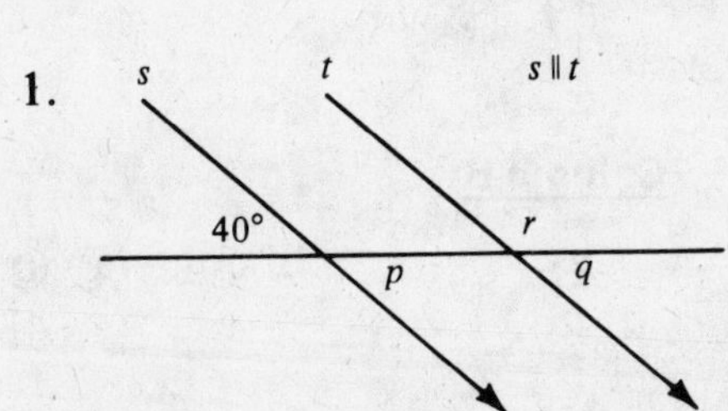

Analysis:
$\measuredangle p = 40°$ vertical angles are equal
$\measuredangle p = \measuredangle q$ corresponding angles are equal
$\measuredangle r + \measuredangle q = 180°$ supplementary angles = 180°
$\measuredangle r + \measuredangle p = 180°$ substitution
$\measuredangle r = 180 - \measuredangle p$

	Column A	Column B	
2.	Triangle I, $\measuredangle r$	Triangle II, $\measuredangle p$	2. Ⓐ Ⓑ Ⓒ Ⓓ

A
K
8
7
I
II
x
y
r
p
6
6
J

Analysis: $\measuredangle r$ is opposite side xK, which has a length of 8. $\measuredangle p$ is opposite side Ky, which has a length of 7. $\measuredangle r > \measuredangle p$ because if two sides are unequal, the greater angle lies opposite the greater side.

	Column A	Column B	
3. $2x + 3 > 5$	x	$+1$	3. Ⓐ Ⓑ Ⓒ Ⓓ

Analysis: Solve: $2x + 3 > 5$

$$\begin{array}{r} 2x + 3 > 5 \\ -3 \quad -3 \\ \hline 2x > 2 \end{array}$$

Divide by 2:

$x > 1$

	Column A	Column B	
4.	$\sqrt{99}$	10	4. Ⓐ Ⓑ Ⓒ Ⓓ

Analysis: $\sqrt{99}$ is between integers 9 and 10:

$$9 < \sqrt{99} < 10$$

$$\sqrt{81} < \sqrt{99} < \sqrt{100}$$

Hence $\sqrt{99} < 10$.

	Column A	Column B	
5.	$\dfrac{\frac{a}{x}}{\frac{b}{x^2}}$	$\dfrac{ax}{b}$	5. Ⓐ Ⓑ Ⓒ Ⓓ

Analysis:

$$\frac{\frac{a}{x}}{\frac{b}{x^2}}$$

$$\frac{a}{x} \cdot \frac{x^2}{b} \quad \text{invert divisor and multiply}$$

$$\frac{a}{\cancel{x}} \cdot \frac{\cancel{x^2}^{\,x}}{b} = \frac{ax}{b} \quad \text{cancel } x\text{'s}$$

	Column A	Column B	
6.	Price of 24 cans of dog food if 3 cans cost 1.26 cents	Price of 30 quarts of milk if 6 quarts cost \$2.02	6. Ⓐ Ⓑ Ⓒ Ⓓ

Analysis: If 3 cans cost \$1.26:
divide $\frac{24}{3} = 8$ and
multiply $8 \times 1.26 = \$10.08$

If 6 quarts cost 2.02:
divide $\frac{30}{6} = 5$ and
multiply $5 \times 2.02 = \$10.10$

	Column A	Column B	
7.	$\$1.89 \div 2\frac{1}{4}$	84%	7. Ⓐ Ⓑ Ⓒ Ⓓ

Analysis: $1.89 \div 2\frac{1}{4} = 1.89 \div \frac{9}{4}$ (improper fraction)

$1.89 \times \frac{4}{9}$ invert divisor and multiply

$\overset{.21}{\cancel{1.89}} \times \frac{4}{\underset{1}{\cancel{9}}} = .84$ cancel out 9's

$= 84\%$ from decimal to percent, move decimal point from left to right two places

	Column A	Column B	
8.	x	y	8. Ⓐ Ⓑ Ⓒ Ⓓ

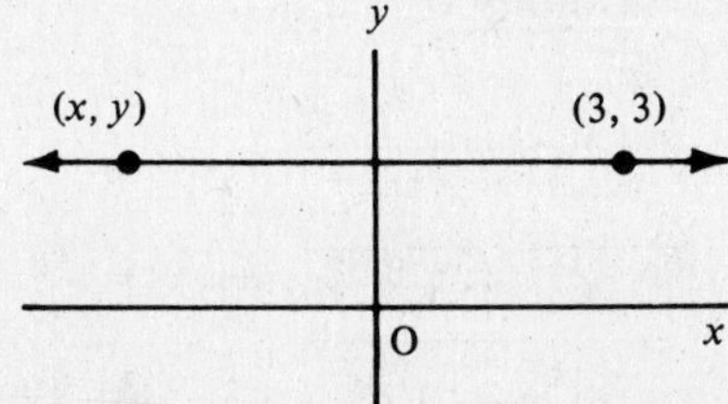

Analysis: The value of x is negative. In the second quadrant and to the left of zero, the value of y is positive 3. Hence $x < y$.

Use this drawing for questions **9** and **10**.

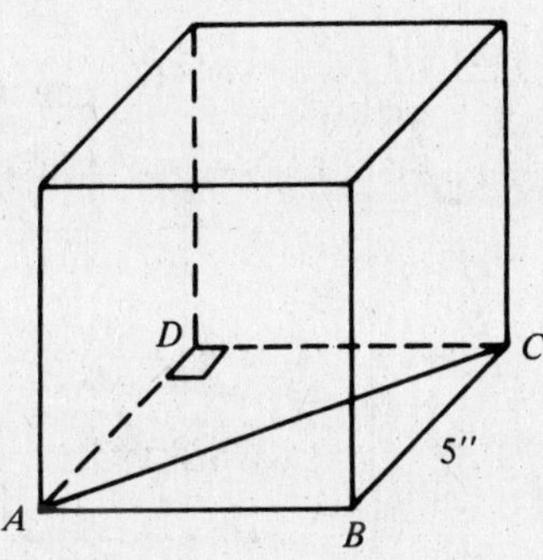

	Column A	Column B	
9.	Volume of cube	Surface area	9. Ⓐ 

Analysis: Volume of cube $v = e^3$ $= (5)^3$ $= 125$ cu in. Area $= 6e^2$ $= 6(25)$ $= 150$ sq in.

	Column A	Column B	
10.	AC	7.07	10. Ⓐ Ⓑ Ⓒ Ⓓ

Analysis:

$$(AB)^2 + (BC)^2 = (AC)^2 \quad \text{(Pythagorean theorem)}$$
$$(5)^2 + (5)^2 = (AC)^2$$
$$25 + 25 = (AC)^2$$
$$50 = (AC)^2$$
$$\sqrt{50} = \sqrt{(AC)^2}$$
$$\sqrt{25} \cdot 2 = AC$$
$$5\sqrt{2} = AC$$
$$5 \times 1.414 = 7.07$$

	Column A	Column B	
1.	$(12 + 4)5 + 8$	$12 + (4 \times 5) + 8$	1. Ⓐ Ⓑ Ⓒ Ⓓ
2.	$(13 \times 8 + 7)2 + 11$	$11 + 2(13 \times 8 + 7)$	2. Ⓐ Ⓑ Ⓒ Ⓓ
3.	$6 \times 5 + 3$	$(6 + 5)3$	3. Ⓐ Ⓑ Ⓒ Ⓓ
4.	54 sq ft	648 sq in	4. Ⓐ Ⓑ Ⓒ Ⓓ
5.	Percentage increase in brand X in 3 years	Percentage increase in brand Y in 3 years	5. Ⓐ Ⓑ Ⓒ Ⓓ

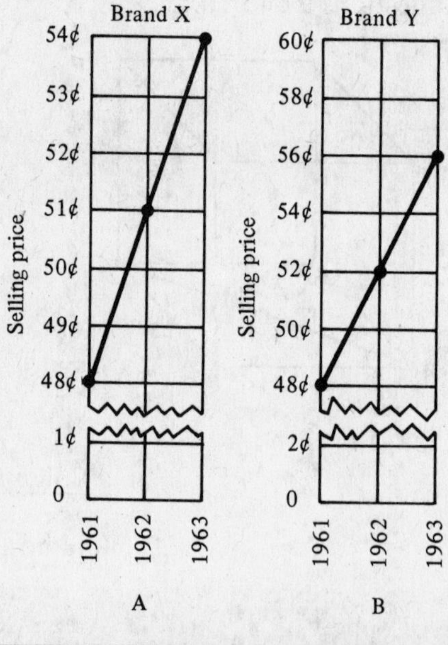

Brand X

Selling price: 54¢, 53¢, 52¢, 51¢, 50¢, 49¢, 48¢, 1¢, 0

1961 1962 1963

A

Brand Y

Selling price: 60¢, 58¢, 56¢, 54¢, 52¢, 50¢, 48¢, 2¢, 0

1961 1962 1963

B

	Column A	Column B	
6.	$.025 \times 1000$	250	6. Ⓐ Ⓑ Ⓒ Ⓓ
7.	7% of 300	210	7. Ⓐ Ⓑ Ⓒ Ⓓ
8.	$\frac{7}{16} \times \frac{5}{7} \times \frac{12}{15}$	$\frac{3}{4} \div 3$	8. Ⓐ Ⓑ Ⓒ Ⓓ

	Column A	Column B	
9.	$6\frac{3}{4} \div \frac{9}{16}$	$\frac{9}{16} \div 6\frac{3}{4}$	9. Ⓐ Ⓑ Ⓒ Ⓓ
10.	10% on a \$350 television set	$.01 \times 350$	10. Ⓐ Ⓑ Ⓒ Ⓓ
11. $p = -2$ $q = 3$	$(5p^2q^3)^2$	7.29×10^4	11. Ⓐ Ⓑ Ⓒ Ⓓ
12.	$x - y$	$y - x$	12. Ⓐ Ⓑ Ⓒ Ⓓ
13. $6x + 7y = 45$	x	y	13. Ⓐ Ⓑ Ⓒ Ⓓ
14. $r = \frac{2}{3}z$ $p = \frac{3}{2}z$	$\frac{p}{\frac{1}{r}}$	z^2	14. Ⓐ Ⓑ Ⓒ Ⓓ
15.	$(y + 3)^2$	$(y + 3)$	15. Ⓐ Ⓑ Ⓒ Ⓓ
16.	$\left(-\frac{3}{5}\right)^2$	$\frac{6}{10}$	16. Ⓐ Ⓑ Ⓒ Ⓓ
17.	a°	1	17. Ⓐ Ⓑ Ⓒ Ⓓ
18.	$\frac{\sqrt{7}}{3}$	$\frac{3}{\sqrt{7}}$	18. Ⓐ Ⓑ Ⓒ Ⓓ
19.	$10b - 17 = 13$	$9z - 27 = 0$	19. Ⓐ Ⓑ Ⓒ Ⓓ
20.	$.2y = .26$	$6y - 5.7 = 5y + 7.3$	20. Ⓐ Ⓑ Ⓒ Ⓓ
21.	Time: 3:36 P.M.	Hour hand is $\frac{3}{5}$ way from 3 o'clock to 4 o'clock.	21. Ⓐ Ⓑ Ⓒ Ⓓ
22. $\frac{1}{3}x + 3 > -6$	x	-18	22. Ⓐ Ⓑ Ⓒ Ⓓ
23.	Reciprocal of x	$\frac{x - 3}{x^2 - 3x}$	23. Ⓐ Ⓑ Ⓒ Ⓓ
24. $\frac{a + b}{b} = \frac{7}{2}$	$a:b$	2.75	24. Ⓐ Ⓑ Ⓒ Ⓓ
25. $x = 3y$	$x:y$	$y:x$	25. Ⓐ Ⓑ Ⓒ Ⓓ

	Column A	Column B	
26.	$\frac{2x^3 - 3x^2}{x^2}$	$2x - 3$	26. Ⓐ Ⓑ Ⓒ Ⓓ
27.	Average of $x - 8$ and $3x + 2$	$\frac{4x^2 - 9}{2x + 3}$	27. Ⓐ Ⓑ Ⓒ Ⓓ
28. $x = \frac{1}{2}$	$x^2 + x$	$\left(\frac{\sqrt{3}}{2}\right)^2$	28. Ⓐ Ⓑ Ⓒ Ⓓ
29.	x	y	29. Ⓐ Ⓑ Ⓒ Ⓓ

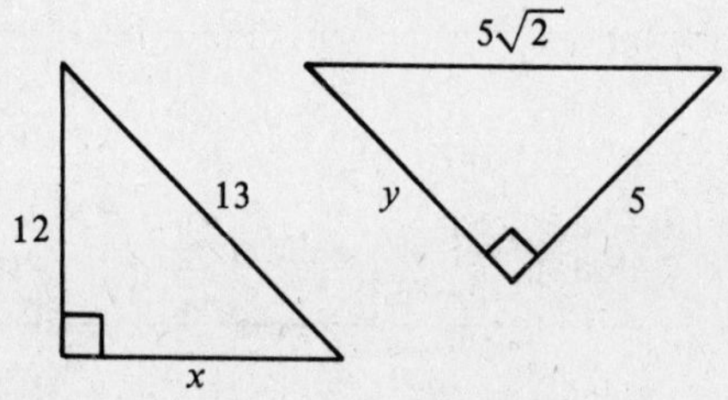

12, 13, x $\quad$ $5\sqrt{2}$, y, 5

	Column A	Column B	
30.	$A(-2, 2)$, $B(-2, -1)$ Length of AB	$E(1, -1)$, $F(1, -3)$ Length of EF	30. Ⓐ Ⓑ Ⓒ Ⓓ
31.	Radius of circle is 10 in. Area of circle.	Diameter of circle is 100 in. Circumference of circle.	31. Ⓐ Ⓑ Ⓒ Ⓓ
32.	x	y	32. Ⓐ Ⓑ Ⓒ Ⓓ

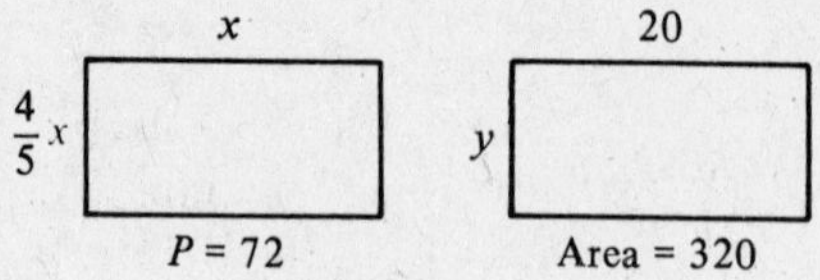

x, $\frac{4}{5}x$, $P = 72$ $\quad$ 20, y, Area = 320

	Column A	Column B	
33.	$r + p$	$t + q$	33. Ⓐ Ⓑ Ⓒ Ⓓ

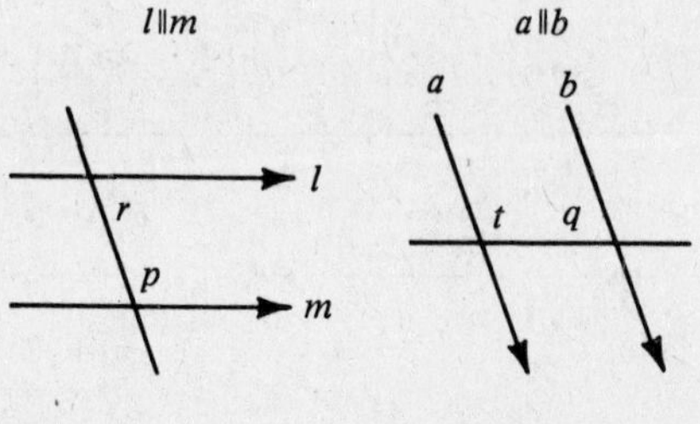

$l \parallel m$ $\quad$ $a \parallel b$

l, m, r, p $\quad$ a, b, t, q

	Column A	Column B	
34.	a	b	34. Ⓐ Ⓑ Ⓒ Ⓓ

$l \parallel m$

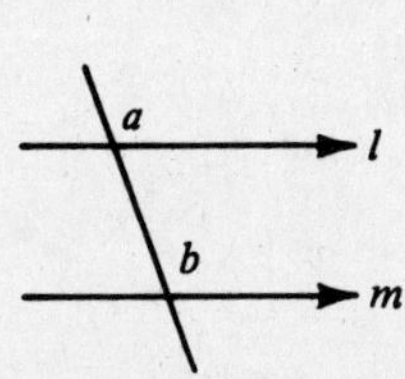

Answers and Analysis

1. **(A)**

$(12 + 4)(5) + 8$	simplify	$12 + 4 \times 5 + 8$	multiply
$(16)(5) + 8$	within	$12 + 20 + 8$	before
$80 + 8$	parentheses	40	adding
88	first		

2. **(C)** The commutative property of addition holds. The reversal of numbers keeps the equality.

$(13 \times 8 + 7)(2) + 11$	$11 + (2)(13 \times 8 + 7)$
$(104 + 7)(2) + 11$	$11 + (2)(104 + 7)$
$(111)(2) + 11$	$11 + (2)(111)$
$222 + 11$	$11 + 222$
232	232

3. **(C)**

$6 \times 5 = 30$	$(6 + 5)(3)$	simplify within
$6 \times 5 + 3 = 33$	$(11)(3)$	parentheses
	33	first

4. **(A)** 1 sq ft = 144 sq in.
$54 \times 144 = 7776$ sq. in.

5. **(A)** A closer examination of the graphs shows that brand X increased from \$0.48 to \$0.54 while brand Y increased from \$0.48 to \$0.56. Brand Y actually had an increase in price \$0.02 greater than brand X.

6. **(B)** $.025 \times 1000 = 25$
To multiply by 1000, move the decimal point from the left to the right three places.

7. **(B)** 7% of $300 = \frac{7}{100} \times 300$

Cancel out 100's:

$$\frac{7}{\cancel{100}} \times \overset{3}{\cancel{300}} = 21$$

8. (C) $\frac{7}{16} \times \frac{5}{7} \times \frac{12}{15}$

$\frac{\cancel{7}^{1}}{\cancel{16}_{4}} \times \frac{\cancel{5}^{1}}{\cancel{7}_{1}} \times \frac{\cancel{12}^{\cancel{3}\,1}}{\cancel{15}_{\cancel{3}\,1}}$ cancel out 7's, 5's, 4's, 3's

$\frac{3}{4} \div 3$ invert divisor and multiply

$\frac{3}{4} \times \frac{1}{3}$

$\frac{\cancel{3}^{1}}{4} \times \frac{1}{\cancel{3}_{1}} = \frac{1}{4}$ cancel out 3's

9. (A) $6\frac{3}{4} \div \frac{9}{16}$

$\frac{27}{4} \div \frac{9}{16}$

$\frac{27}{4} \times \frac{16}{9}$ in proper fraction, invert divisor and multiply

$\frac{\cancel{27}^{3}}{\cancel{4}_{1}} \times \frac{\cancel{16}^{4}}{\cancel{9}_{1}} = 12$ cancel out 4's, 9's

$\frac{9}{16} \div 6\frac{3}{4}$

$\frac{9}{16} \div \frac{27}{4}$

$\frac{9}{16} \div \frac{4}{27}$ in proper fraction, invert divisor and multiply

$\frac{\cancel{9}^{1}}{\cancel{16}_{4}} \times \frac{\cancel{4}^{1}}{\cancel{27}_{3}} = \frac{1}{12}$ cancel out 4's, 9's

10. (A) 10% of 350 =

$\frac{10}{100} \times 350$

$\frac{\cancel{10}^{1}}{\cancel{100}_{\cancel{10}\,1}} \times \cancel{350}^{35}$ cancel out 10's

$1 \times 35 = 35$

$$\begin{array}{r} 350 \\ \times\ .01 \\ \hline 3.50 \end{array}$$

move decimal point from right to left two places

11. (A) Substitute $p = -2$ and $q = 3$

$= [(5)(-2)^2(3)^3]^2$

$= [(5)(4)(27)]^2$

$= [(20)(27)]^2$

$= (540)^2$

$= 291{,}600$

$7.29 \times 10^4 = 72{,}900.$ Move the decimal point four places to the right. Add two zeros.

12. (D) The commutative property of subtraction does not hold. Reversal of numbers does not yield equality. But no relationship can be determined since there are no values for x or y.

13. **(D)** No relationship can be determined between x and y.

14. **(C)** $\frac{p}{\frac{1}{r}}$

$p \cdot \frac{r}{1} = p \cdot r$ invert divisor and multiply

$\frac{2}{3}z \cdot \frac{3}{2}z$ substitute values for p and r

$\frac{\not{2}}{\not{3}} \cdot \frac{\not{3}}{\not{2}} \cdot z \cdot z$ cancel out 2's and 3's

$1z^2 = z^2$

15. **(D)** $(y + 3)^2 = (y + 3)(y + 3)$

Column A has two groups of $(y + 3)$. Column B has one group of $(y + 3)$.

No relationship can be determined since y has no numerical value.

16. **(B)** $\left(-\frac{3}{5}\right)^2 = \left(-\frac{3}{5}\right)\left(-\frac{3}{5}\right)$

$= \frac{9}{25}$

$$\begin{array}{r} .36 \\ 25\overline{)9.00} = 36\% \\ \underline{75} \\ 150 \\ \underline{150} \\ 0 \end{array}$$

$$\frac{6}{10} = \begin{array}{r} .60 \\ 10\overline{)6.00} = 60\% \\ \underline{60} \\ 0 \end{array}$$

17. **(D)** No relationship can be determined.

18. **(B)** $\frac{\sqrt{7}}{3} = \frac{1}{3}\sqrt{7} = .\overline{33}\sqrt{7}$

$\frac{3}{\sqrt{7}}$ can be multiplied by $\frac{\sqrt{7}}{\sqrt{7}} = \frac{3\sqrt{7}}{\sqrt{7}\sqrt{7}} = \frac{3\sqrt{7}}{\sqrt{49}} = \frac{3\sqrt{7}}{7}$

$\frac{3\sqrt{7}}{7} = .\overline{428571}\sqrt{3}$

Hence $\frac{3}{7} > \frac{1}{3}(\sqrt{7})$.

19. **(C)**

$$\begin{array}{r} 10b - 17 = 13 \\ \underline{+17 + 17} \\ 10b = 30 \\ b = 3 \end{array} \quad \text{(additive inverse)}$$

$$\begin{array}{r} 9z - 27 = 0 \\ \underline{+27 + 27} \\ 9z = 27 \\ z = 3 \end{array} \quad \text{(additive inverse)}$$

20. (B) $.2y = .26$

Divide by .2:

$y = 1.3$

$$\begin{array}{r} 6y - 5.7 = 5y + 7.3 \\ -5y + 5.7 = -5y + 5.7 \\ \hline y = 13.0 \end{array}$$ (additive inverse)

21. (C) 3:36 P.M.

$\frac{3}{5}$ of 60 minutes $= \frac{3}{5} \times 60$

Cancel out 5's.

$3 \times 12 = 36$

3:36 P.M.

22. (B) Solve:

$$\begin{array}{r} \frac{1}{3}x + 3 > -6 \\ -3 \quad -3 \\ \hline \frac{1}{3}x > -9 \end{array}$$ (additive inverse)

Multiply by 3: $3 \ \frac{1}{3}x > -9$

$x > -27$

$-27 < -18$

23. (C) Reciprocal of x:

$\frac{1}{x}$

Factor:

$$\frac{x-3}{x^2-3x} = \frac{x-3}{x(x-3)}$$

$= \frac{1}{x}$ cancel out $x - 3$

24. (B) Solve: $\frac{a+b}{b} = \frac{7}{2}$ product of extremes equals product of means

$2(a + b) = 7b$

$2a + 2b = 7b$

$-2b = -2b$ (additive inverse)

$\frac{2a}{2b} = \frac{5b}{2b}$ divide by $2b$

$a{:}b = \frac{a}{b} = \frac{5}{2}$

$a{:}b = \frac{a}{b} = 2.50$

$2.50 < 2.75$

25. (A) Solve: $x = 3y$.

Divide by y:

$\frac{x}{y} = \frac{3}{1}$

$x{:}y = 3{:}1 \qquad y{:}x = 1{:}3$

$\frac{3}{1} > \frac{1}{3}$

26. **(C)** Factor: $\frac{2x^3 - 3x^2}{x^2} = \frac{x^2(2x-3)}{x^2} = 2x - 3$

27. **(C)** Factor: $\frac{x - 8 + 3x + 2}{2}$

$= \frac{4x - 6}{2}$

Factor: $\frac{2(2x-3)}{2}$

Reduced: $2x - 3$

$\frac{4x^2 - 9}{2x + 3} = \frac{(2x-3)(2x+3)}{2x + 3}$

Reduce, cancel out:

$2x - 3 = 2x - 3$

28. **(C)** Substitute $x = \frac{1}{2}$ in

$x^2 + x$

$= \left(\frac{1}{2}\right)^2 + \frac{1}{2}$

$= \frac{1}{4} + \frac{1}{2}$

$= \frac{3}{4}$

$\left(\frac{\sqrt{3}}{2}\right)^2 = \left(\frac{\sqrt{3}}{2}\right)\left(\frac{\sqrt{3}}{2}\right)$

$= \frac{\sqrt{9}}{4}$

$= \frac{3}{4}$

29. **(C)** By the Pythagorean theorem,

$12^2 + x^2 = 13^2$

$144 + x^2 = 169$

$x^2 = 25$

$x = 5$

$5^2 + y^2 = (5\sqrt{2})^2$

$25 + y^2 = 25\sqrt{4}$

$25 + y^2 = 25 \cdot 2$

$25 + y^2 = 50$

$y^2 = 25$

$y = 5$

30. **(A)** The length of the line segment

$\overline{AB} = \sqrt{(x_1 - x_2)^2 + (y_1 - y_2)^2}$

$= \sqrt{(-2 - 2)^2 + [2 - (-1)]^2}$

$= \sqrt{(-4)^2 + (3)^2}$

$= \sqrt{16 + 9}$

$= \sqrt{25}$

$= 5$

$\overline{EF} = \sqrt{(x_1 - x_2)^2 + - (y_1 - y_2)}$

$= \sqrt{(1 - 1)^2 + [-1 - (-3)]^2}$

$= \sqrt{0^2 + (-1 + 3)^2}$

$= \sqrt{(2)^2}$

$= \sqrt{4}$

$= 2$

31. **(C)** $A = \pi r^2$

$= \pi(10)^2$

$= 100\pi$

$C = \pi d$

$= 100\pi$

32. (A)

$$2l + 2w = p$$

$$2\left(\frac{4}{5}x\right) + 2(x) = 72$$

$$\frac{8}{5}x + 2x = 72$$

$$\frac{8}{5}x + \frac{10x}{5} = 72$$

$$\frac{18}{5}x = 72$$

$$y(20) = \text{area}$$

$$20y = 320$$

Divide by 20:

$$y = 16$$

Divide by $\frac{18}{5}$. Invert the divisor and multiply by $\frac{5}{18}$:

$$x = 72 \times \frac{5}{18}$$

Cancel out 18's:

$$x = \frac{\overset{4}{\cancel{72}}}{1} \times \frac{5}{\underset{1}{\cancel{18}}}$$

$$= 20$$

33. (C) $r = p = 180°$ / $t + q = 180°$ — interior angles on same side of transversal are supplementary

34. (C) $\measuredangle a = \measuredangle b$ — corresponding angles are equal

4.

Verbal Review: Antonyms

Each question that follows consists of a word printed in capital letters, followed by five words or phrases lettered A through E. Choose the lettered word or phrase that is most nearly *opposite* in meaning to the word in capital letters. Since some of the questions require you to distinguish fine shades of meaning, be sure to consider all choices before deciding which one is best. The first five questions may be used to review vocabulary.

1. **EBULLIENCE** 1. Ⓐ Ⓑ Ⓒ Ⓓ Ⓔ
   (A) acumen **(B)** palatable **(C)** impunity **(D)** reserve
   (E) glib

Analysis: The word *ebullience* means boiling up or overflow in manner or feeling. *Reserve* is the opposite.

2. **DEPRECATE** 2. Ⓐ Ⓑ Ⓒ Ⓓ Ⓔ
   (A) assault **(B)** praise **(C)** cringe **(D)** insinuate **(E)** supersede

Analysis: The word *deprecate* means belittle or disparage. *Praise* is the opposite.

3. **CAPITULATE** 3. Ⓐ Ⓑ Ⓒ Ⓓ Ⓔ
   (A) formulate **(B)** gather **(C)** accumulate **(D)** separate
   (E) conquer

Analysis: The word *capitulate* means yield or succumb. *Conquer* is the opposite.

4. **SEDITION** 4. Ⓐ Ⓑ Ⓒ Ⓓ Ⓔ
   (A) lie **(B)** fault **(C)** obedience **(D)** placate **(E)** irascible

Analysis: The word *sedition* means insurrection or rebellion. *Obedience* is the opposite.

5. DISSOLUTE — 5. Ⓐ Ⓑ ● Ⓓ Ⓔ
(A) vilify (B) solution (C) virtuous (D) singular (E) challenge

Analysis: The word *dissolute* means dissipated or intemperate. *Virtuous* is the opposite.

1. CHIMERICAL — 1. Ⓐ Ⓑ Ⓒ Ⓓ Ⓔ
(A) resilient (B) morose (C) belligerent (D) factual
(E) enervated

2. OBSEQUIOUS — 2. Ⓐ Ⓑ Ⓒ Ⓓ Ⓔ
(A) haughty (B) declined (C) fawning (D) coherent
(E) elusive

3. CIRCUMLOCUTION — 3. Ⓐ Ⓑ Ⓒ Ⓓ Ⓔ
(A) succinctness (B) consistent (C) railroad (D) initial
(E) hallucination

4. STRATAGEM — 4. Ⓐ Ⓑ Ⓒ Ⓓ Ⓔ
(A) facet (B) sincerity (C) conflict (D) serenity
(E) inactivity

5. QUIESCENT — 5. Ⓐ Ⓑ Ⓒ Ⓓ Ⓔ
(A) malevolent (B) tedious (C) disenchantment
(D) aroused (E) peaceful

6. PRECLUDE — 6. Ⓐ Ⓑ Ⓒ Ⓓ Ⓔ
(A) pseudonym (B) intensify (C) sanction (D) oppose
(E) restore

7. AGGLOMERATE — 7. Ⓐ Ⓑ Ⓒ Ⓓ Ⓔ
(A) obdurate (B) deified (C) separate (D) mitigate
(E) objection

8. INVIDIOUS — 8. Ⓐ Ⓑ Ⓒ Ⓓ Ⓔ
(A) lauded (B) minimal (C) medicinal (D) insidious
(E) approving

9. VENAL — 9. Ⓐ Ⓑ Ⓒ Ⓓ Ⓔ
(A) ensnare (B) inveterate (C) permeable (D) ungainly
(E) incorruptible

10. REPREHENSION — 10. Ⓐ Ⓑ Ⓒ Ⓓ Ⓔ
(A) approval (B) exigency (C) adjure (D) deleterious
(E) casuistry

11. EPITOME — 11. Ⓐ Ⓑ Ⓒ Ⓓ Ⓔ
(A) convivial (B) affable (C) inveterate (D) enlargement
(E) portend

12. REPUDIATE — 12. Ⓐ Ⓑ Ⓒ Ⓓ Ⓔ
(A) prefer (B) abstruse (C) variegate (D) abnegate
(E) impute

13. **PURLOIN**
(A) duplicate (B) expand (C) refund (D) pervade
(E) precede

13. Ⓐ Ⓑ Ⓒ Ⓓ Ⓔ

14. **VITUPERATE**
(A) ameliorate (B) laud (C) negotiate (D) renounce
(E) perceive

14. Ⓐ Ⓑ Ⓒ Ⓓ Ⓔ

15. **MERETRICIOUS**
(A) multifarious (B) modest (C) nefarious (D) sagacious
(E) tempestuous

15. Ⓐ Ⓑ Ⓒ Ⓓ Ⓔ

16. **PLETHORA**
(A) rigor (B) temerity (C) paucity (D) apathy
(E) duplicity

16. Ⓐ Ⓑ Ⓒ Ⓓ Ⓔ

17. **EQUIVOCAL**
(A) positive (B) reluctant (C) justifiable (D) therapeutic
(E) superfluous

17. Ⓐ Ⓑ Ⓒ Ⓓ Ⓔ

18. **FRENETIC**
(A) complex (B) acceptable (C) ominous (D) sedate
(E) general

18. Ⓐ Ⓑ Ⓒ Ⓓ Ⓔ

19. **FIASCO**
(A) production (B) gamut (C) analysis (D) success
(E) allegory

19. Ⓐ Ⓑ Ⓒ Ⓓ Ⓔ

20. **ETIOLATE**
(A) relegate (B) facilitate (C) clean (D) stain (E) discuss

20. Ⓐ Ⓑ Ⓒ Ⓓ Ⓔ

21. **HERETIC**
(A) exorbitant (B) verbal (C) pious (D) clerical (E) stoic

21. Ⓐ Ⓑ Ⓒ Ⓓ Ⓔ

22. **PREDILECTION**
(A) seclusion (B) limpid (C) repulsion (D) anachronism
(E) gibe

22. Ⓐ Ⓑ Ⓒ Ⓓ Ⓔ

23. **LACONIC**
(A) cogent (B) voluble (C) prodigal (D) dulcet (E) acme

23. Ⓐ Ⓑ Ⓒ Ⓓ Ⓔ

24. **MENDACIOUS**
(A) honest (B) adroit (C) theological (D) vituperative
(E) harsh

24. Ⓐ Ⓑ Ⓒ Ⓓ Ⓔ

25. **ANTEDILUVIAN**
(A) foible (B) modern (C) affable (D) pragmatic
(E) foment

25. Ⓐ Ⓑ Ⓒ Ⓓ Ⓔ

26. **MOTLEY**
(A) vermilion (B) levy (C) aphorism (D) fecund
(E) homogeneous

26. Ⓐ Ⓑ Ⓒ Ⓓ Ⓔ

27. **RETROGRESSION**
(A) litigation (B) malaise (C) decline (D) improvement
(E) occipital
27. Ⓐ Ⓑ Ⓒ Ⓓ Ⓔ

28. **COADJUTOR**
(A) conductor (B) opponent (C) adjuster (D) sycophant
(E) parasite
28. Ⓐ Ⓑ Ⓒ Ⓓ Ⓔ

29. **SCINTILLA**
(A) wraith (B) acme (C) mass (D) opening (E) truncheon
29. Ⓐ Ⓑ Ⓒ Ⓓ Ⓔ

30. **PRECIPITOUS**
(A) lugubrious (B) quickly (C) flat (D) sharp (E) sinuous
30. Ⓐ Ⓑ Ⓒ Ⓓ Ⓔ

31. **GULLIBLE**
(A) skeptical (B) birdlike (C) fascinating (D) naive
(E) simpering
31. Ⓐ Ⓑ Ⓒ Ⓓ Ⓔ

32. **SEDULOUS**
(A) destructive (B) poisonous (C) organized (D) tough
(E) careless
32. Ⓐ Ⓑ Ⓒ Ⓓ Ⓔ

33. **PETULANCE**
(A) amiability (B) ennobling (C) vigor (D) tacit
(E) arrogance
33. Ⓐ Ⓑ Ⓒ Ⓓ Ⓔ

34. **PROPINQUITY**
(A) scintilla (B) viable (C) modicum (D) innocuous
(E) remoteness
34. Ⓐ Ⓑ Ⓒ Ⓓ Ⓔ

35. **PROBITY**
(A) commodity (B) loam (C) holiness (D) wickedness
(E) philosophy
35. Ⓐ Ⓑ Ⓒ Ⓓ Ⓔ

36. **GERMANE**
(A) warrant (B) immaterial (C) accomplish (D) slash
(E) implied
36. Ⓐ Ⓑ Ⓒ Ⓓ Ⓔ

37. **FELICITY**
(A) sadness (B) pervade (C) humility (D) vigilante
(E) flattery
37. Ⓐ Ⓑ Ⓒ Ⓓ Ⓔ

38. **COLLIGATE**
(A) survive (B) exaggerate (C) scatter (D) assist
(E) demean
38. Ⓐ Ⓑ Ⓒ Ⓓ Ⓔ

39. **INGENUOUS**
(A) overt (B) interpose (C) sallow (D) cunning
(E) uxorious
39. Ⓐ Ⓑ Ⓒ Ⓓ Ⓔ

40. **DECAMP**
(A) ignoramus (B) relive (C) cooperate (D) desire
(E) appear
40. Ⓐ Ⓑ Ⓒ Ⓓ Ⓔ

Answers and Analysis

1. (D) CHIMERICAL: unreal, fantastic
2. **(A)** OBSEQUIOUS: subservient, slavish
3. **(A)** CIRCUMLOCUTION: redundancy, tautology
4. **(B)** STRATAGEM: device, ruse
5. **(D)** QUIESCENT: dormant, reposed
6. **(C)** PRECLUDE: prevent, forbid
7. **(C)** AGGLOMERATE: unite, amalgamate
8. **(E)** INVIDIOUS: resentful, envious
9. **(E)** VENAL: mercenary, corrupt
10. **(A)** REPREHENSION: reprimand, rebuke
11. **(D)** EPITOME: digest, synopsis
12. **(A)** REPUDIATE: disclaim, refuse
13. **(C)** PURLOIN: pilfer, rob
14. **(B)** VITUPERATE: defame, vilify
15. **(B)** MERETRICIOUS: ostentatious, tawdry
16. **(C)** PLETHORA: oversupply, superabundance
17. **(A)** EQUIVOCAL: conditional, uncertain
18. **(D)** FRENETIC: frantic, excited
19. **(D)** FIASCO: flop, failure
20. **(D)** ETIOLATE: blanch, whiten
21. **(C)** HERETIC: schismatic, sectarian
22. **(C)** PREDILECTION: inclination, liking
23. **(B)** LACONIC: brief, terse
24. **(A)** MENDACIOUS: deceitful, dishonest
25. **(B)** ANTEDILUVIAN: ancient, hoary
26. **(E)** MOTLEY: mixed, variegated
27. **(D)** RETROGRESSION: relapse, decline
28. **(B)** COADJUTOR: associate, colleague
29. **(C)** SCINTILLA: bit, shred
30. **(C)** PRECIPITOUS: sharp, sheer
31. **(A)** GULLIBLE: believing, unsuspecting

32. **(E) SEDULOUS:** industrious, diligent
33. **(A) PETULANCE:** fretfulness, vexation
34. **(E) PROPINQUITY:** nearness, proximity
35. **(D) PROBITY:** integrity, rectitude
36. **(B) GERMANE:** relevant, pertinent
37. **(A) FELICITY:** happiness, bliss
38. **(C) COLLIGATE:** classify, arrange
39. **(D) INGENUOUS:** artless, innocent
40. **(E) DECAMP:** abscond, flee

5.

Verbal Review: Sentence Completions

Each of the sentences that follow has one or more blank spaces, each blank indicating that a word has been omitted. Following the sentence are five lettered words or sets of words. You are to choose the one word or set of words that, when inserted in the sentence, *best* fits in with the meaning of the sentence as a whole. The first eight questions may be used for review.

1. .... music is much more pleasing than............. music. **1.** Ⓐ Ⓑ Ⓒ Ⓓ Ⓔ

(A) propitious .... sentientious
(B) synonymous .... terminus
(C) resonant................. dissonant
(D) prolix.................... viable
(E) lewd...................... nonpareil

Analysis: C is the correct answer because resonant and dissonant are the only choices that refer to musical qualities.

2. His .... made it necessary to .... his basic statement. **2.** Ⓐ Ⓑ Ⓒ Ⓓ Ⓔ

(A) progeny .... supersede
(B) verbosity .... reiterate
(C) foibles .... garble
(D) hallucination............. nullify
(E) seduction................ vilify

Analysis: In other words, he used so many unnecessary words that his basic statement had to be repeated.

3. He had an .... musical talent and singing was his .... 3. Ⓐ Ⓑ Ⓒ Ⓓ Ⓔ
(A) obsolete .... culmination
(B) acerb .... denouement
(C) innate .... forte
(D) illicit .... ethnic
(E) auspicious .... innuendo

Analysis: C is the correct answer. *Innate* means inborn; *forte* means strong point.

4. His writing, though ...., was quite .... 4. Ⓐ Ⓑ Ⓒ Ⓓ Ⓔ
(A) florid .... illusory
(B) fecund .... expedient
(C) dank .... turgid
(D) verbose .... pedestrian
(E) suffuse .... illicit

Analysis: D is the correct answer. The sentence means that even though he used many words his writing was quite commonplace.

5. She found out about the .... and was able to .... him. 5. Ⓐ Ⓑ Ⓒ Ⓓ Ⓔ
(A) presentiment .... rankle
(B) rabble .... personify
(C) tableau .... satiate
(D) tirade .... frizzle
(E) larceny .... blackmail

Analysis: E is the best choice. When she found out about his crime she blackmailed him.

6. The singer's stage fright had an .... effect on the quality of his voice. 6. Ⓐ Ⓑ Ⓒ Ⓓ Ⓔ
(A) insalubrious
(B) ubiquitous
(C) inimical
(D) intractable
(E) adamant

Analysis: Insalubrious is the only word that makes sense.

7. One's lifetime is .... when seen from the viewpoint of .... 7. Ⓐ Ⓑ Ⓒ Ⓓ Ⓔ
(A) laudatory .... prestidigitation
(B) jaded .... youth
(C) superfluous .... transience
(D) ephemeral .... eternity
(E) gauche .... theology

Analysis: D is the only alternative in which *both* words make sense.

8. The primitive emotions of love and hate are found even in the most .... and .... person. 8. Ⓐ Ⓑ Ⓒ Ⓓ Ⓔ

(A) brackish .... mature
(B) banal .... intellectual
(C) visionary .... civilized
(D) beneficent .... stable
(E) vituperative .... healthy

Analysis: D is the only alternative in which *both* words make sense.

1. His .... was .... during the serious conversation. 1. Ⓐ Ⓑ Ⓒ Ⓓ Ⓔ
(A) propinquity .... sylvan
(B) rapacity .... vaunted
(C) scarab .... palpable
(D) travail .... jaded
(E) badinage .... inappropriate

2. Her tendency to .... her success. **2.** Ⓐ Ⓑ Ⓒ Ⓓ Ⓔ
(A) expiate .... repleted
(B) ferret .... superseded
(C) imbibe .... reviled
(D) vacillate .... purloined
(E) procrastinate .... impeded

3. .... and .... are usually studied by those who enjoy language. 3. Ⓐ Ⓑ Ⓒ Ⓓ Ⓔ
(A) liturgy .... pantheism
(B) philology .... etymology
(C) prosody .... ubiquity
(D) tautology .... simony
(E) raillery .... verity

4. When I am............... I am also................ 4. Ⓐ Ⓑ Ⓒ Ⓓ Ⓔ
(A) scintillating .... verbose
(B) quiescent................ succinct
(C) lugubrious .... lachrymose
(D) reviled .... providential
(E) providential.............. rubicund

5. Stealing from the aged is an .... act. 5. Ⓐ Ⓑ Ⓒ Ⓓ Ⓔ
(A) approbrious
(B) unctuous
(C) igneous
(D) ecumenical
(E) euphemistic

6. It is important to .... thoroughly in order to have proper .... 6. Ⓐ Ⓑ Ⓒ Ⓓ Ⓔ
(A) rankle.................. temerity
(B) mitigate .... digestion
(C) transmute .... veneration
(D) query .... progeny
(E) masticate................ digestion

7. Expository prose should be................. 7. Ⓐ Ⓑ Ⓒ Ⓓ Ⓔ
(A) syllogistic
(B) picaresque
(C) lascivious
(D) transverse
(E) perspicuous

8. Although he was an expert in................. he could not prevent the monstrous .... 8. Ⓐ Ⓑ Ⓒ Ⓓ Ⓔ
(A) husbandry .... euphuism
(B) geriatrics .... hyperbole
(C) eugenics................. mutation
(D) homeopathy .... cygnet
(E) ethnology................ collocation

9. Since his lecture was full of........... it became most .... 9. Ⓐ Ⓑ Ⓒ Ⓓ Ⓔ
(A) cliches .... bromidic
(B) gabble .... blatant
(C) foibles .... bombastic
(D) histrionics .... insidious
(E) metaphors .... laconic

10. His .... led him to suspect her .... character. 10. Ⓐ Ⓑ Ⓒ Ⓓ Ⓔ
(A) philology .... valiant
(B) rancor .... secular
(C) vigilance .... petulance
(D) perspicacity.............. fraudulent
(E) vagary .... indolent

11. His................ remarks offended the............... 11. Ⓐ Ⓑ Ⓒ Ⓓ Ⓔ
(A) heretical................ indigent
(B) heinous .... indolent
(C) profane.................. ecclesiastic
(D) ebullient................. commissary
(E) flagrant .... exodus

12. By the fifth year of marriage his sweet young bride had turned into a veritable .... 12. Ⓐ Ⓑ Ⓒ Ⓓ Ⓔ
(A) tyro
(B) agnostic
(C) virago
(D) dilettante
(E) naiad

13. After ruining her dress, I would have preferred her most biting .... to the .... looks she directed at me. 13. Ⓐ Ⓑ Ⓒ Ⓓ Ⓔ

(A) euphemisms .... consummate
(B) anodynes................ feckless
(C) diatribes................. reproachful
(D) effigies.................. refulgent
(E) histrionics .... penitent

14. The foot soldiers................. that they would fight to the end. 14. Ⓐ Ⓑ Ⓒ Ⓓ Ⓔ

(A) ordained
(B) asseverated
(C) presaged
(D) repined
(E) vacillated

15. The spangled, satin gown lent a/an .... quality to her appearance. 15. Ⓐ Ⓑ Ⓒ Ⓓ Ⓔ

(A) meretricious
(B) prefatory
(C) pertinacious
(D) enervated
(E) obsequious

16. There is no greater .... in nature than a bird that cannot fly. 16. Ⓐ Ⓑ Ⓒ Ⓓ Ⓔ

(A) chicanery
(B) malingerer
(C) panacea
(D) fiasco
(E) anomaly

17. They................ God for divine .... 17. Ⓐ Ⓑ Ⓒ Ⓓ Ⓔ

(A) importune .... intervention
(B) impute .... favors
(C) expiate.................. revelation
(D) deprecate................ power
(E) immortalize.............. gifts

18. A................. is always................ favor. 18. Ⓐ Ⓑ Ⓒ Ⓓ Ⓔ

(A) sycophant .... currying
(B) benediction .... eliciting
(C) brigand.................. flouting
(D) facade .... brandishing
(E) tryst .... avowing

19. The .... in the church was a sign of .... 19. Ⓐ Ⓑ Ⓒ Ⓓ Ⓔ

(A) usury .... redress
(B) windfall .... sacrilege
(C) skeptic .... predilection
(D) wraith.................. piety
(E) schism .... sedition

20. The thief moved in a/an.............., ... manner. 20. Ⓐ Ⓑ Ⓒ Ⓓ Ⓔ
(A) sensuous .... tangible
(B) furtive .... surreptitious
(C) phlegmatic............... probing
(D) moribund................. menial
(E) ostentatious.............. patrician

21. The................ had a................ effect on the audience. 21. Ⓐ Ⓑ Ⓒ Ⓓ Ⓔ
(A) martinet................. pernicious
(B) patrimony .... depraved
(C) epilogue.................. salubrious
(D) elixir.................... blatant
(E) cudgel .... brusque

22. The new medicine made her extremely .... and .... 22. Ⓐ Ⓑ Ⓒ Ⓓ Ⓔ
(A) articulate................ copious
(B) doltish .... overt
(C) autocratic .... congruent
(D) torpid................... phlegmatic
(E) ludicrous .... remiss

23. The editor was very ....; he made numerous .... 23. Ⓐ Ⓑ Ⓒ Ⓓ Ⓔ
(A) sedentary................ rifts
(B) fastidious................ emendations
(C) saline .... parables
(D) maudlin.................. orifices
(E) onerous .... idyls

24. His .... were frightening. 24. Ⓐ Ⓑ Ⓒ Ⓓ Ⓔ
(A) spurious................. tacks
(B) transitory................ oblations
(C) turgid .... zephyrs
(D) sporadic................. fulminations
(E) perfidious .... nosegays

25. The................ witch used a tiny doll as a................ 25. Ⓐ Ⓑ Ⓒ Ⓓ Ⓔ
(A) ductile .... missal
(B) eviscerated .... derelict
(C) exacting................. crux
(D) malevolent............... fetish
(E) doughty .... doxology

26. The .... the criminal. 26. Ⓐ Ⓑ Ⓒ Ⓓ Ⓔ
(A) iconoclast .... condoled
(B) bourgeois................ denuded
(C) doggerel................. eulogized
(D) consort.................. imbibed
(E) patriarch .... ostracized

27. Much of romantic music has .... melody. 27. Ⓐ Ⓑ Ⓒ Ⓓ Ⓔ
(A) mellifluous
(B) egregious
(C) flagitious
(D) dogmatic
(E) concomitant

28. His .... led to an .... liver disease. 28. Ⓐ Ⓑ Ⓒ Ⓓ Ⓔ
(A) dipsomania .... ineluctable
(B) avarice.................. auspicious
(C) volition................. unctuous
(D) sojourn.................. audacious
(E) tableau.................. incipient

29. The................ of the two pictures was most................ 29. Ⓐ Ⓑ Ⓒ Ⓓ Ⓔ
(A) sophistry .... hallow
(B) juxtaposition............ esthetic
(C) trappings .... emaciated
(D) pseudonym .... facile
(E) corollary .... extraneous

30. Members of the .... family are .... 30. Ⓐ Ⓑ Ⓒ Ⓓ Ⓔ
(A) bovine .... herbivorous
(B) anthropoid............... adamant
(C) conduit.................. corpulent
(D) congenital .... incarnadine
(E) hieratic.................. chivalrous

31. After rereading the report, they had to .... several charts. 31. Ⓐ Ⓑ Ⓒ Ⓓ Ⓔ
(A) congeal
(B) countermand
(C) interpolate
(D) clack
(E) badger

32. His................ led to a ridiculous................ 32. Ⓐ Ⓑ Ⓒ Ⓓ Ⓔ
(A) collusion .... consanguinity
(B) synthesis .... cordovan
(C) colophon .... temerity
(D) ineptitude .... imbroglio
(E) chauvinism .... quirk

33. He .... the administration by constant .... 33. Ⓐ Ⓑ Ⓒ Ⓓ Ⓔ
(A) admonished............. alacrity
(B) corroborated............ chastisement
(C) duped.................. equivocation
(D) consigned .... cohesion
(E) chaffed................. burgeoning

Answers and Analysis

1. (E) is the only alternative in which both words make sense.
2. (E) is the only alternative in which both words make sense.
3. (B) Philology and etymology both refer to the study of words.
4. (C) When I am sad I am also tearful.
5. (A) Such a crime is considered shameful.
6. (E) Only this choice has two related words.
7. (E) Prose should be clearly written.
8. (C) Only these two have any sensible relationship.
9. (A) Overworked expressions or cliches can be very dull and boring.
10. (D) His keen judgment led him to suspect her phony character.
11. (C) Irreligious remarks would offend a church official.
12. (C) A virago is a nagging woman.
13. (C) Diatribes express anger much more openly than reproachful looks.
14. (B) Asseverated means promised or asserted.
15. (B) Meretricious means attractive in a tawdry way.
16. (E) An anomaly is something which is out of place.
17. (A) This is the only choice where the first word, which means to beg, makes sense.
18. (A) A flatterer gains favors by flattery alone.
19. (E) The split in the church was a sign of rebellion.
20. (B) Two synonyms are needed.
21. (C) A final speech can have a wholesome effect on a play's audience.
22. (D) Two synonyms are needed.
23. (B) The editor was hard to please and made many corrections.
24. (D) His occasional violent explosions were frightening.
25. (D) The evil witch used the doll as a magical object.
26. (E) The leader banished the criminal.
27. (A) Mellifluous means smoothly flowing.
28. (A) An alcoholic inevitably develops liver disease.
29. (B) Placing the pictures side by side was artistically pleasing.
30. (A) Cows are plant eaters.
31. (C) Only this choice makes sense.

32. **(D)** His lack of ability led to a state of confusion.

33. **(C)** He deceived the administration by using unclear language.

6.

Verbal Review: Reading Comprehension

Each passage in this group is followed by questions based on its content. After reading a passage, choose the best answer to each question and blacken the corresponding space on the answer grid. Answer all questions following a passage on the basis of what is *stated* or *implied* in that passage.

Sample Passage One

We do not want to be cantankerous. But we strongly believe that, for reasons to be documented in the succeeding chapters, American civilization tends to stand in such awe of its teen-age segment that it is in danger of becoming a teen-age society, with permanently teen-age standards of thought, culture and goals. As a result, American society is growing down rather than growing up.

This is a creeping disease, not unlike hardening of the arteries. It is a softening of adulthood. It leads to immature goals in music, art and literature. It forces newspapers, television producers and movie-makers to translate the adult English usage into the limited vocabulary of the teen-culture. It opens up vast opportunities for commercial exploitation and thereby sets off a chain reaction which constantly strengthens teen-age tyranny.

It is a tyranny that dominates most brutally the teen-agers themselves. What starts with relatively innocent conforming to the ways of the crowd soon turns into manipulation of those crowd mores by a combination of inept adult leadership and plain commercial exploitation. The longer it continues, the harder it becomes, as in the case of every artificially imposed regime, for dissenters to declare their independence.

We are fully aware that not all teen-agers and their parents have fallen victim to teen-age tyranny. Many have retained their freedom and upheld their standards. But even those who have resisted the trend know that the stronger the tide the harder it becomes to move against it. We hope that our efforts will make it a little easier for them.

One final word of preface: we are not concerned with juvenile delinquency, except where it becomes part of the "general" behavior of a substantial number of teen-agers. The reason we will not deal with

delinquency here is that we strongly feel this to be a different and special problem. It should be treated as such, and by experts far better equipped to diagnose and combat it.

1. What is the authors' attitude toward teen-age cultural standards as opposed to those of adults? — 1. Ⓐ Ⓑ Ⓒ Ⓓ Ⓔ
   A. teen-age standards are, in all things, gross and uncultivated
   B. teen-age standards are to be ignored because they are not based on sufficient experience
   C. when one grows to maturity, one's standards automatically become superior to those of teen-agers
   D. teen-age standards are simply immature in comparison to those of adults
   E. teen-age standards are artificially imposed by commercial interests

Analysis: The references to "American society growing down" rather than "growing up" and "becoming a teen-age society" support the contention on the part of the authors that such a society is immature. *(A)* The authors do not make this generalization. *(B)* The authors do not indicate that such standards are to be ignored, but that they are to be put into proper perspective. *(C)* There is nothing "automatic" about such a development; the authors do not make this claim. *(E)* The authors contend that the process is the other way around—that the teen-age softness pervades the media.

2. The effects of teen-age tyranny on society are initially evinced — 2. Ⓐ Ⓑ Ⓒ Ⓓ Ⓔ
   A. suddenly and catastrophically
   B. in an insidious, unobtrusive manner
   C. as a result of teen-age demands
   D. in such a way as to be truly ineffective
   E. in relatively insignificant areas of concern

Analysis: The topic sentence of the second paragraph bears this out: "This is a creeping disease. . . ." *(A)* This is directly contrary to the authors' contention. *(C)* While this is true, it is an effect that becomes apparent in the insidious manner referred to. *(D)* The authors are pointing out the great effect such "tyranny" does have. *(E)* It is the fact that the effect covers all areas of concern that arouses the authors' fears.

3. The reason for the authors' concern in this matter is that — 3. Ⓐ Ⓑ Ⓒ Ⓓ Ⓔ
   A. today's children are tomorrow's citizens
   B. the voting age has been decreased to eighteen
   C. American civilization itself seems to be threatened
   D. we are becoming the laughingstock of the world
   E. American teen-agers have little political and social knowledge

Analysis: The initial paragraph of the selection displays this concern for American civilization as a whole. *(A)* This, of course, is true, but it is not the major concern of the authors in this selection. *(B)* This is not discussed here. *(D)* There is no indication of this point in the selection. *(E)* This is not broached, although it may be true in many areas.

4. Those most harshly affected by this tyranny are
A. the teen-agers themselves
B. senior citizens
C. the newer generations of teen-agers
D. the parents of the teen-agers
E. the nation at large

4. Ⓐ Ⓑ Ⓒ Ⓓ Ⓔ

Analysis: The topic sentence of the third paragraph states just this: "It is a tyranny that dominates most brutally the teen-agers themselves." *(B), (C), (D),* and *(E)* The statement is specifically made, so these answers are irrelevant.

5. It is clear that the authors will not become involved in a discussion of teen-age crime because
A. they have made only a slight study of the subject
B. they are more interested in other social problems
C. there is enough material about that subject available to readers
D. they feel that teen-age crime should be treated as a part of the problem of crime in general
E. their thought is that teen-age crime is a special and particular problem and should be treated as such

5. Ⓐ Ⓑ Ⓒ Ⓓ Ⓔ

Analysis: The concluding paragraph indicates that just this is true—". . . this [delinquency] to be a different and special problem. It should be treated as such. . . ." *(A)* There is no indication one way or the other in this selection. *(B)* It is simply that the authors feel they cannot, in this work, embrace vast issues in other areas. *(C)* This is not the authors' feeling; it is that they see delinquency as a special problem. *(D)* Actually, this is not the authors' thought.

Sample Passage Two

Good sense is the most equitably distributed thing in the world, for each man considers himself so well provided with it that even those who are most difficult to satisfy in everything else do not usually wish to have more of it than they have already. It is not likely that everyone is mistaken in this; it shows, rather, that the ability to judge rightly and separate the true from the false, which is essentially what is called good sense or reason, is by nature equal in all men, and thus that our opinions differ not because some men are better endowed with reason than others, but only because we direct our thoughts along different paths, and do not consider the same things. For it is not enough to have a good mind: what is most important is to apply it rightly. The greatest souls are capable of the greatest vices; and those who walk very slowly can advance much further, if they always keep to the direct road, than those who run and go astray.

For my part, I have never presumed my mind to be more perfect than average in any way; I have, in fact, often wished that my thoughts were as quick, or my imagination as precise and distinct, or my memory as capacious or prompt, as those of some other men. And I know of no other qualities than these which make for the perfection of the mind; for as to reason, or good sense, inasmuch as it alone makes us men and distinguishes us from the beasts, I am quite willing to believe that it is whole and entire in each of us, and to follow in this the common opinion of the philosophers who say that there are differences of more or less only among the accidents, and not among the forms, or natures, of the individuals of a single species.

1. According to the author, the three elements that comprise the perfect mind are
   A. tenacity of thought, capacious memory, quickness of mind
   B. precise imagination, tenacity of memory, quickness of thought
   C. quickness of wit, ease of conscience, quickness of thought
   D. promptness of memory, distinctness of imagination, quickness of thought
   E. depth of perception, tenacity of faith, intellectual curiosity

1. Ⓐ Ⓑ Ⓒ Ⓓ Ⓔ

Analysis: These are stated directly: "... my thoughts were as quick, ... my imagination as precise and distinct ... my memory as capacious or prompt," and then "... I know of no other qualities than these which make for the perfection of the mind...." The specifics are stated in answer *D*. All the others are, therefore, inapplicable.

2. The basic idea of the first paragraph may be stated as follows:
   A. all persons have an equal portion of good will when they are born
   B. great souls are capable of great evil
   C. good sense, in terms of its distribution among persons, may be called common sense
   D. good sense is the mark of the truly good person
   E. good sense and great knowledge do not necessarily go together

2. Ⓐ Ⓑ Ⓒ Ⓓ Ⓔ

Analysis: Since, according to the topic sentence, "good sense" is the most "equitably distributed thing," the use of the word *common* as meaning "widely distributed" is valid. *(A)* It is not good will that is being discussed, but good sense. *(B)* This is indicated in the paragraph, but it is as a passing reference. *(D)* This is true only when that good sense is rightly applied. *(E)* This may be inferred from what is stated, but it is not the major idea of the first paragraph.

3. About himself, the author states that
   A. he had always sensed his mental superiority over most persons
   B. his awareness of his mental superiority over others was something that grew slowly, with experience
   C. he actually regards his own mental faculties as inferior in many ways to those of the great majority of persons
   D. he has never had an opportunity to compare himself with others mentally
   E. he has never had the feeling that his mind was more than average in any way

3. Ⓐ Ⓑ Ⓒ Ⓓ Ⓔ

Analysis: The topic sentence of the second paragraph states this thought. The specific nature of answer *E* precludes the possibility of any other.

4. The author claims that what sets human beings apart from beasts is
   A. a sense of organization combined with the ability to create
   B. the ability to adapt to the surroundings
   C. a sense of reason coupled with a strong sense of practicality
   D. a sense of reason
   E. the ability to communicate

4. Ⓐ Ⓑ Ⓒ Ⓓ Ⓔ

Analysis: The author states outright: "... reason ... inasmuch as it alone makes us men and distinguishes us from the beasts. . . ." *(A)*, *(B)*, *(C)*, and *(E)* are invalid because of the directness of the statement made by the author.

5. According to the author, the ability to distinguish between the true and the false is
   A. endowed by nature to all creatures
   B. endowed in equal measure to all persons
   C. more heavily present in some persons than in others
   D. an unnatural, cultivated trait in all persons
   E. the basis of morality among human beings

5. Ⓐ Ⓑ Ⓒ Ⓓ Ⓔ

Analysis: The second sentence of the first paragraph establishes this: ". . . the ability to judge rightly and separate the true from the false, is by nature equal in all persons. . . ." The direct quotation makes only one choice possible.

6. One may assume from the tone of the first paragraph that the author
   A. would look favorably upon innovation and breaking away from social norms
   B. would generally favor conformism as opposed to individualism
   C. would accept hasty decisions based upon inspiration
   D. would accept antisocial behavior on the part of the great
   E. feels that possessing a good mind is the greatest achievement

6. Ⓐ Ⓑ Ⓒ Ⓓ Ⓔ

Analysis: The conclusion of the first paragraph points out the perils of those "who run and go astray." *(A)* The author seems to feel that there is too much danger involved in outbursts of innovation. *(C)* Such decisions would go against the recommended themes of walking "very slowly." *(D)* Such behavior would, by implication, be regarded as very dangerous to all. *(E)* This is contrary to the author's feeling that a good mind must be "rightly applied."

Passage One

There is, of course, another side to this thematic origin of scientific thought. Dedicating oneself to some presuppositions or themata means one is likely to exclude others, as Einstein indeed did when he refused to accept the themata that were so basic in the work of the Copenhagen school on Quantum mechanics. Just because they are not contingent on empirical ground, one can expect contrary themata to be vigorously held by opposing sides (as in the case, for example, of the theme-antitheme couple of atomism and the continuum). In the thematic conflict between scientists during the rise of Quantum mechanics in the 1920s, some looked to Erwin Schrödinger's introduction of wave mechanics as "a fulfillment of a long baffled and insuppressible desire" (as one physicist expressed it in 1927). Others abhorred this continuum-based approach and found satisfaction only in fundamental explanations rooted in the themata of discreteness. Both groups faced, on the whole, the same experimental data. But the passionate pursuits of their antithetical quests show the strength which the thematic attachment often has.

When one lists the general themes that have guided the process of scientific discovery of individual scientists and of the profession as a whole, one is struck by the antiquity and relative paucity of themata—by the remarkable fact that while the range and scale of recent theory, experience, and experimental means have multiplied vastly over the centuries, the number and kind of chief thematic elements have changed little. Since Parmenides and Heraclitus, the members of the thematic dyad of Constancy and Change have vied for loyalty, and so have, ever since Pythagoras and Thales, the efficacy of mathematical forms versus the efficacy of materialistic or mechanistic models. The (usually unacknowledged) presuppositions pervading the work of scientists have long included such thematic preconceptions as these: simplicity, order, and symmetry; the primacy of experience versus that of symbolic formalism; reductionism versus holism; discontinuity versus the continuum; hierarchical structure versus unity; the animate versus the inanimate; the use of mechanisms versus teleological or anthropomorphic modes of approach.

1. According to this selection, back in the 1920s a dispute among scientists involved — 1. Ⓐ Ⓑ Ⓒ Ⓓ Ⓔ
   (A) the quantum versus the wave theory
   (B) the Copenhagen school as opposed to the Einsteinian
   (C) Schrödinger's "wave mechanics" as opposed to the quantum theory
   (D) themata as opposed to empiricism
   (E) the themata of the continuum as opposed to the themata of separateness

2. One purpose of the first paragraph of this selection seems to be — 2. Ⓐ Ⓑ Ⓒ Ⓓ Ⓔ
   (A) to point out how difficult and controversial scientific theory can be
   (B) to show that scientific knowledge is frequently based upon human prejudice
   (C) to show how several scientists, handling very much the same basic data, can come to diverse and even antithetical conclusions
   (D) to show the true nature of the brilliance of Einstein's mind
   (E) to show the shortcomings of the scientific approach to problems

3. Which one of the following statements is attested to by the second paragraph? — 3. Ⓐ Ⓑ Ⓒ Ⓓ Ⓔ
   (A) dyads are an important element in scientific research
   (B) the number and varieties of theory and experimentation have far exceeded what appear to be chief thematic elements in science
   (C) the ancient Greeks contributed relatively little to modern scientific theory
   (D) the veins of ancient themata are both rich and fertile
   (E) there is nothing new under the sun

4. Among the following combinations, which one is *not* among the presuppositions pervading the work of scientists? 4. Ⓐ Ⓑ Ⓒ Ⓓ Ⓔ
   (A) constancy and change
   (B) reductionism versus holism
   (C) use of mechanisms versus teleological methods of approach
   (D) use of mechanisms versus anthropomorphic methods of approach
   (E) teleological as opposed to theological modes of approach

Passage Two

Under the microscope, a drop of swamp water resembles a "wonderland" of strange forms and beautiful colors—tiny spheres of green, yellow, or golden brown. Here a strand of bright green beads; there minute stars mingled in a net of delicate green strands. Suddenly a tiny green sphere swims by as it vibrates its slender flagellae.

These fantastic forms belong to tiny plants called algae. Some are 1/25,000 of an inch in diameter. Their bodies consist of a single cell. Others have several cells grouped in chains, spheres, cubes, or flat plates, yet each cell in the colony is independent. Not all algae are microscopic. Some seaweeds are 30 meters long.

Algae live in varied environments all over the world. They are found in fresh and salt water, in hot springs, on ice, on soil, almost anywhere from pole to pole.

All algae have certain things in common. They never have true roots, stems or leaves. They all have chlorophyll and can manufacture food. Different groups of algae are classified according to the presence of pigments that may hide the chlorophyll.

Are algae important? Ecologists estimate that algae in the ocean may be the source of up to 80% of our oxygen supply!

5. The most serious, worldwide effect of bad pollution of ocean waters is that it may 5. Ⓐ Ⓑ Ⓒ Ⓓ Ⓔ
   (A) cause odors
   (B) reduce oxygen supply
   (C) kill clams
   (D) prevent swimming
   (E) cause docks to rot

6. Which could be true of algae? 6. Ⓐ Ⓑ Ⓒ Ⓓ Ⓔ
   (A) they are microscopic
   (B) they can manufacture food
   (C) they are 30 meters long
   (D) they can grow in hot springs
   (E) all of these

7. From this passage we may infer that algae 7. Ⓐ Ⓑ Ⓒ Ⓓ Ⓔ
   (A) live only in water
   (B) require warm climates
   (C) have evolved to produce many adaptations
   (D) do not need sunlight
   (E) always live in single cells

8. What trait do some algae have which shows relationship to animal cells? 8. Ⓐ Ⓑ Ⓒ Ⓓ Ⓔ

(A) they have no true roots
(B) they have cell walls
(C) they manufacture food
(D) they grow on soil
(E) they move around by means of flagellae

Passage Three

Just why some individuals choose one way of adjusting to their difficulties and others choose other ways is not known. Yet what an individual does when he is thwarted remains a reasonably good key to the understanding of his personality. If his responses to thwartings are emotional explosions and irrational excuses, he is tending to live in an unreal world. He may need help to regain the world of reality, the cause-and-effect world recognized by generations of thinkers and scientists. Perhaps he needs encouragement to redouble his efforts. Perhaps, on the other hand, he is striving for the impossible and needs to substitute a worthwhile activity within the range of his abilities. It is the part of wisdom to learn the nature of the world and of oneself in relation to it, and to meet each situation as intelligently and as adequately as one can.

9. Which of the following statements seems best to summarize the author's conclusions? 9. Ⓐ Ⓑ Ⓒ Ⓓ Ⓔ

(A) it is really not difficult to understand why some people adjust to life in one way and other people adjust in another way
(B) it is important to know the nature of the world and to understand one's own relationship to it
(C) without faith and self-knowledge, adjustment to the world and its problems is almost impossible
(D) it is irrational to explode simply because one feels at odds with the world
(E) you can tell much about a person's nature by the way he reacts to difficult situations

10. "Emotional explosions and irrational excuses" seem to indicate 10. Ⓐ Ⓑ Ⓒ Ⓓ Ⓔ

(A) that a person is angry
(B) that a person is basically uncontrolled
(C) that a person tends to live in an unreal world
(D) that a person needs psychiatric assistance
(E) that we all have our problems

11. The way a person reacts under stress may provide a good key to an understanding of 11. Ⓐ Ⓑ Ⓒ Ⓓ Ⓔ

(A) his religious background
(B) his social milieu
(C) his innermost needs
(D) his personality
(E) his basic desires

12. Sometimes a person's difficulties may be caused by 12. Ⓐ Ⓑ Ⓒ Ⓓ Ⓔ
   (A) irrational reactions
   (B) striving for unrealistic goals
   (C) strong emotions
   (D) scientific knowledge
   (E) unknown sources

Passage Four

Hope would promise a foothold out of the nightmare. Beckett's characters, in the main, live nowhere; those in Sartre's play are dead; and Rosencrantz and Guildenstern have no existence except in terms of another dramatic work. In the Absurdist plays the people are characters in someone else's play rather than in real life (such as Pirandello's *Six Characters*). Or else everyone is turning into a rhinoceros. Or time is slowed down for them so that (as in *The Room*) every particle of thought or emotion is relentlessly brought to the surface by microscopic dialogue. Or every day is the same as the day before or after. Or they are in hell. Or in piles of sand or dustbins. Or they are metaphors, images, of a single individual's reality. They are unreal also in having no blood ties or kinship. Marriage is possible, but there are no siblings or children; and in most of the plays, though not all, the main figures are male.

This surreality I take to find its analogue in the T-Group in that the latter, even as it is really practiced, is impossible in a special sense. Two reactions are often forthcoming when one attempts to describe the T-Group form to a layman. One, that people ought to leave. The other, often with some vehemence, that it is nonsense, pointless, of no meaning. Yet this reaction usually comes across as a challenge, of the form, "Go on, prove that it is not nonsense!"

But this is impossible, because it *is* nonsense. It is a Nonsense group. That is, in the extreme form in which I have described it, it can have no purpose in itself beyond that of letting itself exist, and seeing what it is like. It could occur as a natural, fluid result of any other events or relations in secular society. Therefore to use it in dramatic terms must imply some reference to a surreal, allegorical, or metaphysical world. I know of no play where a therapeutic group has been portrayed literally; but if it were it would at once turn into a social problem play. This is because on stage the T-Group could not be a "pure case." It would be a T-Group watched by an audience. Internally, the taskless group can have no witnesses.

13. The relationship that the author establishes between the T-Group and Absurdist plays lies in the fact that 13. Ⓐ Ⓑ Ⓒ Ⓓ Ⓔ
   (A) both are contemporary comments on life, society, and the individual's attempt to adjust
   (B) each has about it a sense of surrealism
   (C) members of T-Groups have written and produced plays of considerable interest and importance
   (D) Sartre and Beckett seemed taken with the notion of the T-Group
   (E) each is another form of the other

14. It would appear from the author's comments that Rosencrantz and Guildenstern 14. Ⓐ Ⓑ Ⓒ Ⓓ Ⓔ
   (A) are characters in a Beckett play
   (B) are playwrights in the surrealist idiom
   (C) are characters in a play
   (D) are philosophical concepts embodied in two characters
   (E) are dead

15. The statement that the T-Group "is a Nonsense group" is meant to be 15. Ⓐ Ⓑ Ⓒ Ⓓ Ⓔ
(A) a derogatory statement
(B) an amusing aside
(C) a statement of fact, according to the author's view
(D) the judgment of contemporary literary philosophers
(E) the feeling of members of the T-Group

16. A fair statement about the characters in Absurdist plays would be 16. Ⓐ Ⓑ Ⓒ Ⓓ Ⓔ
(A) that they represent heroic aspects of the human condition
(B) that they present profound religious convictions of another time
(C) that they are to be identified with problems of our day
(D) that they are not to be interpreted as real, living people
(E) that they have warm interpersonal relationships

17. One would assume that the author refers to the Absurdist plays 17. Ⓐ Ⓑ Ⓒ Ⓓ Ⓔ
(A) to substantiate his discussion of the contemporary theater
(B) to clarify his discussion of the T-Group
(C) to explain the influence of Sartre and Pirandello on modern thought
(D) to illustrate what he means by a "social-problem" play
(E) to change the pace of his discussion of an abstruse idea

Passage Five

Ecology is that branch of science which concerns itself with the relationships between living things (plants and animals) and their natural environments. Human ecology specializes in man's relationship to his natural environment.

Ecology has become of great importance in recent years because of man's devastating impact on his habitat. High schools and colleges across the nation offer special courses in this subject area to make young people aware of the impact of air, water, and land pollution on the quality of man's environment. To the growing pollution of our natural environment we must add soil erosion, destruction of forests, and deposits of large accumulations of solid wastes as causes for concern about the future quality of our natural environment.

Rachel Carson, in her far-reaching book, *Silent Spring,* published in the late fifties, alerted many Americans to the dangers of land and water pollution to the natural wildlife. Man's excessive use of DDT and other pesticides has destroyed much of the bird life and fish in our land. She predicted the wholesale extinction of natural animal life. Many experts have confirmed Rachel Carson's fears that the basic problem of ecology is to determine how far man can go in modifying his environment. In some instances man has changed his environment to such an extent that it has now become a question as to how long life can be preserved on our planet. Whether the problem is real or imaginary, experts agree that man has become the victim of his creativity and genius. Scientists have shown through extensive research that natural habitats are changing because of the spectacular advances in the application of science and industry.

The Great Lakes in the midwestern United States are a living example of ecological disaster. The original balance of nature in the Great Lakes has been drastically upset. Many of the salmon in the area, for instance, have been contaminated by the excessive use of DDT. Attempts to restore the balance of nature will be exceedingly difficult and only partly successful. Scientists warn the Great Lakes may eventually dry up. Even with an all-out effort to improve the Great Lakes, it would take years to restore their original vitality.

18. Ecology is that branch of science which concerns itself with
   (A) climate and soil conditions
   (B) the effect of atmospheric conditions on the weather
   (C) the relationships among the living and nonliving things in an environment
   (D) man and his use of natural resources
   (E) man and his relationship to the animal world

18. Ⓐ Ⓑ Ⓒ Ⓓ Ⓔ

19. Which statement best describes man's basic problem with respect to his environment?
   (A) man has absolutely no control over the natural environment
   (B) man has gone too far in changing his environment
   (C) man has had no effect on his environment
   (D) man has been uninterested in changing his environment
   (E) the natural environment shapes man's life

19. Ⓐ Ⓑ Ⓒ Ⓓ Ⓔ

20. A good title for this passage would be
   (A) Ecology: The New Science
   (B) The Natural Environment Shapes the Life of Man
   (C) Man's Genius Upsets the Balance of Nature
   (D) Man and His Use of Natural Resources
   (E) Man Learns to Live with His Natural Environment

20. Ⓐ Ⓑ Ⓒ Ⓓ Ⓔ

Passage Six

The incidence of new heroin users is going up rapidly in smaller communities. There are now identifiable heroin addiction problems in Racine, Wisconsin; Des Moines, Iowa; and Boulder, Colorado. The problem has even entered some rural areas. It appears that the most rapid growth of heroin usage may be occurring in cities thought to be the strongholds of Middle America that seem immune to such problems as addiction.

This diffusion of heroin from the big cities to the small ones is graphic evidence of the extent to which we have become one nation, one culture. At one time it was conceivable that many parts of the country–the South, the Middle West, small communities–could quarantine themselves from the real and imagined evils of big-city life. Indeed, it was once possible within the big cities to quarantine certain activities by confining them to specialized parts of the city, such as red-light districts, skid row, Chinatown, the "other side of the tracks." Personal mobility, urban growth, the national media, and mass merchandising have changed all that.

No one knows how big the problem may become in the smaller communities, but it is estimated that as many as 200,000 new addicts could be recruited in these areas during the next few years. If that is true, then treatment facilities as well as some law-enforcement efforts will have to be allocated to areas long thought to have no need for such programs.

Concomitant with the shift in the locus of heroin epidemics, there has been a change in the composition of the addict population. The most rapidly growing part of that population is white, both male and female. Indeed, in the United States it would appear that there are more white than black addicts, though the rate for blacks is higher than for whites. Furthermore, whereas the size of the black component is stable, the size of the white component is increasing. This is exactly what one would expect, as heroin epidemics begin in communities without large black ghettos.

21. In addition to the spread of heroin addiction throughout the country, there has also been a notable change in 21. Ⓐ Ⓑ Ⓒ Ⓓ Ⓔ
(A) the quality of heroin purchased on the streets
(B) the intensity of the problem of addiction
(C) the age of the groups involved
(D) the nature of the addict population
(E) the price of obtaining heroin

22. The statements about the use of heroin might support the argument 22. Ⓐ Ⓑ Ⓒ Ⓓ Ⓔ
(A) that drug abuse has always been a problem in the United States
(B) that drug abuse has become a problem only as it has involved the white, middle-class population of the country
(C) that the government has given up in its attempts to solve the the problems of drug abuse
(D) that television exposure has resulted in the increase of drug use
(E) that a culture clash exists in this country

23. In comparison with the size of the white group of drug users 23. Ⓐ Ⓑ Ⓒ Ⓓ Ⓔ
(A) the size of the black group has increased as much
(B) the size of the black group has doubled
(C) the size of the black group remains relatively unchanged
(D) the size of the black group cannot be measured
(E) the size of the black group has diminished

24. One of the results of the increasing mobility in the population of the United States has been 24. Ⓐ Ⓑ Ⓒ Ⓓ Ⓔ
(A) an ability of young people to leave their traditional homes
(B) the breakdown of techniques for quarantining undesirable activities within big cities.
(C) the establishment of metropolitan "red-light" areas
(D) the growth of suburbia
(E) the creation of the nuclear family

Passage Seven

I once made the statement in a room full of college students that the most important thing a young person could acquire in college might be a sense of his own limitations. I realized when I said it that it

was not a very fashionable thing to say. Popular books on do-it-yourself therapy stress the glorious potential of every human being and urge us to accept ourselves, finally, as being only a little lower than angels. I heartily approve any celebration of human potential, but I believe that we must acknowledge our potential for limitless evil as well. We must understand what we can do in the way of evil before we can pretend to be good. This is the beginning of morality, the psychological or spiritual or, in a religious tradition, the mythical basis that makes morality possible. One of the most moral (in this sense) books of the past century is Joseph Conrad's *Heart of Darkness,* because Conrad faces the problem of evil in man. He tells us that a man must recognize in himself the ability to put the head of his enemy on a stick and dance around a fire with it, and only when he recognizes that can he even begin to deal with any moral questions at all. Students who have been nourished on pop psychology and told "I'm OK; you're OK" have some trouble dealing with Conrad, and some of them regard him as perverse.

I am amazed at the number of educated people who believe that we are somehow better, more moral, than our ancestors were. I have seen otherwise intelligent people grow red in the face at the suggestion that human beings are not better now—less cruel, more considerate, less animalistic, more humane—than they were when Nero ruled Rome or when the pharaohs ruled Egypt or when the Druids at Stonehenge readied their sacrifices.

In one way, we may be more likely to become dulled to our potential for evil (and so discover it suddenly and with disastrous consequences) today than we were a few centuries ago. This is because we actively suppress the kind of self-knowledge that makes intelligent moral decisions possible. Sin and guilt are such old-fashioned terms that most of us are embarrassed by the very words.

25. With which of the following statements would the author be most likely to *agree*? — 25. Ⓐ Ⓑ Ⓒ Ⓓ Ⓔ

(A) as time goes on, man and civilization progress at equal rates
(B) man is only slightly lesser than the angels
(C) man is born instinctively good and resistant to evil
(D) Joseph Conrad refused to face the problem of evil in man
(E) we must recognize man's propensity for evil as well as his leanings toward good

26. One would assume from this selection that the author probably taught — 26. Ⓐ Ⓑ Ⓒ Ⓓ Ⓔ

(A) anthropology
(B) advanced literature
(C) English literature
(D) philosophy
(E) science

27. The author's attitude toward popular "do-it-yourself" books could be described as — 27. Ⓐ Ⓑ Ⓒ Ⓓ Ⓔ

(A) critical
(B) approving
(C) apathetic
(D) strongly hostile
(E) sympathetic

28. The mention of Nero, the pharaohs, and the Druids indicates a knowledge of 28. ⒶⒷⒸⒹⒺ
(A) Rome, ancient Egypt, and ancient England
(B) Rome, ancient Greece, and ancient Egypt
(C) Rome, the Far East, and ancient England
(D) Biblical Palestine, Rome, and ancient Egypt
(E) Rome, ancient Egypt, and the British Empire

29. The beginning of morality is based on 29. ⒶⒷⒸⒹⒺ
(A) a strong religious and ethical sense
(B) a knowledge of the possibilities of evil as well as of good
(C) strong family and national ties
(D) a profound sense of tradition
(E) an innate sense of good and evil

30. One would assume that the author favors the knowledge and use of the terms 30. ⒶⒷⒸⒹⒺ
(A) good and evil
(B) moral and immoral
(C) sin and guilt
(D) right and wrong
(E) spiritual and religious

31. The following inference may be drawn from this selection: 31. ⒶⒷⒸⒹⒺ
(A) the author's views are generally accepted in the academic community
(B) students like to hear conflicting and contradictory statements from their professors
(C) it is difficult to make a living through teaching
(D) there are fashionable and unfashionable views within the university classroom
(E) professors generally criticize and condemn the attitudes of their students

Passage Eight

If there used to be nothing more ludicrous than the English people in one of its periodic fits of morality, as Macaulay put it, these have been replaced in this century by the spectacle of the American people—at least a vocal section of it—in one of its periodic fits of self-mortification. If not ludicrous, at any rate, they are vacant; they seem to have no intention; when they are over, they leave no issue. As Philip Guedalla, then one of the liveliest British commentators on the contemporary scene, wrote in 1933: "The fierce alacrity with which American citizens denounce their institutions without the slightest effort to improve them is a perennial surprise." More than intermittently it is also a bore.

I am not speaking of the steady criticism that any nation—and in particular its intellectuals—ought to maintain of its own society, but of a virulence of tone—a kind of bile—which seems to spring from self-doubt into self-hate. In the late 1960's, a British journalist, Ferdinand Mount, who was visiting the United States, said: "You can't stop people hating themselves if that is their preferred choice. . . . [But] even the strain of the Vietnam war does not explain why, for the first time, this cyclically recurrent self-doubt should have weakened the universality of belief in the American ideal." Well, he was wrong in one respect, of course: it was not the first time that the *universality* of this belief had been eroded. But it is true that, during the late 1960's and to some extent since then, whatever the provocations, the repulsion of many Americans for their own country and its total experience has been not merely virulent, not only monotonous, but itself a kind of sickness, which in turn needs diagnosis.

The capacity of Americans for self-criticism has often been noted by outsiders. "Nowhere else is national self-criticism practiced with a severity so relentless and a mockery so bitter," wrote L. P. Jacks in 1933. "Thoughtful people are to be met with all over the country whose minds seem to be constantly exercised in the diagnosis of the national disease." Cyril Connolly said twenty years later: "At a time when the American way, backed by American resources, has made the country into the greatest power the world has known, there has never been more doubting and questioning of the purpose of the American process; the higher up one goes the more searching becomes the self-criticism, the deeper the thirst for a valid mystique of humanity." Twenty years later still, in *Love-Hate Relations,* Stephen Spender has talked of "that passionate hatred of their own country which sometimes affects the most cultivated (and perhaps deeply patriotic) Americans." And the quotations could be multiplied.

32. In what respect does the author link the English and the American people? — 32. Ⓐ Ⓑ Ⓒ Ⓓ Ⓔ
   (A) he cites their similar language and cultures
   (B) he indicates that each has a high sense of morality
   (C) both people, he indicates, are rather ridiculous in their attitudes
   (D) he discusses their similar outbursts of self-denigration and self-mortification
   (E) both people are dedicated to the highest international principles

33. In order to prove his point in this selection, the author cites — 33. Ⓐ Ⓑ Ⓒ Ⓓ Ⓔ
   (A) many native American historians and critics
   (B) an assortment of foreign diplomats and business people
   (C) several French, German, and English analysts
   (D) several British journalists and writers
   (E) many contemporary newspaper editorials and accounts

34. Which of the following statements is borne out by the selection? — 34. Ⓐ Ⓑ Ⓒ Ⓓ Ⓔ
   (A) such self-criticism on the part of citizens is common to every nation
   (B) the Americans actually look upon themselves and their actions with a kind of wry humor
   (C) foreign observers tend to accept as valid the Americans' sense of self-hatred
   (D) such self-hatred as Americans feel is really a healthy state for a nation
   (E) such self-hatred as the Americans feel may well become a disease in and of itself

35. In the opinion of Ferdinand Mount — 35. Ⓐ Ⓑ Ⓒ Ⓓ Ⓔ
   (A) the Americans were completely right in manifesting their hatred for their institutions

(B) there was no reason to lose faith in the basic American ideal
(C) there was ample evidence that the basic ideals of America had proved inadequate
(D) a movement to replace American institutions and beliefs would have great impact at this moment
(E) foreign observers were really amused by this American display

36. One reaction to all the American displays of self-hatred can be — 36. Ⓐ Ⓑ Ⓒ Ⓓ Ⓔ
(A) an equal hatred on the observer's part
(B) a sense of boredom on the part of the observer
(C) a desire to reassure the Americans of their basic goodness
(D) a wish to express a feeling of triumph over the American hypocrisy
(E) an international feeling of repugnance toward Americans

Passage Nine

Between ten and midnight the United States is politically leaderless—there is no center of information anywhere in the nation except in the New York headquarters of the great broadcasting companies and the two great wire services. No candidate and no party can afford their investment on election night to match the news-gathering resources of the mass media; and so, as every citizen sits in his home watching his TV set or listening to his radio, he is the equal of any other in knowledge. There is nothing that can be done in these hours, for no one can any longer direct the great strike for America's power; the polls have closed. Good or bad, whatever the decision, America will accept the decision—and cut down any man who goes against it, even though for millions the decision runs contrary to their own votes. The general vote is an expression of the national will, the only substitute for violence and blood. Its verdict is to be defended as one defends civilization itself.

There is nothing like this American expression of will in England or France, India or Russia or China. Only one other major nation in modern history has ever tried to elect its leader directly by mass, free, popular vote. This was the Weimar Republic of Germany, which modeled its unitary vote for national leader on the American practice. Out of its experiment with the system it got Hitler. Americans have had Lincoln, Wilson, two Roosevelts. Nothing can be done when the voting returns are flooding in; the White House and its power will move to one or another of the two candidates, and all will know about it in the morning. But for these hours history stops.

37. The "power" referred to in the beginning of the essay is — 37. Ⓐ Ⓑ Ⓒ Ⓓ Ⓔ
(A) physical power
(B) political power
(C) military power
(D) electrical power
(E) power, in general

38. The author seems to admire — 38. Ⓐ Ⓑ Ⓒ Ⓓ Ⓔ
(A) the waiting candidates
(B) Roman and Athenian philosophers
(C) the American system for transferring power
(D) the troops, guns, and conspirators
(E) none of the above

39. If troops and guns were commonly used on election day, that may indicate that **39.** Ⓐ Ⓑ Ⓒ Ⓓ Ⓔ

(A) a military man would win
(B) power is transferred peacefully
(C) free elections are guaranteed
(D) there is no election
(E) force was used to determine the election

40. Between ten P.M. and midnight the United States has no leader because **40.** Ⓐ Ⓑ Ⓒ Ⓓ Ⓔ

(A) the President has resigned
(B) the strike for power has ended
(C) the polls have closed and the results are not in
(D) there has been a revolution
(E) the networks have shut down

41. "The great strike for America's power" in the third sentence refers to **41.** Ⓐ Ⓑ Ⓒ Ⓓ Ⓔ

(A) the strike of the mass media
(B) the great coal strike
(C) striking while the iron is hot
(D) the election campaign
(E) the strike after the election

Passage Ten

The first aim of this satire, it would appear, is to explode the myth of hardhat virility. Did you think that those strong, inarticulate louts were comfortable with their animal natures? You couldn't be more wrong. Archie's sexual life is limited by inhibition and narrowness, as witness his discomfort when his wife proposes they return to their honeymoon hotel for a twenty-fifth wedding anniversary. Archie is, furthermore, a blusterer and an ignoramus, who can get out no idiom but that it is mangled, no proverb but that it is turned upside down, no word of more than two syllables but that it is mispronounced. (Many of these manglings and mispronunciations are reminiscent indeed of the black-face violence perpetrated on the King's English by Amos n' Andy, back in that unenlightened past which is now to the enlightened an embarrassment to recall: "Wait a minute heah Andy! Whut is you doin? Is you mulsiflyin or revidin?") Archie is also a World War II veteran, a factor integral to his status as a reactionary. He has only to narrow his small blue eyes at his peace-marching son-in-law and deliver a prideful reference to "double-yew double-yew two" in order to induce laughter from a studio audience that *knows* how the failures of our past, of our elders, of everything we have become are inextricably linked with the proto-fascist type of the veteran.

42. The author's purpose in writing this selection might be summed up as **42.** Ⓐ Ⓑ Ⓒ Ⓓ Ⓔ

(A) a desire to expose the shallowness of television writing
(B) an attempt to point out the similarities between current entertainment and that of the past
(C) a wish to excoriate the use of dialect in entertainment
(D) a desire to analyze what appears to be a popular program
(E) a desire to label the political slant of a television program

43. One would assume from this selection that the character Archie is represented as — 43. Ⓐ Ⓑ Ⓒ Ⓓ Ⓔ
   (A) being truly patriotic in his attitudes
   (B) proud of his masculinity
   (C) proud of his national background
   (D) pleased and proud of the accomplishments of his wife
   (E) a typical middle-class father

44. What reason is alluded to that would make the "enlightened" embarrassed to recall the *Amos n' Andy Show*? — 44. Ⓐ Ⓑ Ⓒ Ⓓ Ⓔ
   (A) the portrayal of underprivileged people in their home milieu
   (B) the use of dialect for purposes of stereotypical humor
   (C) the use of black-face comedians to portray the roles
   (D) the use of atypical situations as a source of humor
   (E) the use of malapropisms for purposes of humor

45. The fact that Archie is a veteran of World War II is used — 45. Ⓐ Ⓑ Ⓒ Ⓓ Ⓔ
   (A) in order to establish him as reactionary
   (B) to prove his manliness
   (C) to establish his real patriotism
   (D) to explain his inability to think clearly
   (E) to establish his age

Answers and Analysis

1. **(E)** The first paragraph indicates the nature of the debate of the 1920s as being between "wave mechanics ... the continuum-based approach" as opposed to the "themata of discreteness" (separateness). *(A)* The quantum theory involved both the wave and the discrete approaches. *(B)* There is no discussion of the opposition of two such "schools." There is mention only of Einstein's rejecting the basic themata of the Copenhagen school. *(C)* Again, it is apparent that this is simply one of the approaches used in handling the larger issue of the quantum theory itself. *(D)* This dispute is not mentioned at all.

2. **(C)** The last two sentences of the first paragraph support this conclusion: "Both groups faced . . . the same experimental data. But the passionate pursuits of their antithetical quests show the strength which the thematic attachment has." *(A)* That this is true is implied in the selection, but it is not the point the author is striving to elucidate. *(B)* It is not human prejudice the author points to, but differing approaches to the same material. *(D)* There is no attempt to pursue this theme in the selection. *(E)* The author points to conflicting results, not to shortcomings or faults with the scientific approach.

3. **(B)** This is the basic content of the long topic sentence of the second paragraph; it is indeed the concluding phrase of that sentence. *(A)* There are references to and illustrations of dyads, but there is no attempt to indicate their particular importance in scientific research. *(C)* There is nothing to indicate this. As a matter of fact, the implications and references might point to just the opposite. But this is not the point of the selection. *(D)* There is no judgment expressed about the ancient themata, merely the mention that they have not changed much over the centuries. *(E)* This is much too simple a conclusion, and it is not representative of the author's view.

4. **(E) This is not offered as a combination at all. *(A), (B), (C), (D)* Each of these *is* specifically mentioned.**

5. (B) Loss of oxygen would obviously have the worst worldwide effects. The others are serious but may be remediable.

6. (E) All are correct. *(A)* They are 1/25,000 of an inch in diameter, visible only with a microscope. *(B)* All have chlorophyll, used in photosynthesis. *(C)* Some seaweeds are 30 meters long. *(D)* This is a remarkable adaptation. Most organisms would die in hot springs.

7. (C) Five different environments are explicitly listed "from pole to pole." This infers many adaptations for different environments. *(A), (B), (D)* and *(E)* are wrong. *(A)* Algae live on land or water. *(B)* They live from pole to pole, in great variations of temperature. *(D)* Chlorophyll needs sunlight for manufacture of food. *(E)* Algae may be in chains, spheres, flat plates, and be 30 meters long.

8. (E) Moving around is distinctly a trait ordinarily associated with animals. The other choices are not ordinarily considered as animal traits important for classification.

9. **(B) This is the author's conclusion to the paragraph—"It is the part of wisdom to learn the nature of the world and of oneself in relation to it." *(A)* This is directly contradictory to the opening sentence—the topic sentence—of the paragraph. *(C)* There is no actual discussion of faith as an attribute of adjustment to the world. *(D)* There is mention of "irrational excuses," but no statement that it is "irrational" to explode. *(E)* This is a statement borne out by the paragraph, but it is not representative of the overall meaning of the selection.**

10. (C) This is directly stated in the sentence "If his responses . . . he is tending to live in an unreal world." Each of statements *(A), (B), (D),* and *(E) may be inferred* from the paragraph, but answer *(C)* is *directly stated.* Therefore, it takes precedence over the other responses.

11. **(D) This is directly stated in *sentence 2. (A)* This may be true, but it is not stated within the paragraph. *(B)* Again, there is nothing within the paragraph that indicates that this is a point in the author's mind. *(C)* While one may make this assumption in terms of ordinary knowledge, there is nothing to show that the author feels this way. *(E)* Ordinary knowledge may support this view, but it is not a matter of discussion within this paragraph.**

12. (B) This answer is indicated by the statement that "he is striving for the impossible. . . ." The specific nature of answer *(B)* precludes *(A), (C), (D),* and *(E)* from being correct.

13. **(B) After the author establishes the "surreality" of the Absurdist plays, he indicates, in the topic sentence of the second paragraph, that "This surreality I take to find its analogue in the T-Group. . . ." *(A)* This is true in the selection, but the item the author chooses to examine further is the surreality, not the broader similarities. *(C)* This is not indicated in the selection. *(D)* Again, there is no indication of this in the selection. *(E)* That there are differences of kind is indicated in the selection.**

14. **(C) The statement that Rosencrantz and Guildenstern have no existence "except in terms of another dramatic work" reveals that they must therefore be in some dramatic work. In addition, the opening statement deals with plays and characters in plays. *(A)* This is obviously not so, since the author discusses Beckett's characters in general terms. *(B)* Since they are characters, they cannot be actual playwrights. *(D)* While this may be so, it is apparent that they are alluded to as characters. *(E)* This does not appear to be so, from the author's comments.**

15. **(C)** The author uses the term in the sense of non-sense, not in the sense of being ridiculous. *(A)* The author avoids making judgments here. He is discussing the entire matter seriously. *(B)* Again, this is central to his theme, therefore not to be treated as an aside. *(D)* This is the author's opinion. *(E)* It would appear contrary to what the members would state and feel.

16. **(D)** The second part of the opening paragraph emphasizes the fact that characters in Absurdist plays are, indeed, not to be viewed as "real-life" characters. *(A)* While this may be true, it is only within the context of the overall "unreal" aspect of such characters. *(B)* This is also true, but it is not, within the framework of the selection, the basic point of the author. *(C)* This is true only if we recall their "unreality" and lack of connection with the present world. *(E)* Since they are depicted as having no "blood-tie or kinship," such relationships would be hard to assume as correct.

17. **(B)** He draws his illustration of the T-Group from the allusions to the Absurdist plays. *(A)* He is not concerned with the contemporary theater as such. *(C)* Again, he alludes to Sartre and Pirandello only to sharpen his focus on the concept of the T-Group. *(D)* These plays would not be probable as illustrations of such "real-world" problems or commentaries. *(E)* This is not so, since the discussion of the Absurdist plays is in itself somewhat abstruse.

18. (C) is the correct answer. See the opening statement in the first paragraph.

19. (B) is the correct answer. See the second paragraph, which specifically states this point in the opening statement. The remainder of the passage is made up of supporting ideas to prove the validity of the problem.

20. (C) is the correct answer. This can be concluded from reading the passage. Check the first two paragraphs for main and supporting ideas. The third paragraph gives us specific evidence to prove the point.

21. **(D)** The topic sentence of the final paragraph indicates the emphasis on this phase of the problem. *(A)* There is no discussion of the quality of the drug itself. *(B)* It is the spread of the addiction, not its intensity, that is under discussion here. *(C)* There is no discussion or comparison of the ages of the groups involved in this addiction. *(E)* This aspect of the problem is not mentioned in the selection.

22. **(B)** The statement that at one time such problems as addiction could be and were confined to certain sections of cities, and that now "the most rapidly growing part of that population is white. . . ." would lead to the inference indicated in this question. *(A)* This selection does not discuss the problem of addiction from the historical point of view. *(C)* There is actually no discussion of the government's role in tackling this problem. *(D)* While the word *media* is used, there is no discussion of the relative responsibilities of either TV, radio, or the films. *(E)* There is no indication of such a discussion herein.

23. (C) This is specifically stated: ". . . whereas the size of the black component is stable. . . ." Because of the specific nature of the answer, choices *(A)*, *(B)*, *(D)*, and *(E)* are invalid.

24. **(B)** The second paragraph indicates that "personal mobility . . ." has "changed all that. . . . ," referring to the ability to quarantine such problems into specialized parts of the city. *(A)* While this may be true, there is no indication of it in the selection. It is an irrelevant point. *(C)* This is actually contrary to the author's point. *(D)* This problem is not central to the selection. *(E)* This matter is not alluded to at all in the selection.

25. **(E)** The author states directly that "Man must understand what he can do in the way of evil before he can even pretend to be good." *(A)* This is actually contrary to what the author feels, as indicated by his examples mentioned in the second paragraph. *(B)* This is a Shakespearean judgment

with which the author does not appear to agree as being necessarily true. *(C)* The author feels that man actually has as much propensity toward evil as toward good. *(D)* This is actually contrary to what the author specifically states.

26. **(D)** It would appear, although there are references from the areas of history and literature, that the author teaches a subject that embraces many areas and that attempts to arrive at an understanding of man's knowledge of himself and his motives. Philosophy is a broader subject than the others indicated. A good teacher of philosophy must have knowledge of areas *(A)*, *(B)*, *(C)*, and *(E)* of learning in order to be more effective in his specific branch of learning.

27. **(A)** The mention of the author's being against the fashion of thinking espoused in "popular books on do-it-yourself therapy," and the use of the term "pop psychology," make it appear that the author does not approve of such works. *(B)* This would appear to be contrary to the author's view. *(C)* Apathetic means indifferent; this the author is not. *(D)* While the author is "critical"—disapproving—there is nothing to indicate so strong an emotion as hostility. *(E)* Again, the author is not sympathetic to such works.

28. **(A)** Nero fiddled while Rome burned; the pharaohs were the pyramid builders of ancient Egypt; the Druids were a priestly sect of ancient Britain. Because of the specific nature of the correct answer, *(B)*, *(C)*, *(D)*, and *(E)* are incorrect.

29. **(B)** This is the conclusion one draws from the author's statement: "Man must understand . . . to be good. This is the beginning of morality. . . ." *(A)* This is a correct assumption in terms of general thought and discussion, but it does not suit the meaning of this specific discussion. *(C)* Again, in general terms this may prove to be a correct assumption, but it does not fit in with *this author's* discussion. *(D)* Here, too, is a valid point of argument that is irrelevant to this particular selection. *(E)* This might be argued in a discussion of morality, but this author does not broach this particular matter.

30. **(C)** The implication is that, in the author's view, the knowledge and use of the terms *sin* and *guilt* help man to identify matters of good and evil and, therefore, are desirable. Each of the terms paired in *(A)*, *(B)*, *(D)*, and *(E)* is currently in use. The author would not, therefore, be inclined to advocate their use, since such use is already present in society.

31. **(D)** *Sentence 2* indicates that the professor was aware that the point of view he espoused was not fashionable on campus. This indicates that there are such things as fashionable or unfashionable points of view. *(A)* This is obviously not true in view of the fact that the author's opinions were looked upon as unpopular. *(B)* The implications of the selection, though not expressed specifically, are that the students are disturbed by such contradictory, thought-provoking alternatives. *(C)* This is completely irrelevant to the discussion. *(E)* There is nothing within the selection to justify this generalization.

32. **(D)** The opening paragraph establishes the theme that the Americans seem to have replaced the British in the quality of self-criticism and moral self-castigation. *(A)* This aspect of similarity is not brought up. *(B)* There is an implication that this might be so, but the stress is placed on the almost "ludicrous" extent of self-recrimination. *(C)* Since he does not discuss attitudes at large, this is not an accurate conclusion. *(E)* This, of course, is not broached at all.

33. **(D)** The people whom he cites are frequently identified as "British commentator" or "British journalist." Each of the others is, by implication, British. *(A)* There are no Americans identified as such. *(B)* The people cited are usually journalists and observers rather than diplomats or business people as such. *(C)* None of these is cited or identified. *(E)* It is the people, not the articles or journals, that are cited.

34. **(E)** The conclusion of the second paragraph bears this out: "... a kind of sickness, which in turn needs diagnosis." *(A)* The point is made that this type of criticism—to this degree—is uncommon. *(B)* The point is made that there is bitterness rather than humor involved. *(C)* The consensus of these statements is that such harshness is not necessary or justified. *(D)* The contrary point is made.

35. **(B)** The point is made by Mr. Mount that, despite the horror of the Vietnam war, there was no need to lose faith in the *basic ideals* of America. *(A)* The indication is that such hatred—to the degree it was manifested—was not right. *(C)* This is not borne out by the judgment of Mr. Mount. *(D)* No such idea seems to be in the mind of the writer quoted. *(E)* The reaction of foreign observers was rather more serious than mere amusement.

36. **(B)** The concluding statement of the initial paragraph indicates just this point. *(A)* There is nothing to substantiate this conclusion. *(C)* While this may be implied, the major emphasis—in that the concluding statement makes the point clearly—is that this self-criticism can become boring. *(D)* It is understanding and sympathy rather than a desire to feel triumphant that come through in this selection. *(E)* This is not borne out at all, nor does it seem suggested.

37. (B) is correct. The powers named are all part of the executive power of the President. The end of the first paragraph also mentions "election day." *(E)* is too general.

38. (C) is correct. The author states that America has had the best and longest lasting system for peaceful transfer of power. *(A)* and *(B)* are mentioned but there is no indication of admiration. *(D)* is incorrect. The author states that these things are *absent* on election day.

39. (E) is correct. The implication of using troops and guns during an election is that the voters are being forced to vote or behave in a particular way. *(A)* is not necessarily true. *(B)* is wrong because if power is transferred peacefully, troops and guns would not be used. *(C)* is false because the use of troops and guns usually indicates that the election is not free. *(D)* is not a logical conclusion.

40. (C) is correct. Between the time the polls close and the results are tallied, no one knows who the next President will be. *(A)*, *(D)* and *(E)* are untrue. *(B)* is true, but it is not the reason the author says the U.S. is leaderless.

41. (D) is correct. The author indicates that on election day the long campaign for power ends. The other answers are not relevant.

42. **(D)** The topic sentence of the paragraph sets forth the purpose of discussing a problem which, it develops, is the TV show *All in the Family.* *(A)* Actually, it is the *character* that is being analyzed, not the writing nor any other phase of the program. *(B)* This parallel is pointed out, but only in terms of furthering the analysis of the program under discussion. *(C)* This is not apparent in the piece. *(E)* The political aspect of the program is not under discussion, although one might deduce certain characteristics from what is presented.

43. **(B)** Since the purpose of the satire is stated as being "to explode the myth of hardhat virility" and most of the focus is on the character of Archie, one may conclude that Archie is indeed proud of his "hardhat virility." *(A)* Actually, this aspect of the character is labelled as "bluster." In addition, the conclusion seems to label such types as "proto-fascist." *(C)* It is his veteran's status that is emphasized here, not the overall national pride. *(D)* There is no indication of this attitude on Archie's part. *(E)* Middle class is not usually equated with "hardhat."

44. **(B)** It is the use of "black-face violence perpetrated on the King's English" as a basis of humor that is referred to. *(A)* This is not alluded to in the discussion. *(C)* There appears to be no objection to

black-face actors in such roles. *(D)* Since atypical situations are frequently used for this purpose, it is not valid to object to them here. *(E)* There is no objection to this standard device in humor.

45. **(A)** Since the portrayal, for purposes of this program, is that of the veteran as a "proto-fascist type," Archie is branded as reactionary in his thinking. *(B)* There is no link established between veteran status and being "a man." *(C)* Actually, in this selection, just the opposite is established. *(D)* The direction of this characteristic is to establish a general line of thought and approach, not the quality of the thinking itself. *(E)* This is only one phase of the establishing of the age of the character; it is the nature of thinking, however, which is emphasized.

7.

Verbal Review: Analogies

An analogy can use either words or symbols. The following are three forms of the same analogy:

(a) man is to boy as woman is to girl
(b) man : boy : : woman : girl
(c) man : boy as woman : girl

In all cases an analogy indicates that there is a relationship between two terms which is also found between the other two terms. In the above examples, man and boy are related because one is the adult male and the other the young male of the human species. Similarly, woman is the adult female and girl is the young female. Notice both pairs mention the adult first, the young second. Notice one pair is male, the other female.

When an analogy problem is given, one term or pair of terms is left out and the test-taker must choose the term which best completes the analogy. The form of the analogy question can vary:

1. **MAN** is to **BOY** as **WOMAN** is to _____
   (A) girl **(B)** lady **(C)** male **(D)** person
   Here the last term is missing.

2. **MAN : BOY** : : _____ : _____
   (A) woman : girl **(B)** rooster : hen **(C)** woman : lady **(D)** boy : girl
   Here one *pair* of terms is missing.

3. **MAN : BOY** : : _____ **:GIRL**
   (A) woman **(B)** baby **(C)** male **(D)** rooster
   Here *any one* of the four terms can be missing.

Solving the Analogy Problem

1. First look for relationships among the terms of the analogy:

   A. Look for the relationship between the terms separated by a single colon. Find the same relationship between the other pair:

   TEETH : CHEW : : _____ : HEAR

   (A) listen **(B)** drum **(C)** ear **(D)** noise

   Relationship: Teeth are a part of body whose function is chewing. Therefore the correct choice is a part of the body whose function is to hear. Notice the two aspects of the relationship–part of the body *and* function: **(C)** ear is correct.

   B. Look for the relationship between the first (1) and third (3) terms in the analogy. Find the same relationship between (2) and (4):

1	2	3	4
GOD :		**: : GOOD :**	**EVIL**

   (A) angel **(B)** fairy **(C)** witch **(D)** sin

   Relationship: God is a religious figure who is associated with good. Therefore, the correct choice is a religious figure who is associated with evil. Notice the two aspects of the relationship — a religious figure and an abstract quality. Study the choices. An angel usually represents good. So does a fairy. A witch is usually wicked or evil but is *not* a religious figure. Sin is an act of behavior that is evil. Of the four choices, (C), witch, is best because it is a *figure* (though not religious) and represents evil.

   C. Look for the relationship between the second (2) and fourth (4) terms. Find the same relationship between (1) and (3):

1	2	3	4
	: PARE	**: : BERRY :**	**PEAR**

   (A) fruit **(B)** bury **(C)** blueberry **(D)** dig

   Relationship: "Pare" and "pear" are homonyms. "Pare" is a verb; "pear" is a noun. Therefore, the correct choice should be a homonym of "berry" and a verb since "berry" is a noun. The only choice that fits both aspects is "bury."

2. Usually the incorrect options seem plausible–*choose carefully!*

3. If you can't find the relationships, guess intelligently:

   A. Often an answer which introduces a third part of speech to the analogy is incorrect.

   B. Eliminate all the answers that you *know* are wrong. Choose from those that remain.

4. If you can't guess intelligently, guess anyway — do *not* leave out any answers in the S.A.T.

5. If the directions ask for the *best* choice, be careful. There may be more than one *correct* choice, but only *one* is *best*.

Three Important Don'ts

1. *Don't* look for relationships between the first (1) and fourth (4) terms, or between the second (2) and third (3) terms. This type of reasoning is faulty and does not solve the analogy problem:

   1 2 3 4

   DOG: PUPPY : : ______ : KITTEN

   (A) meow **(B)** canine **(C)** cat **(D)** kitty

   Notice how this faulty reasoning might lead you to pick **(D)** kitty or **(B)** canine, while the correct choice is **(C)** cat.

   The same faulty reasoning occurs when you try to find the relationship between the second (2) and third (3) terms:

   1 2 3 4

   COAT : WOOL : : DRESS :

   A) wool **(B)** cotton **(C)** cover **(D)** shirt

   Notice how through faulty reasoning you might choose **(A)** wool or **(C)** cover while **(B)** cotton is correct.

2. Don't use reverse sequence in your answer:

   DOG : COLLIE : : ______ : HUMAN BEING

   (A) homo sapiens **(B)** boy **(C)** species **(D)** mammal

   The relationship of the first pair is one of type of animal–dog–to a specific breed–collie. The order must be maintained. Type of animal–**(D)** mammal–to specific kind–human being. Don't reverse the order by choosing **(B)** boy, which would put specific kind first.

3. Don't expect the second pair of terms to always be of the same type, class or species as the first. However, the nature of the relationship must be the same.

   CALF : COW : : SAPLING : TREE

   The first pair refers to animals; the second to plants. Notice that each pair has a relationship of young to mature. A calf is a young cow; a sapling is a young tree.

   Now try the following samples before practicing on the review questions that follow.

In each of the following questions, a related pair of words or phrases is followed by five lettered pairs of words or phrases. Select the lettered pair that best expresses a relationship similar to that expressed in the original pair.

1. STRING : GUITAR :: **1.** Ⓐ Ⓑ ● Ⓓ Ⓔ

(A) key : piano
(B) harp : finger
(C) reed : oboe
(D) violin : case
(E) music : instrument

Analysis: The vibration of a guitar's strings produces music; the vibration of an oboe's reed produces music.

2. ARC : CIRCLE :: 2. Ⓐ Ⓑ Ⓒ Ⓓ Ⓔ

(A) number : count
(B) pie : slice
(C) segment : line
(D) fraction : percent
(E) algebra : geometry

Analysis: A segment is part of a line, as an arc is part of a circle, i.e., a part of a whole.

3. KICK : FOOTBALL :: 3. Ⓐ Ⓑ Ⓒ Ⓓ Ⓔ

(A) dust : rag
(B) mop : sweep
(C) flowers : pick
(D) wash : dishes
(E) bake : cook

Analysis: One kicks a football as one washes the dishes. Each shows action that is done to an object.

4. SILENCE : NOISE :: 4. Ⓐ Ⓑ Ⓒ Ⓓ Ⓔ

(A) quiet : peace
(B) talk : whisper
(C) baldness : hair
(D) sing : dance
(E) giggle : laugh

Analysis: Silence is the absence of noise; baldness is the absence of hair.

5. OBESE : OVERWEIGHT :: 5. Ⓐ Ⓑ Ⓒ Ⓓ Ⓔ

(A) run : race
(B) jump : skip
(C) hilarious : funny
(D) heavy : mighty
(E) big : large

Analysis: The first word in the matching analysis is an extreme. Notice that in choice *E* there are two synonyms with no difference in degree.

In each of the following questions, a related pair of words or phrases is followed by five lettered pairs of words or phrases. Select the lettered pair that best expresses a relationship similar to that expressed in the original pair.

1. ASKEW : STRAIGHT :: 1. Ⓐ Ⓑ Ⓒ Ⓓ Ⓔ

(A) smooth : soft
(B) rough : smooth
(C) tall : high
(D) rough : tough
(E) often : frequent

2. INCOHERENT : INCONSISTENT :: 2. Ⓐ Ⓑ Ⓒ Ⓓ Ⓔ

(A) male : man
(B) deserve : award
(C) train : track
(D) plant : seed
(E) understandable : logical

3. ARTHUR MILLER : GEORGE BERNARD SHAW :: 3. Ⓐ Ⓑ Ⓒ Ⓓ Ⓔ

(A) Gary Cooper : Robert Redford
(B) Saul Bellow : Charles Dickens
(C) Marc Chagall : Paul Cezanne
(D) Agnes DeMille : Isadora Duncan
(E) Isaac Newton : Albert Einstein

4. RAIN : DROP :: 4. Ⓐ Ⓑ Ⓒ Ⓓ Ⓔ

(A) milk : bucket
(B) ice : skid
(C) water : icicle
(D) snow : flake
(E) pudding : bowl

5. ARCHIPELAGO : ISLANDS :: 5. Ⓐ Ⓑ Ⓒ Ⓓ Ⓔ

(A) sand : beach
(B) sky : cloud
(C) mounds : rocks
(D) constellation : stars
(E) bakery : bread

6. ANTWERP : BELGIUM :: 6. Ⓐ Ⓑ Ⓒ Ⓓ Ⓔ

(A) Russia : Yugoslavia
(B) Italy : Sicily
(C) Lima : Peru
(D) New York : New York City
(E) England : Ireland

7. BLADE : SKATE :: 7. Ⓐ Ⓑ Ⓒ Ⓓ Ⓔ

(A) car : gas
(B) chair : leg
(C) table : knife
(D) wheel : bike
(E) bowl : soup

8. PHILOSOPHY : WISDOM :: 8. Ⓐ Ⓑ Ⓒ Ⓓ Ⓔ

(A) classics : Greece
(B) concert : music
(C) theology : minister
(D) psychology : mind
(E) earthly : temporal

9. **BARREL : VIAL ::**
(A) honey : milk
(B) shovel : hoe
(C) key : door
(D) pit : peach
(E) volume : monograph

9. Ⓐ Ⓑ Ⓒ Ⓓ Ⓔ

10. **BAT : TAB ::**
(A) fin : end
(B) but : tub
(C) and : also
(D) one : won
(E) success : joy

10. Ⓐ Ⓑ Ⓒ Ⓓ Ⓔ

11. **ARROW : ROCKET ::**
(A) bow : arrow
(B) Ford : car
(C) sand : glass
(D) bottle : container
(E) stagecoach : jet

11. Ⓐ Ⓑ Ⓒ Ⓓ Ⓔ

12. **IGLOO : ESKIMO ::**
(A) house : man
(B) tree : bark
(C) cabin : hunter
(D) tent : camping
(E) tepee : Indian

12. Ⓐ Ⓑ Ⓒ Ⓓ Ⓔ

13. **CUP : LIP ::**
(A) revenge : sadist
(B) inch : mile
(C) monocle : eye
(D) wood : carve
(E) chalk : write

13. Ⓐ Ⓑ Ⓒ Ⓓ Ⓔ

14. **CHURCH : STATE ::**
(A) confusion : adaptation
(B) priest : official
(C) time : minutes
(D) team : player
(E) breeze : sunshine

14. Ⓐ Ⓑ Ⓒ Ⓓ Ⓔ

15. **APPLE : PIE ::**
(A) dentist : teeth
(B) milk : cake
(C) sin : evil
(D) potato : salad
(E) eat : bread

15. Ⓐ Ⓑ Ⓒ Ⓓ Ⓔ

16. **BRITTLE : BREAK ::**
(A) glass : crack
(B) sharp : scratches
(C) tree : wind
(D) flexible : bend
(E) ice : melt

16. Ⓐ Ⓑ Ⓒ Ⓓ Ⓔ

17. **SATELLITE : ORBIT ::**
(A) projectile : trajectory
(B) protuberance : swell
(C) arrow : range
(D) bullet : barrel
(E) elevator : shaft

17. Ⓐ Ⓑ Ⓒ Ⓓ Ⓔ

18. **ALUMNI : ALUMNAE ::**
(A) girl : boy
(B) school : schools
(C) roosters : hens
(D) boredom : ennui
(E) mothers : fathers

18. Ⓐ Ⓑ Ⓒ Ⓓ Ⓔ

19. **SHEEP : FLOCK ::**
(A) deer : horses
(B) flowers : bunch
(C) group : crowd
(D) cows : herd
(E) eggs : dozen

19. Ⓐ Ⓑ Ⓒ Ⓓ Ⓔ

20. **BORROW : LEND ::**
(A) lengthen : abridge
(B) pretty : ugly
(C) in : out
(D) people : animal
(E) cat : dog

20. Ⓐ Ⓑ Ⓒ Ⓓ Ⓔ

21. **LAWYER : JUDGE ::**
(A) message : messenger
(B) capitalist : interest
(C) mother : daughter
(D) reporter : editor
(E) lieutenant : army

21. Ⓐ Ⓑ Ⓒ Ⓓ Ⓔ

22. **RAISIN : GRAPE ::**
(A) bread : toast
(B) orange : kumquat
(C) prune : plum
(D) apple : berry
(E) wash : hang

22. Ⓐ Ⓑ Ⓒ Ⓓ Ⓔ

23. **SADIST : MASOCHIST ::**
(A) citizen : people
(B) jailer : prisoner
(C) teacher : school
(D) alarm : warning
(E) governor : mayor

23. Ⓐ Ⓑ Ⓒ Ⓓ Ⓔ

24. **PLUTOCRACY : WEALTHY ::**
(A) democracy : vote
(B) theocracy : Bible
(C) residency : alien
(D) monarchy : king
(E) usury : money

24. Ⓐ Ⓑ Ⓒ Ⓓ Ⓔ

25. **BIOCHEMISTRY : SCIENCES ::**
(A) dance : theatre
(B) behavior : psychology
(C) philosophy : humanities
(D) handcuffs : criminology
(E) green : envy

25. Ⓐ Ⓑ Ⓒ Ⓓ Ⓔ

26. **STARVATION : FAMINE ::**
(A) energy : resistance
(B) ship : harbor
(C) dissect : join
(D) disease : epidemic
(E) surgeon : operation

26. Ⓐ Ⓑ Ⓒ Ⓓ Ⓔ

27. **ICHTHYOLOGIST : FISH ::**
(A) synthesis : essay
(B) scissors : hand
(C) ornithologist : bird
(D) introduction : index
(E) philologist : stamps

27. Ⓐ Ⓑ Ⓒ Ⓓ Ⓔ

28. **COURT : JUSTICE ::**
(A) camp : counselor
(B) hospital : health
(C) school : books
(D) palace : royal
(E) airport : hangar

28. Ⓐ Ⓑ Ⓒ Ⓓ Ⓔ

29. **RUNG : LADDER ::**
(A) notch : belt
(B) logs : cabin
(C) step : stairway
(D) bricks : concrete
(E) limbs : body

29. Ⓐ Ⓑ Ⓒ Ⓓ Ⓔ

30. **AFTERNOON : DUSK ::**
(A) spring : fall
(B) 2 P.M. : 5 P.M.
(C) Sunday : Friday
(D) light : dark
(E) sun : moon

30. Ⓐ Ⓑ Ⓒ Ⓓ Ⓔ

31. **REEF : LIGHTHOUSE ::**
(A) traffic : red light
(B) eyes : sleep
(C) speech : slander
(D) ships : commerce
(E) cane : limp

31. Ⓐ Ⓑ Ⓒ Ⓓ Ⓔ

32. **EXPLOSION : HINDENBURG ::**
(A) bridge : collapse
(B) election : president
(C) iceberg : Titanic
(D) lap : water
(E) union : labor

32. Ⓐ Ⓑ Ⓒ Ⓓ Ⓔ

33. **VIBRATION : SOUND ::**
(A) ring : bell
(B) staff : stick
(C) courage : strength
(D) dust : chalk
(E) gravity : pull

33. Ⓐ Ⓑ Ⓒ Ⓓ Ⓔ

34. **HYDROGEN : GAS ::**
(A) oxygen : breathe
(B) gold : jewelry
(C) mercury : liquid
(D) plant : grow
(E) steel : solid

34. Ⓐ Ⓑ Ⓒ Ⓓ Ⓔ

35. **BOMB : TARGET ::**
(A) aim : miss
(B) train : station
(C) brow : forehead
(D) ball : throw
(E) vest : suit

35. Ⓐ Ⓑ Ⓒ Ⓓ Ⓔ

36. **KINETIC : MOTION ::**
(A) piscatorial : fish
(B) tree : branch
(C) kernel : corn
(D) dog : bone
(E) snake : bite

36. Ⓐ Ⓑ Ⓒ Ⓓ Ⓔ

37. **GOURMAND : GOURMET ::**
(A) monster : scare
(B) response : answer
(C) gossip : raconteur
(D) fat : obese
(E) negligent : careless

37. Ⓐ Ⓑ Ⓒ Ⓓ Ⓔ

38. **DICHOTOMY : SCHISM ::**
(A) careful : remiss
(B) duty : obligation
(C) dissemble : feign
(D) cautious : injury
(E) cogent : task

38. Ⓐ Ⓑ Ⓒ Ⓓ Ⓔ

39. **ECUMENICAL : CHURCH ::**
(A) court : judge
(B) culinary : kitchen
(C) mechanic : tools
(D) smoke : factory
(E) sphinx : desert

39. Ⓐ Ⓑ Ⓒ Ⓓ Ⓔ

40. **ATOM : MOLECULE ::**
(A) toothpick : tooth
(B) ocean : lake
(C) bark : tree
(D) raspberry : apple
(E) star : galaxy

40. Ⓐ Ⓑ Ⓒ Ⓓ Ⓔ

41. **PAMPAS : ARGENTINA ::**
(A) hill : climb
(B) stalactite : cave
(C) steppes : Russia
(D) oil : Texas
(E) Alps : Switzerland

41. Ⓐ Ⓑ Ⓒ Ⓓ Ⓔ

42. **SPOTS : MEASLES ::**
(A) clamp : hold
(B) fire : flames
(C) dollar : penny
(D) trail : path
(E) swellings : mumps

42. Ⓐ Ⓑ Ⓒ Ⓓ Ⓔ

43. **NAIAD : SWIM ::**
(A) star : heavens
(B) fish : catch
(C) daughter : father
(D) nimrod : hunt
(E) life : pills

43. Ⓐ Ⓑ Ⓒ Ⓓ Ⓔ

44. **TRANSPARENT : TRANSLUCENT ::**
(A) warmth : heat
(B) blocked : opened
(C) transmigration : inertia
(D) passage : highway
(E) translucent : opaque

44. Ⓐ Ⓑ Ⓒ Ⓓ Ⓔ

45. **FEVER : INFECTION ::**
(A) height : weight
(B) one : many
(C) symbol : sign
(D) sorrow : death
(E) thunderhead : storm

45. Ⓐ Ⓑ Ⓒ Ⓓ Ⓔ

46. **BIBLIOPHILE : LIBRARY ::**
(A) dog : biscuit
(B) neutron : scientist
(C) philatelist : post office
(D) machinist : repair
(E) infant : adult

46. Ⓐ Ⓑ Ⓒ Ⓓ Ⓔ

47. **GALLEY : KITCHEN ::**
(A) fabric : yarn
(B) teeth : stomach
(C) ship : house
(D) box : package
(E) roof : walls

47. Ⓐ Ⓑ Ⓒ Ⓓ Ⓔ

48. **RETINA : EYE ::**
(A) wagon : car
(B) chair : leg
(C) sun : earth
(D) piston : engine
(E) spur : horse

48. Ⓐ Ⓑ Ⓒ Ⓓ Ⓔ

49. **BALLET : CHOREOGRAPHER ::**
(A) paper : ream
(B) people : elect
(C) pistol : trigger
(D) play : director
(E) dove : peace

49. Ⓐ Ⓑ Ⓒ Ⓓ Ⓔ

50. **ATHLETE : TRAINING ::**
(A) mercenary : money
(B) porpoise : sea
(C) student : studying
(D) child : parent
(E) adult : child

50. Ⓐ Ⓑ Ⓒ Ⓓ Ⓔ

Answers and Analysis

1. **(B)** Only *B* contains two opposites.

2. **(E)** If something is incoherent, it is usually inconsistent. If something is understandable, it is usually logical. Moreover, both sets of words are adjectives.

3. **(B)** Arthur Miller is a contemporary playwright. George Bernard Shaw is not contemporary. Saul Bellow is a contemporary novelist. Charles Dickens is not contemporary. All four are writers.

4. **(D)** Rain falls in drops; snow falls in flakes.

5. **(D)** An archipelago is a group of islands. A constellation is a group of stars.

6. **(C)** Antwerp is a city in Belgium. Lima is a city in Peru. Both Belgium and Peru are countries.

7. **(D)** A blade on a skate touches the ground. A wheel on a bike touches the ground.

8. **(D)** Philosophy is concerned with wisdom as psychology is concerned with the mind.

9. **(E)** A barrel is a large container; a vial is a small one. A volume is a lengthy written work; a monograph is a short written work.

10. **(B)** *Tab* is *bat* backwards; *tub* is *but* backwards.

11. **(E)** A rocket is a modern projectile; a jet is a modern means of transportation.

12. **(E)** An igloo is the precise name for an Eskimo house just as tepee is for an Indian house. Notice that (A) is too general.

13. **(C)** A cup is put to the lip as a monocle is put to the eye.

14. **(B)** The head of a church is a priest; the head of a state is an official.

15. **(D)** Apples are made into pie; potatoes are made into salad. Also both pairs are commonly found together—apple pie and potato salad.

16. **(D)** When something is brittle it breaks; when it is flexible it bends. In (B), a sharp object scratches something else.

17. **(A)** A satellite travels along an orbit while any projectile travels along a trajectory.

18. (C) Alumni are male graduates and alumnae are female graduates. *Roosters* is also male and plural; *hens* is female and plural.

19. **(D)** Sheep travel in a flock as cows travel in a herd.

20. **(A)** The opposite of borrow is lend; the opposite of lengthen is abridge. These words are verbs.

21. **(D)** A lawyer becomes a judge as a reporter becomes an editor.

22. **(C)** A raisin is a dried grape. A prune is a dried plum.

23. **(B)** A sadist is the opposite of a masochist. A jailer is the opposite of a prisoner. All four are nouns.

24. **(D)** A plutocracy is government by the wealthy. A monarchy is government by a king.

25. **(C)** Biochemistry is part of the sciences as philosophy is part of the humanities.

26. **(D)** Starvation is associated with a famine as disease is associated with an epidemic.

27. **(C)** An ichthyologist studies fish as an ornithologist studies birds.

28. **(B)** One seeks justice in court and health in a hospital.

29. **(C)** A rung is part of a ladder as step is part of a stairway. They are both used to go up and down.

30. **(B)** Afternoon is to dusk as 2 P.M. is to 5 P.M. 2 P.M. is usually afternoon; 5 P.M. is usually dusk.

31. **(A)** A sailor is warned of a reef by a lighthouse. A pedestrian is warned of traffic by a red light.

32. **(C)** An explosion destroyed the Hindenburg. An iceberg destroyed the Titanic.

33. **(E)** Vibrations cause sound. Gravity causes a pull.

34. **(C)** Hydrogen is a gas as mercury is a liquid. Both hydrogen and mercury are elements. In (E) steel is not an element.

35. **(B)** A bomb travels to a target as a train travels to a station.

36. **(A)** *Kinetic* is associated with motion as *piscatorial* is with fish.

37. **(C)** A sophisticated, knowledgeable gourmand is a gourmet. In the same way, a gossip can become a raconteur.

38. **(C)** Synonyms are needed as the answer.

39. **(B)** *Ecumenical* refers to the church as *culinary* refers to the kitchen.

40. **(E)** An atom is part of a molecule. A star is part of a galaxy.

41. **(C)** Pampas are the plains of Argentina. The steppes are the plains of Russia.

42. (E) One of the symptoms of measles is spots. One of the symptoms of mumps is swellings.

43. **(D)** A naiad is a swimmer. A nimrod is a hunter.

44. **(E)** Each of these adjectives refers to a smaller and smaller amount of light passing through an object.

45. **(E)** A fever is a sign of infection. A thunderhead is a sign of a storm.

46. **(C)** A bibliophile, one who loves books, will spend time in the library. A philatelist, one who collects stamps, will spend time in the post office.

47. **(C)** A galley is a kitchen, but on a ship, not in a house.

48. **(D)** The retina helps the eye function. A piston helps an engine work.

49. **(D)** A choreographer directs a ballet as a director directs a play.

50. **(C)** An athlete needs training to succeed. A student needs studying to succeed.

8.

Posttest

The format of this posttest is similar to the pretest you took at the beginning of this book. The purpose of this examination is to evaluate your progress. It is important for you to use the review sections presented in the book, and to practice on the sample questions in each chapter. Essentially, you should now be prepared to take the Scholastic Aptitude Test and obtain higher scores.

If you still find weaknesses after taking this test, you should refer to a textbook or consult with your teachers.

Work on this examination as if it were the real thing. Answer every question, and work steadily. Good luck!

SECTION ONE: MATHEMATICS

Directions: In this section solve each problem, using any available space on the page for scratchwork. Then indicate the *best* answer by blackening the corresponding space on the answer grid. *Note:* Figures that accompany problems in this test are intended to provide information useful in solving the problems. They are drawn as accurately as possible EXCEPT when it is stated in a specific problem that its figure is not drawn to scale. All figures lie in a plane unless otherwise indicated. All numbers used are real numbers.

1. The product of $\frac{2}{3}$ and its reciprocal is: 1. Ⓐ Ⓑ Ⓒ Ⓓ Ⓔ

   (A) 1 (B) $\frac{4}{9}$ (C) 0 (D) -1 (E) $\frac{9}{4}$

2. How many integers greater than 100 can be formed from the digits 0, 2, and 3 if no digit is repeated in any number? 2. Ⓐ Ⓑ Ⓒ Ⓓ Ⓔ

   (A) 12 (B) 30 (C) 18 (D) 4 (E) 8

3. If the length of a square is doubled, then: 3. Ⓐ Ⓑ Ⓒ Ⓓ Ⓔ
   (A) The perimeter and area are both doubled.
   (B) The perimeter and the area are each multiplied by 4.
   (C) The area is multiplied by 4 and the perimeter is doubled.
   (D) The perimeter is multiplied by 4 and the area is doubled.
   (E) None of the above.

4. The average of A, B, C, and D is: 4. Ⓐ Ⓑ Ⓒ Ⓓ Ⓔ

   (A) $A + B + C + \frac{D}{4}$ (B) $\frac{A + B + C + D}{4}$ (C) $\frac{4A + 4B + 4C + 4D}{4}$

   (D) $4(A + B + C + D)$ (E) $\frac{ABCD}{4}$

5. Express the fraction $\frac{N^2 + N - 6}{2N + 6}$ in lowest terms: 5. Ⓐ Ⓑ Ⓒ Ⓓ Ⓔ

   (A) $\frac{N-1}{N}$ (B) $\frac{N-2}{2}$ (C) $\frac{N+2}{2}$ (D) $\frac{N}{2}$ (E) $\frac{N}{2} + N - 6$

6. A merchant buys 285 suits at $30.47 per suit. The approximate cost of these suits to the merchant is: 6. Ⓐ Ⓑ Ⓒ Ⓓ Ⓔ

   (A) $870 (B) $8700 (C) $87,000 (D) $87 (E) $870,000

7. How many different paths can one take to go from N to F (without reversing one's steps)? 7. Ⓐ Ⓑ Ⓒ Ⓓ Ⓔ

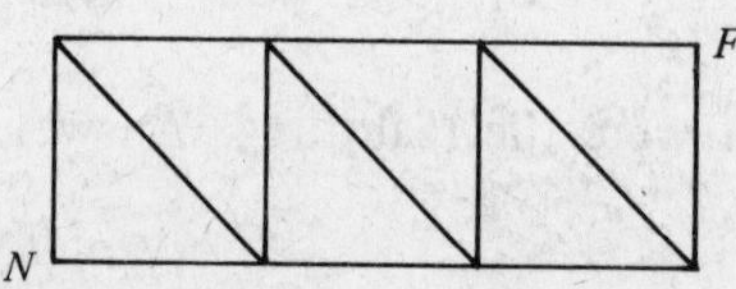

   (A) 15 (B) 28 (C) 13 (D) 21 (E) 45

8. A freight train and a passenger train leave at the same time from the same station and travel in opposite directions. The average rate of the passenger train is 55 miles per hour and that of the freight train is 45 miles per hour. At the end of 3 hours, how many miles are they from each other? 8. Ⓐ Ⓑ Ⓒ Ⓓ Ⓔ

   (A) 250 (B) 150 (C) 200 (D) 100 (E) 300

9. A salesperson had a piece of fabric 16 yards long. She sold the following amounts: $5\frac{1}{4}$ yards, $7\frac{3}{4}$ yards, and $2\frac{1}{3}$ yards. What was left from the original piece? 9. Ⓐ Ⓑ Ⓒ Ⓓ Ⓔ

   (A) $\frac{3}{4}$ yd (B) $3\frac{2}{3}$ yd (C) $\frac{2}{3}$ yd (D) $2\frac{1}{3}$ yd (E) $1\frac{1}{3}$ yd

10. Radius $OA = 3$. Calculate the area of the shaded region. **10.** Ⓐ Ⓑ Ⓒ Ⓓ Ⓔ

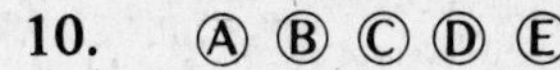

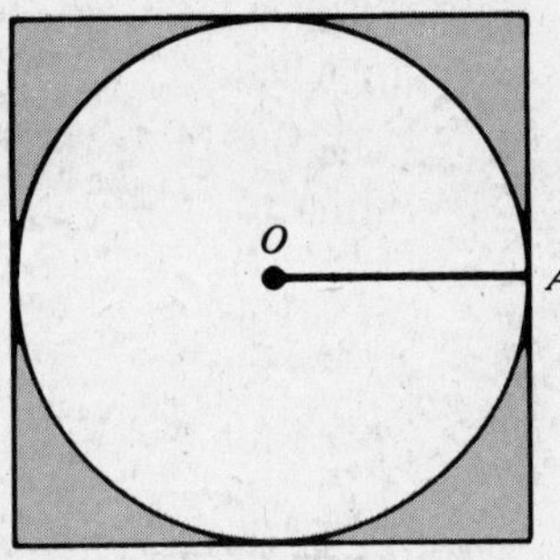

(A) 9 **(B)** $36 - 36\pi$ **(C)** 36π **(D)** $36 - 9\pi$ **(E)** 9π

Use the accompanying graph for questions **11** and **12**.

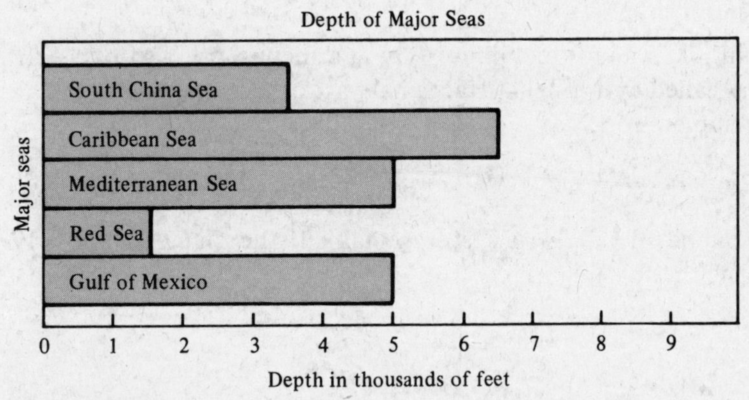

11. What is the approximate ratio of the depth of the South China Sea to the depth of the Red Sea? **11.** Ⓐ Ⓑ Ⓒ Ⓓ Ⓔ
(A) 7:10 **(B)** 3:1 **(C)** 7:3 **(D)** 7:5 **(E)** 1:3

12. Approximately, what is the depth of the Caribbean Sea? **12.** Ⓐ Ⓑ Ⓒ Ⓓ Ⓔ
(A) 6.5 **(B)** 65 **(C)** 650 **(D)** 6500 **(E)** 65,000

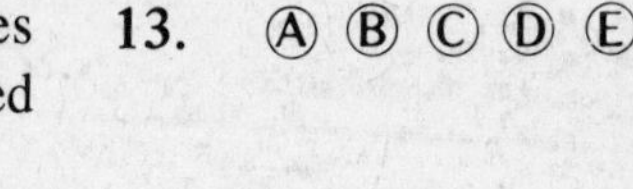

13. The larger rectangle has been divided into a square and three rectangles with areas K^2, $8K$, and $4K$. What is the numerical value of the shaded rectangle? **13.** Ⓐ Ⓑ Ⓒ Ⓓ Ⓔ

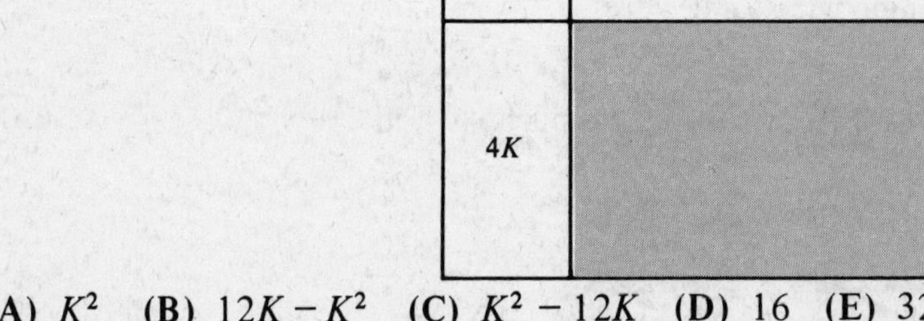

(A) K^2 **(B)** $12K - K^2$ **(C)** $K^2 - 12K$ **(D)** 16 **(E)** 32

14. In triangle ABC, line DE is parallel to AC. Find the length of DE. **14.** 

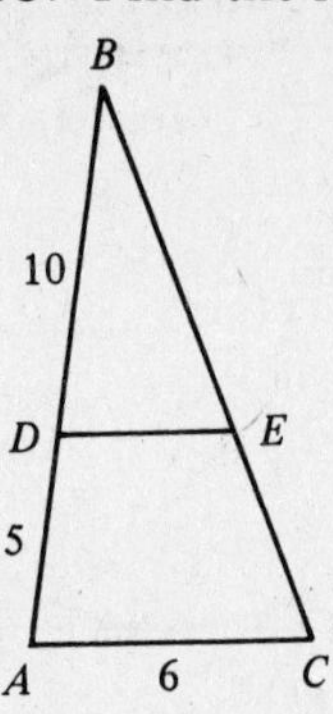

(A) 10 **(B)** 5 **(C)** 15 **(D)** 6 **(E)** 4

15. The sum of three consecutive integers is 33. Find the largest integer. **15.** Ⓐ Ⓑ Ⓒ Ⓓ Ⓔ

(A) −10 **(B)** 10 **(C)** −11 **(D)** 11 **(E)** 12

16. It takes Ms. Smith Y hours to complete typing a manuscript. After 2 hours, she was called away. What fractional part of the assignment was left to be completed? **16.** Ⓐ Ⓑ Ⓒ Ⓓ Ⓔ

(A) $\frac{2-Y}{Y}$ **(B)** $\frac{Y}{2}$ **(C)** $Y-2$ **(D)** $\frac{Y-2}{2}$ **(E)** $\frac{Y-2}{Y}$

17. Calculate the volume of a spherical storage tank if the diameter is 2.4 feet long using the formula **17.** Ⓐ Ⓑ Ⓒ Ⓓ Ⓔ

$$\text{volume} = \frac{4}{3}\pi r^3 \qquad \left(\pi = \frac{22}{7}\right)$$

(A) 3.6 cu ft **(B)** 7.2 cu ft **(C)** 3.4 cu ft **(D)** 8.3 cu ft
(E) 9.7 cu ft

18. How long is chord AB of circle O? **18.** Ⓐ Ⓑ Ⓒ Ⓓ Ⓔ

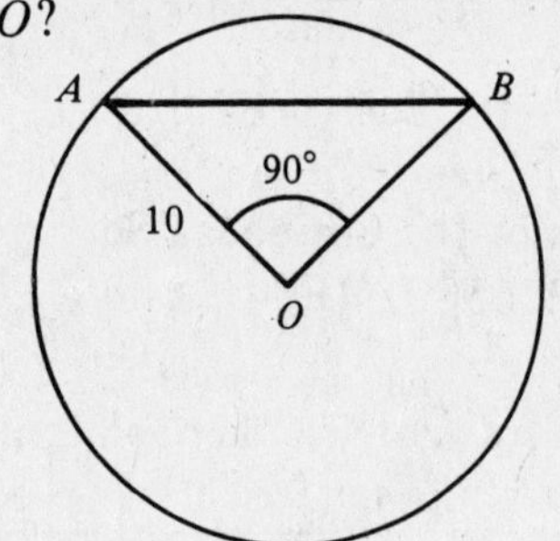

(A) $2\sqrt{10}$ **(B)** $10\sqrt{2}$ **(C)** 100 **(D)** 10 **(E)** $2\sqrt{50}$

19. It is impossible to construct a triangle whose sides are: **19.** Ⓐ Ⓑ Ⓒ Ⓓ Ⓔ

(A) 7, 7, 16 **(B)** 5, 7, 12 **(C)** 4, 8, 13 **(D)** 5, 6, 10 **(E)** 5, 5, 10

20. In triangle ABC, altitude CD divides angle C into two parts, X and Y. **20.** Ⓐ Ⓑ Ⓒ Ⓓ Ⓔ

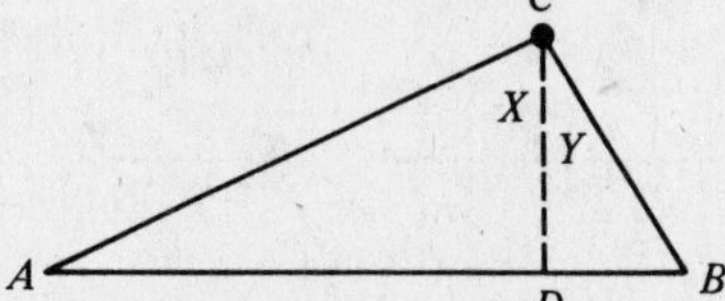

Then:
(A) $\measuredangle X + \measuredangle Y = \measuredangle A + \measuredangle B$
(B) $\measuredangle X - \measuredangle Y = \measuredangle A - \measuredangle B$
(C) $\measuredangle X + \measuredangle A = \measuredangle Y + \measuredangle B$
(D) $\measuredangle X + \measuredangle B = \measuredangle Y + \measuredangle A$
(E) $\measuredangle X + \measuredangle A = \measuredangle Y + \measuredangle B$

21. If the fractions $\frac{x+y}{3}$ and $\frac{x-y}{4}$ are combined, the result is: 21. Ⓐ Ⓑ Ⓒ Ⓓ Ⓔ

(A) $\frac{7x+y}{12}$ (B) $\frac{2x}{7}$ (C) $\frac{7x-y}{12}$ (D) $\frac{5x+4y}{12}$ (E) $\frac{x^2-y^2}{7}$

22. Find the coordinates of point D. 22. Ⓐ Ⓑ Ⓒ Ⓓ Ⓔ

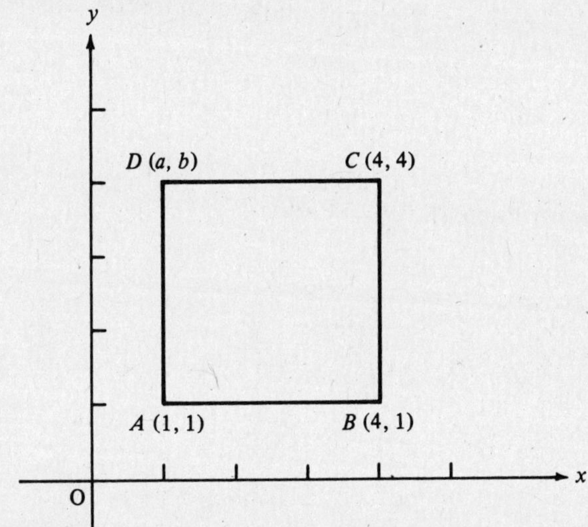

(A) (1, 4) (B) (4, 1) (C) (4, 4) (D) (1, 1) (E) (1, 3)

23. When $\frac{x^2-9}{x}$ is divided by $\frac{x-3}{5x}$, the quotient is: 23. Ⓐ Ⓑ Ⓒ Ⓓ Ⓔ

(A) $\frac{(x-3)^2(x+3)}{5x^2}$ (B) $5x(x+3)$ (C) $5(x+3)$ (D) $5(x-3)$

(E) $\frac{5x}{x-3}$

24. The solution set of the inequality $3x - 4 > 8$ is: 24. Ⓐ Ⓑ Ⓒ Ⓓ Ⓔ
(A) $x > 4$ (B) $x < 4$ (C) $x \geqslant 4$ (D) $x = 4$ (E) $x = -4$

25. In rectangle $ABCD$, E is the midpoint of AB and F is the midpoint of AD. What is the length of BD? 25. Ⓐ Ⓑ Ⓒ Ⓓ Ⓔ

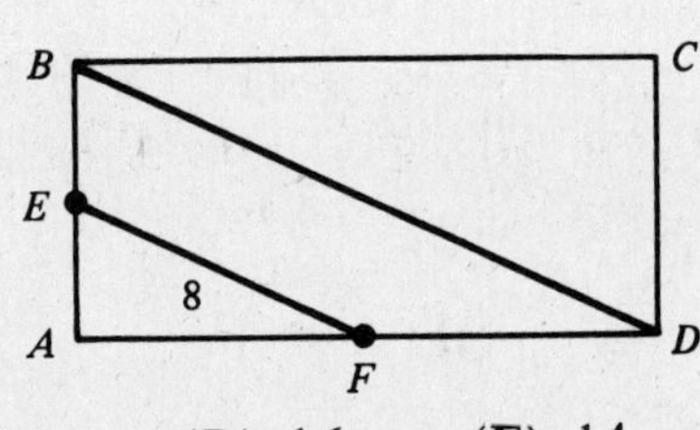

(A) 8 (B) 10 (C) 12 (D) 16 (E) 14

SECTION TWO: VERBAL

Antonyms

Each question that follows consists of a word printed in capital letters, followed by five words or phrases lettered A through E. Choose the lettered word or phrase that is most nearly *opposite* in meaning to the word in capital letters. Since some of the questions require you to distinguish fine shades of meaning, be sure to consider all the choices before deciding which one is best.

1. **INDUBITABLE** 1. Ⓐ Ⓑ Ⓒ Ⓓ Ⓔ
(A) putative (B) doubtful (C) trenchant (D) repine
(E) lampoon

2. **UNGAINLY** 2. Ⓐ Ⓑ Ⓒ Ⓓ Ⓔ
(A) livid (B) indiscriminate (C) tacky (D) dexterous
(E) garble

3. **ENNUI** 3. Ⓐ Ⓑ Ⓒ Ⓓ Ⓔ
(A) ken (B) noisome (C) vigor (D) preclude
(E) languish

4. **SUBJOIN** 4. Ⓐ Ⓑ Ⓒ Ⓓ Ⓔ
(A) impeach (B) grimace (C) detach (D) diffidence
(E) turpor

5. **CAPRICIOUS** 5. Ⓐ Ⓑ Ⓒ Ⓓ Ⓔ
(A) steadfast (B) peaceful (C) conceptual (D) disposed
(E) arrogance

6. **EXPIATE** 6. Ⓐ Ⓑ Ⓒ Ⓓ Ⓔ
(A) divest (B) pardon (C) punish (D) infer
(E) calculate

7. **CAPTIOUS** 7. Ⓐ Ⓑ Ⓒ Ⓓ Ⓔ
(A) blunt (B) laudatory (C) mediate (D) cheating
(E) absolute

8. **LASSITUDE** 8. Ⓐ Ⓑ Ⓒ Ⓓ Ⓔ
(A) energy (B) practical (C) acumen (D) ethical
(E) forgiveness

9. **IMPUTE** 9. Ⓐ Ⓑ Ⓒ Ⓓ Ⓔ
(A) refute (B) elevate (C) love (D) comfort (E) change

10. **WINSOME** 10. Ⓐ Ⓑ Ⓒ Ⓓ Ⓔ
(A) sincere (B) rebuilt (C) ugly (D) factious
(E) graceful

Sentence Completions

Each of the sentences that follow has one or more blank spaces, each blank indicating that a word has been omitted. Following the sentence are five lettered words or sets of words. You are to choose the one word or set of words that, when inserted in the sentence, *best* fits in with the meaning of the sentence as a whole.

11. Man's .... is responsible for many .... acts. 11. Ⓐ Ⓑ Ⓒ Ⓓ Ⓔ
(A) cupidity .... rapacious
(B) recalcitrance .... circumscribed
(C) monogamy .... anachronistic
(D) cupidity .... obstreperous
(E) antipathy .... rapacious

12. The .... may also become a .... 12. Ⓐ Ⓑ Ⓒ Ⓓ Ⓔ
(A) dynasty .... jetty
(B) sybarite .... connoisseur
(C) corona .... cult
(D) miscreant .... ghoul
(E) etude .... fiord

13. His .... analysis showed great .... 13. Ⓐ Ⓑ Ⓒ Ⓓ Ⓔ
(A) bovine .... casuistry
(B) docile .... turbulence
(C) prolix .... adulation
(D) endogenous .... conniving
(E) erudite .... acumen

14. His .... statements are too ridiculous to be taken .... 14. Ⓐ Ⓑ Ⓒ Ⓓ Ⓔ
(A) saturnine .... rabidly
(B) recalcitrant .... synonymously
(C) trenchant .... preposterously
(D) craven .... elatedly
(E) puerile .... seriously

15. The .... girl won the .... of all. 15. Ⓐ Ⓑ Ⓒ Ⓓ Ⓔ
(A) titled .... emissary
(B) scintillating .... attention
(C) beauteous .... erudition
(D) epigrammatic .... vanguard
(E) crass .... tranquility

16. The . . . . around the moon was an . . . . sign.
(A) parody .... audacious
(B) oblation .... impalpable
(C) hiatus .... onerous
(D) corona .... auspicious
(E) dregs .... organic

16. Ⓐ Ⓑ Ⓒ Ⓓ Ⓔ

17. Her poetry was . . . . and . . . .
(A) maudlin .... surreptitious
(B) pectoral .... mnemonic
(C) platonic .... rote
(D) recondite .... transitory
(E) banal .... bland

17. Ⓐ Ⓑ Ⓒ Ⓓ Ⓔ

18. A . . . . is used to show something is missing in a line of print.
(A) pogrom
(B) tableau
(C) trachea
(D) reproof
(E) caret

18. Ⓐ Ⓑ Ⓒ Ⓓ Ⓔ

19. The . . . . troop appeared over the . . . .
(A) equestrian .... butte
(B) albino .... heyday
(C) exorbitant .... pendant
(D) diabolic .... ventricle
(E) incendiary .... rhesus

19. Ⓐ Ⓑ Ⓒ Ⓓ Ⓔ

20. The . . . . hopes to gain much by . . . .
(A) presbyter .... oligarchy
(B) apostle .... recrimination
(C) licentiate .... query
(D) sycophant .... flattery
(E) sagacious .... transmutation

20. Ⓐ Ⓑ Ⓒ Ⓓ Ⓔ

Reading Comprehension

Each passage in this group is followed by questions based on its content. After reading a passage, choose the best answer to each question and blacken the corresponding space on the answer grid. Answer all questions following a passage on the basis of what is *stated* or *implied* in that passage.

Passage One

If I am right it will be a slow business for our people to reach rational views, assuming that we are allowed to work peaceably to that end. But as I grow older I grow calm. If I feel what are perhaps an old man's apprehensions, that competition from new races will cut deeper than working men's disputes and

will test whether we can hang together and can fight; if I fear that we are running through the world's resources at a pace that we cannot keep; I do not lose my hopes. I do not pin my dreams for the future to my country or even to my race. I think it probable that civilization somehow will last as long as I care to look ahead—perhaps with smaller numbers, but perhaps also bred to greatness and splendor by science. I think it not improbable that man, like the grub that prepares a chamber for the winged thing it never has seen but is to be—that man may have cosmic destinies that he does not understand. And so beyond the vision of battling races and an impoverished earth I catch a dreaming glimpse of peace.

The other day my dream was pictured to my mind. It was evening. I was walking homeward on Pennsylvania Avenue near the Treasury, and as I looked beyond Sherman's statue to the west the sky was aflame with scarlet and crimson from the setting sun. But, like the note of downfall in Wagner's opera, below the sky line there came from little globes the pallid discord of the electric lights. And I thought to myself the *Götterdämmerung* will end, and from those globes clustered like evil eggs will come the new masters of the sky. It is like the time in which we live. But then I remembered the faith that I partly have expressed, faith in a universe not measured by our fears, a universe that has thought and more than thought inside of it, and as I gazed, after the sunset and above the electric lights, there shone the stars.

21. Which of the following statements best sums up the author's attitude or general outlook? 21. Ⓐ Ⓑ Ⓒ Ⓓ Ⓔ

(A) he remains calm because he is an old man and will not see what is to come
(B) he continues, despite his age, to nurse the fears and resentments of his youth
(C) he is afraid that invasions by other races will lead to the downfall of our society
(D) he is reassured by his faith in a universe that is beyond even the greatest measurements of man
(E) he is actually indifferent to the future; he merely hopes that future generations will be able to handle their problems

22. Which of the following conclusions can *not* be drawn from the selection? 22. Ⓐ Ⓑ Ⓒ Ⓓ Ⓔ

(A) man will go on in increasing numbers and with greater stature until the end of time
(B) civilization will continue in numbers on a somewhat lesser scale
(C) science will enable civilization to become great and splendid
(D) the author reveals considerable faith in the powers of science
(E) the author is generally optimistic about the future

23. There is a feeling expressed by the author that the severest competition to our society will come from 23. Ⓐ Ⓑ Ⓒ Ⓓ Ⓔ

(A) the class struggle
(B) other political ideologies
(C) new races
(D) contradictions within our society itself
(E) other worlds

24. One may assume that the author lived in 24. Ⓐ Ⓑ Ⓒ Ⓓ Ⓔ
A. New York City
B. Los Angeles
C. the state of Washington
D. Washington, D. C.
E. London

25. The author's hopes for the future are not specifically limited to 25. Ⓐ Ⓑ Ⓒ Ⓓ Ⓔ
A. the human race
B. his own country and race
C. science and man
D. faith in the future
E. incomprehensible cosmic destinies

Passage Two

While carbohydrates, fats and proteins make up more than 90% of our diets, we cannot live without the tiny quantities of other nutrients. Vitamins and minerals are needed in quantities as small as millionths of a pound daily.

For many years, vitamins were known because of the diseases their deficiency caused. Now more is known about why such tiny quantities affect the body so profoundly.

The need for calcium to maintain healthy bones is only one of its important functions. The movement of calcium into and out of cells is vital to many cells, including muscles. It triggers the function of these cells. Sodium ions move in and out of the bloodstream and bathe the cells in a liquid that maintains osmotic pressure. The water balance of the body is maintained with the help of these ions.

We eat foods in quantities, measured by pounds, to produce and maintain trillions of cells in the body. But we must have that tiny quantity of Vitamin C to help hold the cells in tissues together. Capillary cells will disintegrate without Vitamin C.

Vitamin B_{12}, the blood cell vitamin, is one of the most powerful of the nutrients in its effect per molecule. The daily need for most vitamins and minerals is measured in thousandths of a gram (milligrams). Look at your vitamin bottle. Vitamin B_{12} is measured in mcg., which represents millionths of a gram (micrograms).

Because so many of our foods are processed, many people take supplementary vitamin pills to insure their intake of sufficient quantities of vitamins and minerals.

26. The main idea of this passage is that 26. Ⓐ Ⓑ Ⓒ Ⓓ Ⓔ
(A) people should eat balanced diets
(B) people should be sure of getting enough vitamins and minerals
(C) vitamins are needed for healthy capillaries
(D) we cannot be healthy without calcium
(E) water balance requires salt in the diet

27. About how many times as great is the effect, per molecule, of Vitamin B_{12} when compared to other vitamins? 27. Ⓐ Ⓑ Ⓒ Ⓓ Ⓔ
(A) 10 times
(B) 100 times
(C) 200 times
(D) 1000 times
(E) 100,000 times

28. Vitamins and minerals produce their effects 28. Ⓐ Ⓑ Ⓒ Ⓓ Ⓔ

I. outside of cells
II. inside of cells
III. only inside of cells

(A) I only
(B) II only
(C) III only
(D) I and II only
(E) I and III only

29. According to the passage, which materials are needed in greatest quantities for nourishment, growth, and repair of muscle cells? 29. Ⓐ Ⓑ Ⓒ Ⓓ Ⓔ

(A) carbohydrates
(B) fats
(C) proteins
(D) (A), (B) and (C)
(E) calcium

30. According to the passage, it may be inferred that processed foods 30. Ⓐ Ⓑ Ⓒ Ⓓ Ⓔ

(A) are better because they are pure
(B) are better because vitamins are added
(C) are inferior because chemicals are added
(D) are better because harmful ingredients are carefully removed
(E) may be inferior because vitamins and minerals have been removed

Analogies

In each of the following questions, a related pair of words or phrases is followed by five lettered pairs of words or phrases. Select the lettered pair that best expresses a relationship similar to that expressed in the original pair.

31. **BACCHUS : DRINK ::** 31. Ⓐ Ⓑ Ⓒ Ⓓ Ⓔ
(A) Orpheus : Eurydice
(B) Amazon : ruler
(C) Diana : hunt
(D) Zeus : Olympus
(E) Plato : Aristotle

32. **PRESIDENT : NATION ::** 32. Ⓐ Ⓑ Ⓒ Ⓓ Ⓔ
(A) snake : bite
(B) frog : swim
(C) mayor : city
(D) student : college
(E) land : man

33. **TEPID : BOILING ::** 33. Ⓐ Ⓑ Ⓒ Ⓓ Ⓔ
    (A) car : tire
    (B) fast : long
    (C) charcoal : flame
    (D) cool : freezing
    (E) light : dark

34. **FRICTION : WAR ::** 34. Ⓐ Ⓑ Ⓒ Ⓓ Ⓔ
    (A) pleasure : enjoyment
    (B) prologue : play
    (C) water : reservoir
    (D) discontent : strike
    (E) teacher : grammar

35. **DEPRESSION : SUICIDE ::** 35. Ⓐ Ⓑ Ⓒ Ⓓ Ⓔ
    (A) crime : prison
    (B) emulate : mimic
    (C) paranoia : delusions
    (D) express : imply
    (E) complain : condemn

36. **CATERPILLAR : BUTTERFLY ::** 36. Ⓐ Ⓑ Ⓒ Ⓓ Ⓔ
    (A) star : flag
    (B) face : head
    (C) mountain : field
    (D) tadpole : frog
    (E) animal : fur

37. **NORTH AMERICA : CANADA ::** 37. Ⓐ Ⓑ Ⓒ Ⓓ Ⓔ
    (A) land : lake
    (B) valley : hill
    (C) wolf : dog
    (D) Europe : France
    (E) New York : Rochester

38. **RUSTIC : URBAN ::** 38. Ⓐ Ⓑ Ⓒ Ⓓ Ⓔ
    (A) surround : ring
    (B) dry : wet
    (C) sink : float
    (D) country : city
    (E) river : stream

39. **PEDIATRICS : GERIATRICS ::** 39. Ⓐ Ⓑ Ⓒ Ⓓ Ⓔ
    (A) sociology : anthropology
    (B) medicine : law
    (C) history : biology
    (D) obstetrics : thanatology
    (E) geology : chemistry

40. **BOOKKEEPER : ACCOUNTANT ::** 40. Ⓐ Ⓑ Ⓒ Ⓓ Ⓔ
(A) player : coach
(B) farmer : cowboy
(C) senator : congressman
(D) typist : stenographer
(E) janitor : engineer

SECTION FOUR: VERBAL

Antonyms

Each question that follows consists of a word printed in capital letters, followed by five words or phrases lettered A through E. Choose the lettered word or phrase that is most nearly *opposite* in meaning to the word in capital letters. Since some of the questions require you to distinguish fine shades of meaning, be sure to consider all the choices before deciding which one is best.

1. **PROLIX** 1. ⒶⒷⒸⒹⒺ
(A) reject (B) nominate (C) unequal (D) alert (E) pithy

2. **PARITY** 2. ⒶⒷⒸⒹⒺ
(A) paralyze (B) bizarre (C) disproportion (D) intrigue
(E) ability

3. **BUCOLIC** 3. ⒶⒷⒸⒹⒺ
(A) remote (B) well-to-do (C) skittish (D) urban
(E) scheming

4. **CATACLYSM** 4. ⒶⒷⒸⒹⒺ
(A) grace (B) elegance (C) disharmony (D) appearance
(E) benefit

5. **PRIMORDIAL** 5. ⒶⒷⒸⒹⒺ
(A) recent (B) saucy (C) blithe (D) injurious
(E) insistent

6. **ONEROUS** 6. ⒶⒷⒸⒹⒺ
(A) straight (B) pleasant (C) alone (D) buxom
(E) miserable

7. **NEBULOUS** 7. ⒶⒷⒸⒹⒺ
(A) heavenly (B) precise (C) reckless (D) playful
(E) offering

8. **MUTATION** 8. ⒶⒷⒸⒹⒺ
(A) permanence (B) attempt (C) repair (D) anticipation
(E) tension

9. **CATEGORICAL** 9. ⒶⒷⒸⒹⒺ
(A) approval (B) deny (C) equivocal (D) camel
(E) terminal

10. **AGGLOMERATE:** **(A)** obdurate **(B)** deified **(C)** separate **(D)** mitigate **(E)** objection — 10. Ⓐ Ⓑ Ⓒ Ⓓ Ⓔ

11. **INVIDIOUS:** **(A)** offensive **(B)** minimal **(C)** medicinal **(D)** insidious **(E)** approved — 11. Ⓐ Ⓑ Ⓒ Ⓓ Ⓔ

12. **VENAL:** **(A)** ensnare **(B)** inveterate **(C)** permeable **(D)** ungainly **(E)** incorruptible — 12. Ⓐ Ⓑ Ⓒ Ⓓ Ⓔ

13. **REPREHENSION:** **(A)** approval **(B)** exigency **(C)** adjure **(D)** deleterious **(E)** casuistry — 13. Ⓐ Ⓑ Ⓒ Ⓓ Ⓔ

14. **EPITOME:** **(A)** convivial **(B)** affable **(C)** inveterate **(D)** enlargement **(E)** portend — 14. Ⓐ Ⓑ Ⓒ Ⓓ Ⓔ

15. **REPUDIATE:** **(A)** prefer **(B)** abstruse **(C)** variegate **(D)** abnegate **(E)** impute — 15. Ⓐ Ⓑ Ⓒ Ⓓ Ⓔ

Sentence Completions

Each of the sentences that follow has one or more blank spaces, each blank indicating that a word has been omitted. Following the sentence are five lettered words or sets of words. You are to choose the one word or set of words that, when inserted in the sentence, *best* fits in with the meaning of the sentence as a whole.

16. The king was both .... and .... which made him an effective ruler. — 16. Ⓐ Ⓑ Ⓒ Ⓓ Ⓔ
    (A) covetous .... malevolent
    (B) benign .... ascetic
    (C) puissant................. benign
    (D) austere.................. bucolic
    (E) chivalrous .... bovine

17. A............. man is mainly concerned with the............. aspects of life. — 17. Ⓐ Ⓑ Ⓒ Ⓓ Ⓔ
    (A) resilient .... moribund
    (B) specious................. fallow
    (C) taciturn .... secular
    (D) various.................. lascivious
    (E) parsimonious .... pecuniary

18. We certainly do not have a .... of energy sources; therefore we must .... what we have. — 18. Ⓐ Ⓑ Ⓒ Ⓓ Ⓔ
    (A) microcosm............... mitigate
    (B) plethora................. husband
    (C) gamut................... obfuscate
    (D) defection .... pervade
    (E) dearth................... libel

19. When giving directions it is best to be .... but .... 19. Ⓐ Ⓑ Ⓒ Ⓓ Ⓔ
(A) redundant .... trenchant
(B) droll .... esoteric
(C) definitive .... eclectic
(D) facetious .... baleful
(E) laconic .... accurate

20. The explanation was .... ; no one could understand it. 20. Ⓐ Ⓑ Ⓒ Ⓓ Ⓔ
(A) abstruse
(B) dissonant
(C) wanton
(D) flamboyant
(E) effete

21. The propellor plane is now .... 21. Ⓐ Ⓑ Ⓒ Ⓓ Ⓔ
(A) desultory
(B) covert
(C) ductile
(D) obsolete
(E) endemic

22. A .... and a .... work closely together. 22. Ⓐ Ⓑ Ⓒ Ⓓ Ⓔ
(A) crag .... crux
(B) duenna .... dryad
(C) bigamist .... atheist
(D) parole .... recluse
(E) terpsichorean .... choreographer

23. His .... made him extremely .... 23. Ⓐ Ⓑ Ⓒ Ⓓ Ⓔ
(A) sagacity .... coniferous
(B) conclave .... averse
(C) concupiscence .... salacious
(D) grimace .... flaccid
(E) corpulence .... fustian

24. During the long illness she showed great...................... 24. Ⓐ Ⓑ Ⓒ Ⓓ Ⓔ
(A) felicity
(B) fortitude
(C) hegemony
(D) palaver
(E) assault

25. Proper............... care often............... complications during birth. 25. Ⓐ Ⓑ Ⓒ Ⓓ Ⓔ
(A) overt.................. nurtures
(B) pastoral .... iterates
(C) prenatal .... precludes
(D) parietal .... proffers
(E) thoracic .... reviles

Reading Comprehension

Each passage in this group is followed by questions based on its content. After reading a passage, choose the best answer to each question and blacken the corresponding space on the answer grid. Answer all questions following a passage on the basis of what is *stated* or *implied* in that passage.

Passage One

There were many reasons why the whole character of the twentieth century should be very different from that of the nineteenth. The great wave of vitality and national expansion, which, during the Victorian period, swept both England and America to a high-water mark of national prosperity, left in its ebb a highly developed industrial civilization and a clear path for all the currents of scientific and mechanistic thought that were to flood the new century. However, literature, which had been nourished by the general vigor of the time but not at all by the practical interests of the period, declined as the spirit itself dispersed. Before the end of the century, that positive, homogeneous, energetic social culture that collaborated with the great Victorian writers had disintegrated. The literary coterie of the nineties already marked the arrival of an entirely new idea. Art had begun to be created for Art's sake. The great age of groups and "movements" began. The eighteenth-century poets did not call themselves classicists, nor did the nineteenth-century poets call themselves romanticists; their poetic coloring was simply the quality of their whole response to the whole of life. But the literary history of the late nineteenth and early twentieth centuries is full of theories and "isms"—Symbolism, Futurism, Imagism, Vorticism, Expressionism, Dadaism, Surrealism—which provided artistic creeds for various groups and set the individual artist apart from the community in the popular opinion.

26. Which of the following statements is a valid conclusion to draw from the implications of the author? 26. Ⓐ Ⓑ Ⓒ Ⓓ Ⓔ

(A) national vitality and expansionism have little or no impact on national prosperity and well-being
(B) the great sense of homogeneity that characterized Victorian England had no real effect on the work of the authors of the time
(C) literature is not always affected favorably by the practical interests and improvements of any particular area
(D) one aspect of the greatness of Victorian authors was that they were able to divorce themselves from the social currents of their age
(E) the effects of the Victorian era that were revealed in England were not duplicated in America

27. There is a general feeling in this selection that when artists are labeled and categorized 27. Ⓐ Ⓑ Ⓒ Ⓓ Ⓔ

(A) they develop a strong sense of identity
(B) they seem to lose contact with the community at large
(C) they are raised in importance within the social structure
(D) they know what is expected of them by their patrons
(E) life becomes easier for those artists who have not yet "arrived"

28. According to the selection, the terms *classicists* and *romantics* were applied to the poets of

28. Ⓐ Ⓑ Ⓒ Ⓓ Ⓔ

(A) the eighteenth and nineteenth centuries respectively
(B) the late nineteenth and early twentieth centuries respectively
(C) the Expressionist and Vorticist schools respectively
(D) the Greek period and the nineteenth century respectively
(E) almost any era

29. The statement "Art had begun to be created for Art's sake" implies

29. Ⓐ Ⓑ Ⓒ Ⓓ Ⓔ

(A) that Art is basically untrue and unreal for most people
(B) that there were malicious forces at work among the artists
(C) that Art is basically to be created for society
(D) that the author is critical of art and artists in general
(E) that there had been a steady movement of art toward Art

30. Which of the combined statements that follow seem to be borne out by the selection?

30. Ⓐ Ⓑ Ⓒ Ⓓ Ⓔ

(A) literary "isms" provide identity for the artist and give him a sense of purpose
(B) literary "isms" seem to be limited to relatively modern times, and they follow on the heels of great imperialist movements
(C) literary "isms" provide political creeds for groups and set the artist apart from the community
(D) literary "isms" provide artistic creeds for groups and set the artist apart from the community
(E) literary "isms" lead to artistic autonomy and individual irresponsibility

Passage Two

The intellect is usually defined as a separate human faculty in human beings—the ability to think about facts and ideas and to put them in order. The intellect is usually contrasted with the emotions, which are thought to distort facts and ideas, or contrasted with the imagination, which departs from facts.

As a result, it is often assumed that intellectuals are people who think, who have the facts and the ideas, and that the rest of society is composed of nonintellectuals and anti-intellectuals who don't. This is of course not the case, and it is possible to be an intellectual and not be intelligent, and to be a nonintellectual and think very well.

It is also assumed that there are basic differences between science and art, between scientists and artists; it is assumed that scientists are rational, objective, abstract, concerned with the intellect and with reducing everything to a formula, and that artists, on the other hand, are temperamental, subjective, irrational, and concerned with the expression of the emotions. But we all know temperamental, irrational, scientists and abstract, cold-blooded artists. We know, too, that there is a body of knowledge in art. There are as many facts and ideas in art as there are in any other field, and there are as many kinds of art as there are ideas—abstract or concrete, classical, romantic, organized, unorganized, expressionist, surrealist, intuitive, intellectual, sublime, ridiculous, boring, exciting, and dozens of others. The trouble lies in thinking about art the way most people think about the intellect. It is not what they think it is.

This would not be quite so serious a matter if it were not taken so seriously, especially by educators, and those who urge their views upon educators—that is, I suppose, the rest of mankind. If thinking is an activity which takes place in a separate faculty of the intellect, and if the aim of education is to teach people to think, it is therefore natural to assume that education should train the intellect through the academic disciplines. These disciplines are considered to be the subject-matter for intellectual training, and they consist of facts and ideas from the major fields of human knowledge, organized in such a way that the intellect can deal with them, that is to say, they are organized in abstract, conceptual, logical terms. It is assumed that learning to think is a matter of learning to recognize and understand these concepts. Educational programs in school and college are therefore arranged with this idea in mind, and when demands for the improvement of education are made, they usually consist in demands for more academic material to be covered and more academic discipline of this kind to be imposed. It is a call for more organization, not for more learning.

One of the most unfortunate results of this misunderstanding of the nature of the intellect is that the practice of the arts and the creative arts themselves are too often excluded from the regular curriculum of school and college or given such a minor role in the educational process that they are unable to make the intellectual contribution of which they are supremely capable.

31. The three aspects of man are — 31 Ⓐ Ⓑ Ⓒ Ⓓ Ⓔ
- **(A)** imagination, thinking, distorting
- **(B)** emotions, distorting, departing
- **(C)** intellect, facts, ideas
- **(D)** abilities, thinking, emotions
- **(E)** imagination, emotions, intellect

32. The author — 32. Ⓐ Ⓑ Ⓒ Ⓓ Ⓔ
- **(A)** agrees that artists and scientists are basically different
- **(B)** thinks that artists and scientists are *not* basically different
- **(C)** agrees with the way most people think about the intellect
- **(D)** feels all intellectuals are intelligent
- **(E)** feels all scientists are rational

33. The unfortunate result of the erroneous thinking about art and intellect is that 33. Ⓐ Ⓑ Ⓒ Ⓓ Ⓔ
- **(A)** the academic disciplines are less and less organized
- **(B)** intellectual training has lost its importance
- **(C)** art has broken down into many ideas
- **(D)** they are not taken seriously by educators
- **(E)** the practice of the creative arts is left out of the regular curriculum

34. The author says that 34. ⒶⒷⒸⒹⒺ
   (A) emotions distort facts; imagination departs from facts
   (B) artists are concerned with the expression of the emotions
   (C) it is impossible to be a temperamental, irrational scientist
   (D) it is impossible to be an abstract, cold-blooded artist
   (E) artists and scientists must unite

35. The author probably wants to 35. ⒶⒷⒸⒹⒺ
   (A) urge a change in curriculum
   (B) support the status quo
   (C) gain power for the scientist
   (D) return to an earlier type of education
   (E) provide education only for the intellectual

Analogies

In each of the following questions, a related pair of words or phrases is followed by five lettered pairs of words or phrases. Select the lettered pair that best expresses a relationship similar to that expressed in the original pair.

36. **ANGLE : DEGREE ::** 36. ⒶⒷⒸⒹⒺ
   (A) high : low
   (B) straight : crooked
   (C) line : inches
   (D) circle : square
   (E) ruler : protractor

37. **BLADE : GRASS ::** 37. ⒶⒷⒸⒹⒺ
   (A) air : gas
   (B) grain : sand
   (C) metal : rod
   (D) plant : leaves
   (E) roof : house

38. **TONE : DEAF ::** 38. ⒶⒷⒸⒹⒺ
   (A) arm : lift
   (B) touch : smell
   (C) paint : brush
   (D) sight : sound
   (E) color : blind

39. **RADIUS : DIAMETER ::** 39. ⒶⒷⒸⒹⒺ
   (A) 3 : 8
   (B) 4 : 6
   (C) 12 : 15
   (D) 5 : 10
   (E) 9 : 13

40. **OAK : ACORN ::**
(A) stable : barn
(B) tree : branch
(C) tulip : bulb
(D) library : book
(E) ruler : line

40. Ⓐ Ⓑ Ⓒ Ⓓ Ⓔ

41. **12½% : ⅛ ::**
(A) decade : century
(B) 100% : 1
(C) 6/10 : ½
(D) 66⅔% : ⅔
(E) second : minute

41. Ⓐ Ⓑ Ⓒ Ⓓ Ⓔ

42. **FUR : COAT ::**
(A) secrete : conceal
(B) cotton : nylon
(C) fly : swim
(D) silk : blouse
(E) kittens : cats

42. Ⓐ Ⓑ Ⓒ Ⓓ Ⓔ

43. **COTTON : POLYESTER ::**
(A) climate : cyclone
(B) disagreement : adaptation
(C) minutes : day
(D) wool : acrilan
(E) United States : North America

43. Ⓐ Ⓑ Ⓒ Ⓓ Ⓔ

44. **BACON : POUND ::**
(A) gun : lead
(B) dime : silver
(C) ceiling : chandelier
(D) eggs : dozen
(E) puppet show : puppet maker

44. Ⓐ Ⓑ Ⓒ Ⓓ Ⓔ

45. **HORN : BLOW ::**
(A) anarchy : democracy
(B) game : play
(C) reprove : denounce
(D) harp : pluck
(E) pocket : pants

45. Ⓐ Ⓑ Ⓒ Ⓓ Ⓔ

SECTION FIVE: MATHEMATICS

Part A

Directions: In this section solve each problem, using any available space on the page for scratchwork. Then indicate the *best* answer in the appropriate space on the answer grid.
Note: Figures that accompany problems in this test are intended to provide information useful in solving the problems. They are drawn as accurately as possible *except* when it is stated in a specific

problem that its figure is not drawn to scale. All figures lie in a plane unless otherwise indicated. All numbers used are real numbers.

1. How many 14.4 centimeter strips can be cut from a board 216 centimeters long? 1. Ⓐ Ⓑ Ⓒ Ⓓ Ⓔ

(A) 1.5 (B) 15 (C) 150

(D) 201.6 (E) none of these

2. Express as a trinomial: $(3a + 5)(2a - 3)$ 2. Ⓐ Ⓑ Ⓒ Ⓓ Ⓔ

(A) $5a^2 - 15$
(B) $6a^2 + 15$
(C) $6a^2 - 4a - 15$
(D) $6a^2 + a - 15$
(E) $6a^2 - a + 15$

3. Which expression represents the number of cents, c, that a customer received in change from a \$1 bill after buying n articles each costing 5 cents? 3. Ⓐ Ⓑ Ⓒ Ⓓ Ⓔ

(A) $c = 1 - 5n$ (B) $c = 100 - 5n$ (C) $c = 95n$

(D) $c = 100 - \frac{n}{5}$ (E) $c = 1 - \frac{n}{5}$

4. If $4x - 3 = 17$, then $x =$ 4. Ⓐ Ⓑ Ⓒ Ⓓ Ⓔ

(A) -5 (B) 5 (C) $-3\frac{1}{2}$

(D) $32\frac{1}{2}$ (E) none of these

5. Find 3 consecutive odd integers whose sum is -57. 5. Ⓐ Ⓑ Ⓒ Ⓓ Ⓔ

(A) 17, 19, 21 (B) 18, 19, 20 (C) $-18, -19, -20$

(D) $-18, -29$ (E) none of these

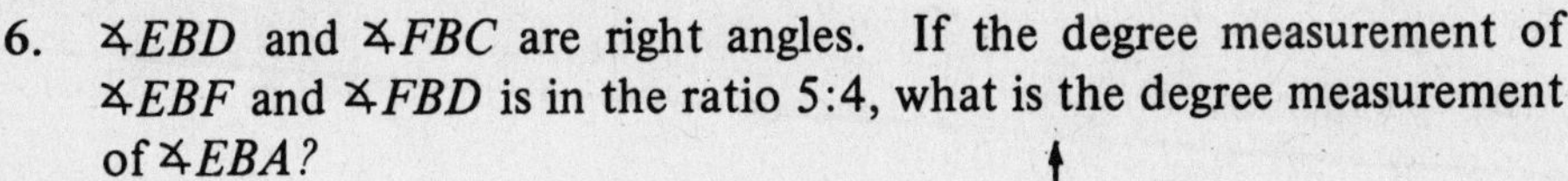

6. ∡EBD and ∡FBC are right angles. If the degree measurement of ∡EBF and ∡FBD is in the ratio 5:4, what is the degree measurement of ∡EBA?

6. Ⓐ Ⓑ Ⓒ Ⓓ Ⓔ

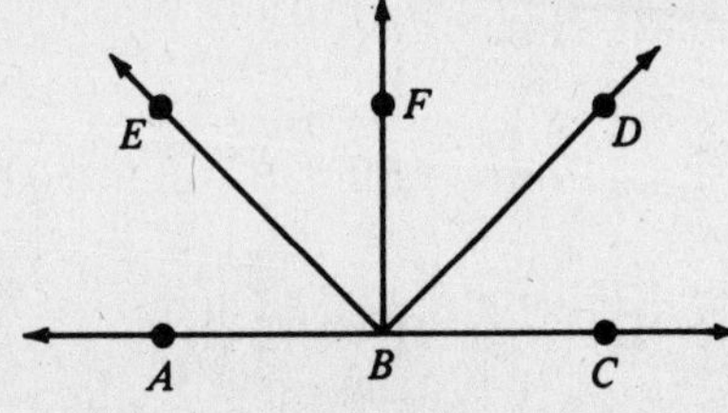

(A) 40° (B) 50° (C) 55° (D) 60° (E) 45°

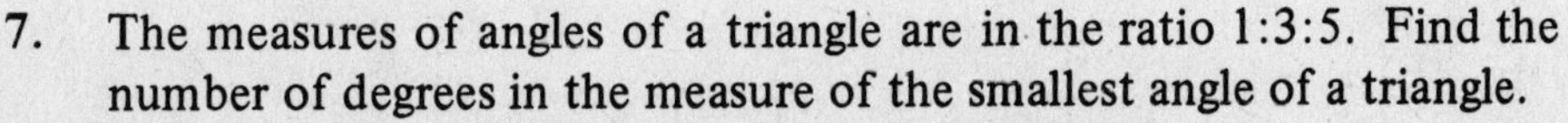

7. The measures of angles of a triangle are in the ratio 1:3:5. Find the number of degrees in the measure of the smallest angle of a triangle. 7. Ⓐ Ⓑ Ⓒ Ⓓ Ⓔ

(A) 20° (B) 60° (C) 100° (D) 180° (E) 40°

8. In triangle ABC, $AB = AC$ and the measure of angle A is twice the measure of angle B. Find the number of degrees in the measure of the exterior angle at C.
(A) 145° **(B)** 135° **(C)** 125° **(D)** 95° **(E)** 45° — 8. Ⓐ Ⓑ Ⓒ Ⓓ Ⓔ

Use this line graph for questions 9 and 10.

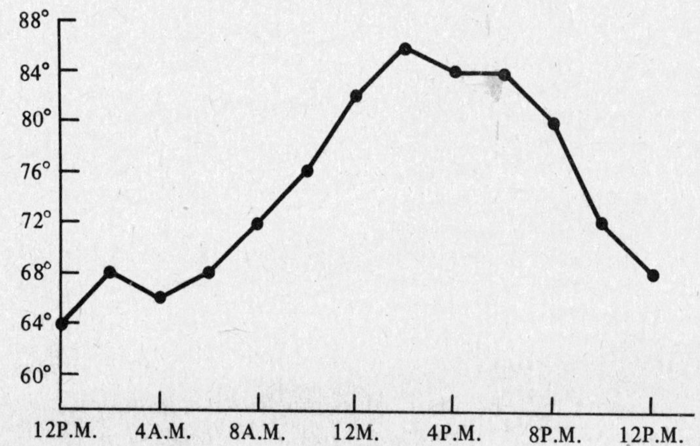

9. During what 2-hour period was the temperature constant?
(A) 2 A.M.–4 A.M. **(B)** 8 A.M.–10 A.M. **(C)** 12 noon–2 P.M. **(D)** 4 P.M.–6 P.M. **(E)** 6 P.M.–8 P.M. — 9. Ⓐ Ⓑ Ⓒ Ⓓ Ⓔ

10. At what two times of the day was the temperature 76°?
(A) 10 A.M. and 10 P.M. **(B)** 8 A.M. and 8 P.M. **(C)** 10 A.M. and 9 P.M. **(D)** 10 A.M. and 12 P.M. **(E)** 12 noon and 10 P.M. — 10. Ⓐ Ⓑ Ⓒ Ⓓ Ⓔ

11. Find the length of a leg of a right triangle whose hypotenuse is 40 inches and whose other leg is 24 inches. — 11. Ⓐ Ⓑ Ⓒ Ⓓ Ⓔ

(A) 64 inches **(B)** 16 inches **(C)** 8 inches
(D) 32 inches **(E)** none of these

12. The circumference of a circle whose diameter is 9 inches is approximately: — 12. Ⓐ Ⓑ Ⓒ Ⓓ Ⓔ

(A) 28 inches **(B)** 32 inches **(C)** 42 inches
(D) 254 inches **(E)** none of these

13. How far does a rolling wheel with a 4-inch radius travel in eight revolutions? — 13. Ⓐ Ⓑ Ⓒ Ⓓ Ⓔ

(A) 8π ft **(B)** $5\frac{1}{3}\pi$ ft **(C)** 12π ft **(D)** 4π ft **(E)** $10\frac{1}{3}\pi$ ft

14. Find the value of $\frac{8}{3-x}$ if $x = -1$. — 14. Ⓐ Ⓑ Ⓒ Ⓓ Ⓔ

(A) $\frac{8}{5}$ **(B)** $\frac{1}{4}$ **(C)** 4 **(D)** 2 **(E)** $\frac{1}{2}$

15. The reciprocal of $\frac{5}{x-2}$ is: 15. Ⓐ Ⓑ Ⓒ Ⓓ Ⓔ

(A) -5 (B) $\frac{5}{2-x}$ (C) $\frac{1}{5}$ (D) $\frac{x-2}{5}$ (E) $\frac{-5}{x+2}$

Part B

Directions: Each question in this section consists of two quantities, one in Column A and one in Column B. You are to compare the two quantities and on the answer grid blacken space

(A) if the quantity in Column A is the greater;

(B) if the quantity in Column B is the greater;

(C) if the two quantities are equal;

(D) if the relationships cannot be determined from the information given.

Common Information: In a question, information concerning one or both of the quantities to be compared is centered above or to the left of the two columns. A symbol that appears in both columns represents the same thing in Column A as it does in Column B.

Numbers: All numbers used are real numbers.

Figures: Position of points, angles, regions, etc., can be assumed to be in the order shown.

Lines shown as straight can be assumed to be straight.

Figures are assumed to lie in the plane unless otherwise indicated.

Figures that accompany questions are intended to provide information useful in answering the questions. However, unless a note states that a figure is drawn to scale, you should solve these problems NOT by estimating the sizes by sight or by measurement, but by using your knowledge of mathematics.

	Column A	Column B	
16.	$5\sqrt{2}$	$2\sqrt{5}$	16. Ⓐ Ⓑ Ⓒ Ⓓ
17.	$4m - 3n - (3m + 2n)$	$m + 5n$	17. Ⓐ Ⓑ Ⓒ Ⓓ
18.	$4:6 = m:15$	10	18. Ⓐ Ⓑ Ⓒ Ⓓ
19.	$(5-\sqrt{3})(5+\sqrt{3})$	16	19. Ⓐ Ⓑ Ⓒ Ⓓ
20. $x^2 + 3x + y^2 = x^2 + 2y + y^2$	$x:y$	$y:x$	20. Ⓐ Ⓑ Ⓒ Ⓓ
21. $a > 0$	$1 - \frac{1}{a}$	$1 + \frac{1}{a}$	21. Ⓐ Ⓑ Ⓒ Ⓓ
22. $\sqrt{.09x^2} = 81$	x	250	22. Ⓐ Ⓑ Ⓒ Ⓓ
23.	$\frac{1}{2}x = \frac{7}{6}$	$\frac{2}{3}y = \frac{7}{6}$	23. Ⓐ Ⓑ Ⓒ Ⓓ
24. $s = 4p,\ s = \frac{3}{2}m$	$p:m$	3:8	24. Ⓐ Ⓑ Ⓒ Ⓓ

	Column A	Column B	
25.	Price of 32 envelopes if purchased at rate of two for 5 cents	Price of 1 lb of coffee if a $3\frac{2}{3}$-lb can costs $3.30	**25.** Ⓐ Ⓑ Ⓒ Ⓓ

Use this chart for questions 26 and 27.

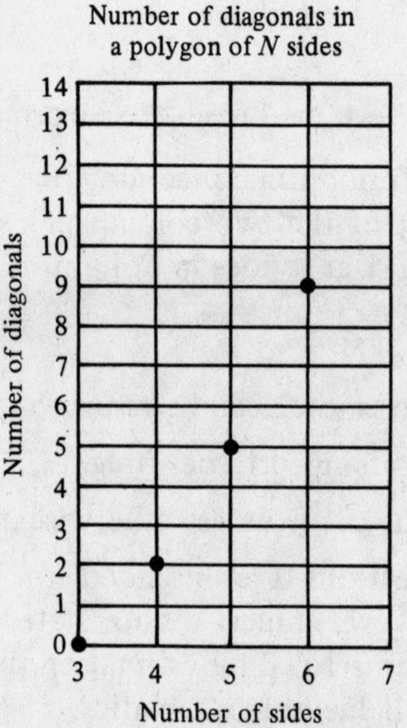

	Column A	Column B	
26.	Number of diagonals in a parallelogram	Number of diagonals in a trapezoid	**26.** Ⓐ Ⓑ Ⓒ Ⓓ
27.	Number of diagonals in a hexagon	Number of diagonals in a rhombus	**27.** Ⓐ Ⓑ Ⓒ Ⓓ
28.	Find the radius when the circumference of the circle is 9π.	Find the radius when the area of the circle is 25π.	**28.** Ⓐ Ⓑ Ⓒ Ⓓ
29.	Area of triangle	Perimeter of triangle	**29.** Ⓐ Ⓑ Ⓒ Ⓓ

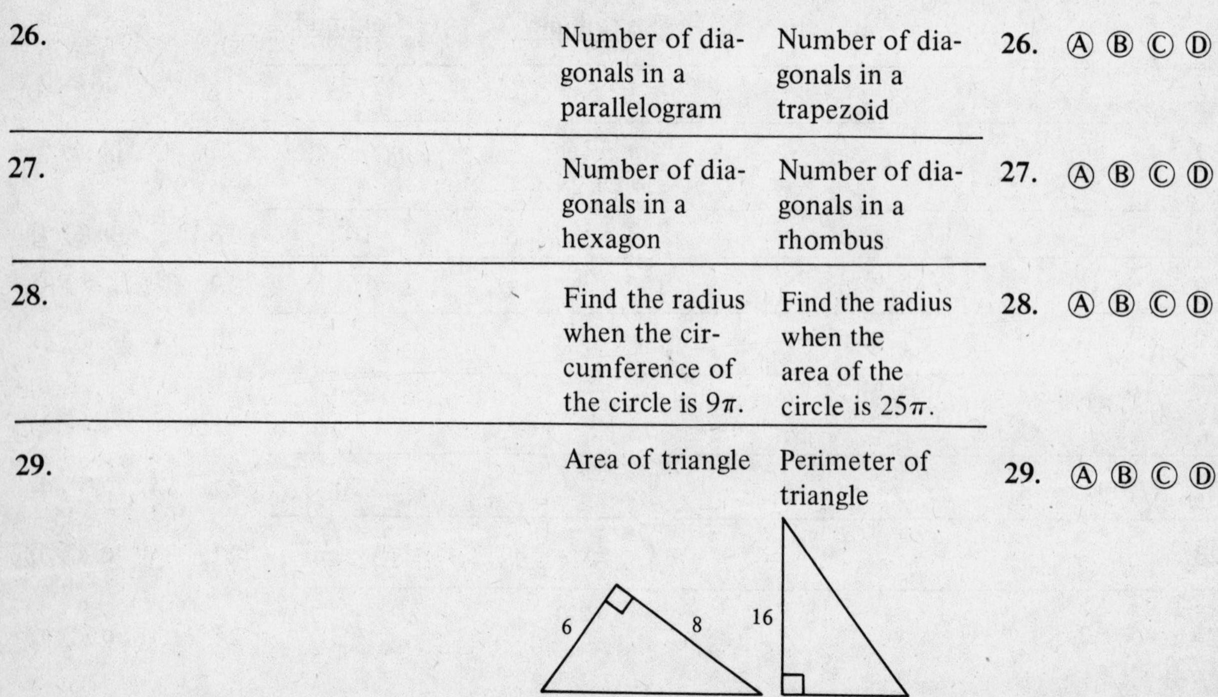

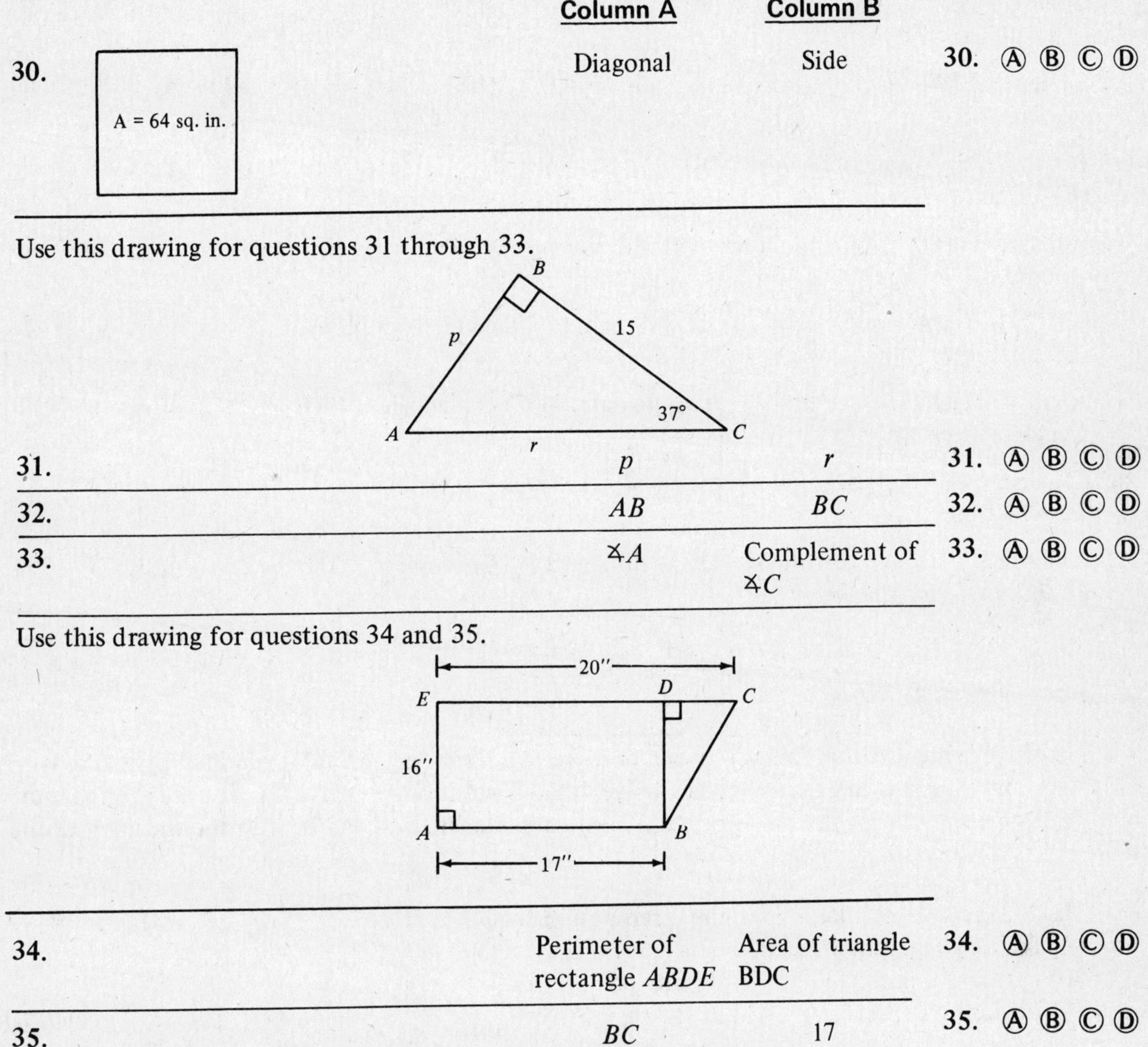

	Column A	Column B	
30.	Diagonal	Side	30. Ⓐ Ⓑ Ⓒ Ⓓ

Use this drawing for questions 31 through 33.

	Column A	Column B	
31.	p	r	31. Ⓐ Ⓑ Ⓒ Ⓓ
32.	AB	BC	32. Ⓐ Ⓑ Ⓒ Ⓓ
33.	$\measuredangle A$	Complement of $\measuredangle C$	33. Ⓐ Ⓑ Ⓒ Ⓓ

Use this drawing for questions 34 and 35.

	Column A	Column B	
34.	Perimeter of rectangle $ABDE$	Area of triangle BDC	34. Ⓐ Ⓑ Ⓒ Ⓓ
35.	BC	17	35. Ⓐ Ⓑ Ⓒ Ⓓ

SECTION SIX: VERBAL

Antonyms

Each questions consists of a word printed in capital letters, followed by five words or phrases lettered (A) through (E). Choose the lettered word or phrase that is most nearly *opposite* in meaning to the word in capital letters. Some of the questions require you to distinguish fine shades of meaning, so be sure to consider all the choices before deciding which one is best.

1. **SEDITION**: **(A)** lie **(B)** fault **(C)** obedience **(D)** placate **(E)** irascible — 1. Ⓐ Ⓑ Ⓒ Ⓓ Ⓔ
2. **INTREPID**: **(A)** scurrilous **(B)** pusillanimous **(C)** propitious **(D)** mellifluent **(E)** militate — 2. Ⓐ Ⓑ Ⓒ Ⓓ Ⓔ

3. **EFFRONTERY**: **(A)** timidity **(B)** palpable **(C)** raillery **(D)** libel **(E)** forensic — 3. Ⓐ Ⓑ Ⓒ Ⓓ Ⓔ

4. **TURBULENT**: **(A)** quiescent **(B)** cursory **(C)** extol **(D)** gyrate **(E)** imbibe — 4. Ⓐ Ⓑ Ⓒ Ⓓ Ⓔ

5. **PIQUANT**: **(A)** docile **(B)** sweet **(C)** insipid **(D)** captious **(E)** affable — 5. Ⓐ Ⓑ Ⓒ Ⓓ Ⓔ

6. **EFFULGENT**: **(A)** corpulent **(B)** dormant **(C)** adamant **(D)** gloomy **(E)** impervious — 6. Ⓐ Ⓑ Ⓒ Ⓓ Ⓔ

7. **VACUOUS**: **(A)** incorrigible **(B)** replete **(C)** pixilated **(D)** nebulous **(E)** tractable — 7. Ⓐ Ⓑ Ⓒ Ⓓ Ⓔ

8. **ABERRATION**: **(A)** verity **(B)** palliate **(C)** maladroit **(D)** trenchant **(E)** normalcy — 8. Ⓐ Ⓑ Ⓒ Ⓓ Ⓔ

9. **JOCOSE**: **(A)** jovial **(B)** plethora **(C)** serious **(D)** quiescent **(E)** mordant — 9. Ⓐ Ⓑ Ⓒ Ⓓ Ⓔ

10. **RETICENT**: **(A)** garrulous **(B)** willingness **(C)** misery **(D)** deciduous **(E)** shady — 10. Ⓐ Ⓑ Ⓒ Ⓓ Ⓔ

Sentence Completions

Each of the sentences that follow has one or more blank spaces, each blank indicating that a word has been omitted. Following the sentence are five lettered words or sets of words. You are to choose the one word or set of words that, when inserted in the sentence, *best* fits in with the meaning of the sentence as a whole.

11. His .... humor gave him a reputation for .... — 11. Ⓐ Ⓑ Ⓒ Ⓓ Ⓔ
    (A) factious .... homage
    (B) mordant .... insensitivity
    (C) flagrant .... contrition
    (D) esthetic .... fecundity
    (E) blithe .... altercation

12. The .... begged for .... — 12. Ⓐ Ⓑ Ⓒ Ⓓ Ⓔ
    (A) coterie .... adulation
    (B) factotum .... commiseration
    (C) buffoon .... latitude
    (D) reprobate .... absolution
    (E) chattel .... recrimination

13. The loser of the .... was forced to pay .... — 13. Ⓐ Ⓑ Ⓒ Ⓓ Ⓔ
    (A) tautology .... homage
    (B) culmination .... subsidy
    (C) confrontation .... restitution
    (D) shamble .... diadem
    (E) vicissitude .... credence

14. It was snowing, hailing, and sleeting at the same time; what a .... of .... **14.** Ⓐ Ⓑ Ⓒ Ⓓ Ⓔ

(A) pottage .... culminations
(B) matrix .... evacuations
(C) paroxysm .... hallucinations
(D) modicum .... gestations
(E) conglomeration .... precipitation

15. She is very .... and, therefore, easily .... **15.** Ⓐ Ⓑ Ⓒ Ⓓ Ⓔ

(A) decorous .... affronted
(B) garrulous .... gratified
(C) disinterested .... biased
(D) euphoric .... ingratiated
(E) debilitated .... impassioned

Reading Comprehension

Each passage in this group is followed by questions based on its content. After reading a passage, choose the best answer to each question and blacken the corresponding space on the answer grid. Answer all questions following a passage on the basis of what is *stated* or *implied* in that passage.

Passage One

Dr. Schweitzer said, "Each patient is his own best doctor." But most people benefit by having a doctor help the "doctor within." It is estimated that 90% of human ailments have mental aspects to the disease. Getting better is helped by an operation, an anti-toxin or a special medicine, but the mind must want to get better. It is this mind action that often works "miracle cures" or death from "unknown causes."

Part of the brain is the hypothalamus, which controls the secretion of hormones from the pituitary glands. The pituitary's hormone response may affect every function and every part of the body. Therefore, if a patient has great confidence in his doctor, this inner force gets to work, perhaps from the brain to the hypothalamus to all parts of the body.

In one study, two groups of patients in very severe pain were treated. One group was given morphine and the pain was relieved. The other group was given placebos made of milk sugar. Seventy-seven per cent of this group obtained as much relief as the morphine group. Some heroin addicts were relieved of "cold turkey" symptoms by injections of salt solution. Ulcers have been cured with sugar pill placebos.

For many years, scientists had little respect for the work of faith healers, herb doctors, and freak diet enthusiasts. Now we know that any one of these may help a person with an ailment resulting from stress. How about Laetrile? Some cancer patients definitely have been cured by this "useless" drug.

16. According to the passage, most human ailments involve **16.** Ⓐ Ⓑ Ⓒ Ⓓ Ⓔ

(A) foods
(B) stress
(C) bacteria
(D) fungi
(E) toxins

17. The main idea of the passage is that 17. Ⓐ Ⓑ Ⓒ Ⓓ Ⓔ
(A) mental reaction to treatment is a very important factor in the cure
(B) operations are necessary for some diseases
(C) special medicines are necessary for some diseases
(D) drug addicts can be relieved by placebos
(E) herb doctors cannot cure diseases

18. It can be inferred from this passage that cures of some ailments can be brought about by 18. Ⓐ Ⓑ Ⓒ Ⓓ Ⓔ
I. hypnotism
II. placebos
III. herbs
(A) I only
(B) II only
(C) III only
(D) I and III only
(E) I, II and III

19. The pituitary gland exerts its effect by means of 19. Ⓐ Ⓑ Ⓒ Ⓓ Ⓔ
(A) nerves
(B) serum
(C) hormones
(D) vitamins
(E) antibiotics

20. Although Laetrile has been judged "useless" by medical authorities, it can be inferred from this passage that some cures by Laetrile are a result of 20. Ⓐ Ⓑ Ⓒ Ⓓ Ⓔ
I. mental reaction
II. antibiotics
III. herbs
(A) I only
(B) II only
(C) III only
(D) I and III only
(E) I, II and III only

Passage Two

The Naval Observatory this week asked the Cerro Tololo Interamerican Observatory at La Serena, Chile, to help in confirming their find. The Cerro Tololo astronomers promptly turned their powerful 158-inch telescope on Pluto and confirmed yesterday that the Naval Observatory had indeed found a Pluto satellite.

The Pluto moon has been officially designated 1978-P-1, but its discoverer, Mr. Christy, has proposed the permanent name of Charon. Aside from its similarity to the name of Mr. Christy's wife Charlene, Charon was the name of the boatman in Greek mythology who ferried the souls of the dead across the river Styx into the underworld. Pluto was the god of the underworld.

The solar system's natural satellites now number thirty-three known moons and three suspected ones. They include one for Earth, two for Mars (which were both discovered by the Naval Observatory 101 years ago), thirteen certain and one possible for Saturn, five for Uranus, two for Neptune and one for Pluto. Neither Venus nor Mercury is known to have a satellite.

In calculating the orbit, ephemeris, and other properties of Charon, Robert S. Harrington, a Naval Observatory astronomer, made some startling discoveries, he said yesterday.

For one, Charon's orbit is apparently only 12,000 miles above the surface of Pluto—too close for the Naval Observatory telescope to see the planet and its satellite as separate objects.

Dr. Thomas van Flandern of the observatory said he hoped that the Kitt Peak National Observatory and Hale Observatory's 200-inch telescope on Mount Palomar, California, would quickly take up the search for a visible separation between Pluto and Charon.

21. Which of the following statements bears out an allusion to international cooperation among astronomers? — 21. Ⓐ Ⓑ Ⓒ Ⓓ Ⓔ
   (A) the Kitt Peak National Observatory entered the search for a visible separation between Pluto and Charon
   (B) the name for the new moon was taken from Greek mythology
   (C) the Cerro Tololo astronomers confirmed the finding of the new moon
   (D) Mrs. Christy is foreign-born
   (E) the Hale Observatory refused to cooperate in this venture

22. The logical connection between the name Pluto and the name Charon is that — 22. Ⓐ Ⓑ Ⓒ Ⓓ Ⓔ
   (A) Pluto was the god of the underworld
   (B) the Greeks had a well-developed science of astronomy long before the modern era
   (C) Charon was the ferryman of the Styx, and Pluto was the god of the underworld
   (D) both names reflect a superstitious attitude on the part of modern astronomers
   (E) the discoverer's wife has a name similar to Charon

23. The name of the discoverer of the new moon is — 23. Ⓐ Ⓑ Ⓒ Ⓓ Ⓔ
   (A) Harrington
   (B) unknown
   (C) Cerro Tololo
   (D) Mr. Christy
   (E) Dr. Thomas van Flandern

24. Which of the following statements is true, according to the selection? — 24. Ⓐ Ⓑ Ⓒ Ⓓ Ⓔ
   (A) the equipment of the United States Naval Observatory is too antiquated for modern observation
   (B) an observer on the far side of Pluto would have a better view of the new moon
   (C) there is a strong possibility of life on Pluto
   (D) Charon's orbit is too close to the surface of Pluto to permit separate identification by the Naval Observatory
   (E) information from other nations about the new moon was too late in arriving

25 . The following fact has been ascertained by the astronomers: 25. Ⓐ Ⓑ Ⓒ Ⓓ Ⓔ

(A) there are 36 established moons in our solar system
(B) there are several moons whose existence is only suspected
(C) there are moons known to be or suspected to be around all the planets of our solar system
(D) there is a vast difference between the satellite of a planet and its moon
(E) Pluto originated as a planet in and of itself

Passage Three

Many people love songbirds and would like to do something to attract them, so that their habits of nesting and rearing and feeding the young can be studied. Growth of the young can be observed from emergence from the eggs to time of departure from parental care. The birds are fascinating to look at and listen to.

Building a bird house can lead to an immensely rewarding hobby–bird watching–and at the same time satisfy an urge to attract our feathery friends. Many types of designs for bird houses are available, including several that are simple to build. Almost anyone with a simple design and a minimum of tools and materials can complete such a project. Choice of specific design for the bird house is essential, however, as certain types will attract certain species of birds, whereas others will not.

If a bird house is not used the first season, it is no indication of faulty construction or improper placement. There may already be more nesting facilities than the resident bird population can occupy.

Failure to attract feathered tenants can often be attributed to the following faults: (1) entrance holes too small for the birds desired; (2) boxes put up in dense woods; (3) boxes placed in trees, and therefore accessible to birds' enemies, instead of on posts or poles; and (4) no care taken to protect birds nesting in boxes. Three of these faults concern site–the second and third obviously, and the fourth indirectly–for it is manifestly easier to protect a bird house and its occupants if it is readily reached.

To be easily accessible, bird boxes should not be beyond the reach of an available ladder; those placed higher inevitably will be neglected. Houses on poles seem more acceptable than others to certain birds, probably because they impress the birds as being safer. Isolated trees can actually be made safe with tree guards, but perhaps they do not seem safer to the birds.

Houses should be fairly low, away from dense woods, and on poles rather than in trees. If possible, they should be placed in partial sunlight, the opening facing away from prevailing winds.

It is not good to have a large number of boxes in a limited area; birds insist on territorial rights, especially in competition with other individuals of the same species. If houses are too close together, conflicts between prospective tenants may result in none of the houses being occupied. The purple martin is the only native gregarious species that nests in bird boxes, and houses for colonies of these birds should be on poles, well separated from trees or buildings. Tree swallows are sociable and several individual boxes for them may be built near each other.

26. Bird houses are better placed on poles than on trees because 26. Ⓐ Ⓑ Ⓒ Ⓓ Ⓔ

(A) poles are close together
(B) birds' enemies cannot reach them as easily
(C) poles can be higher than a ladder
(D) trees are hit by lightning
(E) trees are too flexible

27. The author uses the last paragraph
(A) to discuss social conflicts of birds
(B) to end the selection
(C) to change the subject
(D) to compare different birds
(E) to give directions for building bird houses

27. Ⓐ Ⓑ Ⓒ Ⓓ Ⓔ

28. The most important idea in the selection is that
(A) site and construction make a good bird house
(B) building a bird house makes bird watching a rewarding hobby
(C) birds like their own territory
(D) too many nests in one area are not good
(E) songbirds are fascinating

28. Ⓐ Ⓑ Ⓒ Ⓓ Ⓔ

29. Building a bird house
(A) requires a professional
(B) is a waste of time
(C) provides something to attract birds
(D) can be dangerous
(E) results in conflicts between tenants

29. Ⓐ Ⓑ Ⓒ Ⓓ Ⓔ

30. "Purple martin" refers to a
(A) famous birdwatcher
(B) color for a bird house
(C) type of bird house
(D) type of bird
(E) type of nest

30. Ⓐ Ⓑ Ⓒ Ⓓ Ⓔ

Analogies

In each of the following questions, a related pair of words or phrases is followed by five lettered pairs of words, numbers or phrases. Select the lettered pair that best expresses a relationship similar to that expressed in the original pair.

31. **GOLD : MIDAS ::**
(A) bird : eagle
(B) devil : Satan
(C) hero : conquest
(D) Wisdom : Athena
(E) genius : Shakespeare

31. Ⓐ Ⓑ Ⓒ Ⓓ Ⓔ

32. **BALD : HIRSUTE ::**
(A) small : tiny
(B) broad : fat
(C) anemic : robust
(D) fatuous : loud
(E) mercurial : redundant

32. Ⓐ Ⓑ Ⓒ Ⓓ Ⓔ

33. **LUNG : AIR : :** 33. Ⓐ Ⓑ Ⓒ Ⓓ Ⓔ
(A) finger : nail
(B) picture : T.V.
(C) leaf : branch
(D) axle : wheel
(E) heart : blood

34. **FEATHERS : BIRDS : :** 34. Ⓐ Ⓑ Ⓒ Ⓓ Ⓔ
(A) scales : fish
(B) jacket : man
(C) icing : cake
(D) stone : moss
(E) window : house

35. **LIMOUSINE : CAR : :** 35. Ⓐ Ⓑ Ⓒ Ⓓ Ⓔ
(A) house : cave
(B) railroad : bus
(C) fur : animal
(D) mansion : house
(E) stone : pebble

36. **DIAMOND : ROCK : :** 36. Ⓐ Ⓑ Ⓒ Ⓓ Ⓔ
(A) pearl : oyster
(B) tea : coffee
(C) ice : cold
(D) gold : metal
(E) slipper : boot

Answers and Analysis

SECTION ONE: MATHEMATICS

1. **(A)** When the product of any two numbers is 1, one of the numbers is the multiplicative inverse or reciprocal of the other number. Hence the reciprocal of $\frac{2}{3}$ is $\frac{3}{2}$.

$$\text{Multiply } \frac{2}{3} \times \frac{3}{2} = 1.$$

2. **(D)** Since none of the digits can be repeated, all three of the digits must be used to write a number of three digits.

   (1) To select the first number, only 2 or 3 can be selected since 0 cannot be used in the hundred's place. (2 choices)

   (2) For the second digit, only 0 or either 2 or 3 can be selected for the ten's place. (2 choices)

(3) For the third digit, only 1 number from the list that had not been previously selected can be used in the one's place. (1 choice)

Then by the principle of selecting one thing in M different ways and if chosen in N different ways:

$M;N$ = different ways
2;2;1 = 4 different numbers

3. (C) Doubled means to be multiplied by 2.

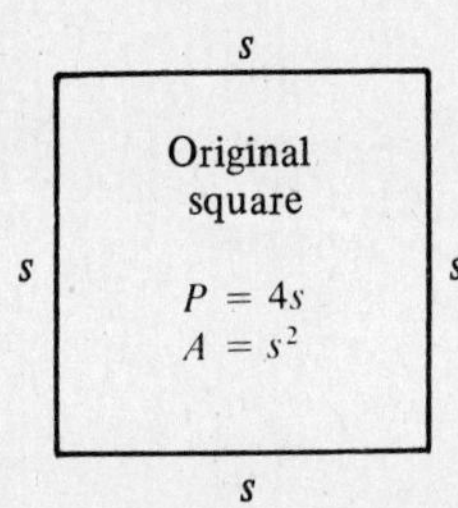

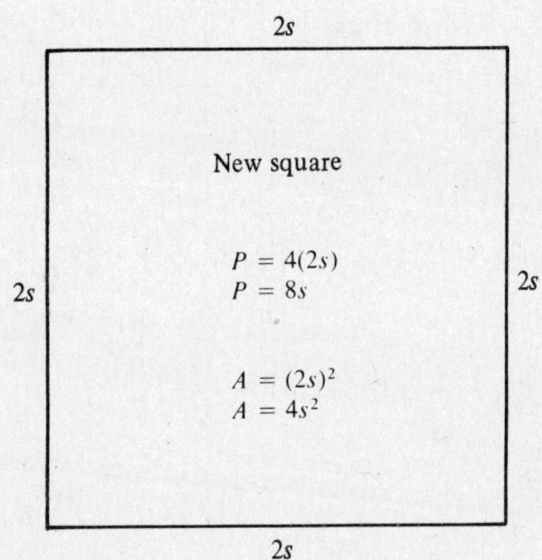

Original		*New*
$P = 4s$	=	$8s$ → mult. by 2
$A = s^2$	=	$4s^2$ → mult. by 4

4. (B) To find the average, add their sum and divide the total by the number of items:

$$\frac{A + B + C + D}{4}$$

5. (B) $N^2 + N - 6$ is factored into: $(N + 3)(N - 2)$. $2N + 6$ is factored into: $2(N + 3)$

$$\frac{\cancel{(N+3)}(N-2)}{2\cancel{(N+3)}}$$

$$\frac{N-2}{2}$$ cross out common factor $(N + 3)$ in numerator and denominator

6. (B) Multiply:

```
   30.47
  X 285
 8683.95 → approximately 8700
```

7. (D)

To go from N to 1	1 path
To go from N to 2	2 paths
To go from N to 3	3 paths
To go from N to 4	5 paths
To go from N to 5	8 paths
To go from N to 6	13 paths
To go from N to F	21 paths

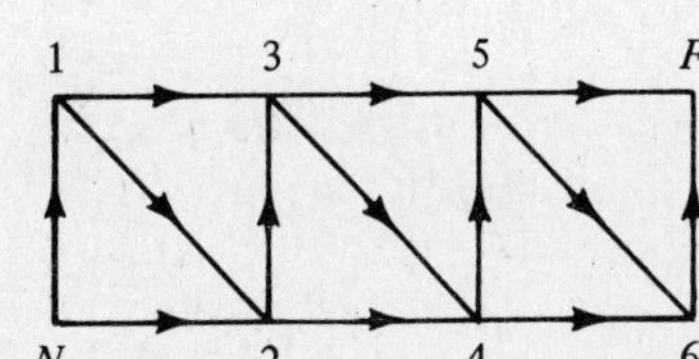

Recognize the pattern:

1, 2, 3, 5, 8, 13, 21, . . .
1 + 2 = 3
2 + 3 = 5
3 + 5 = 8
8 + 5 = 13
8 + 13 = 21

8. **(E)** Let d = total number of miles.

Passenger train   Freight train

rate × time = distance
(mph) (hours) (miles)

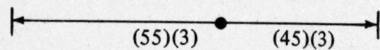

|—— (55)(3) ——•—— (45)(3) ——|

$$(55)(3) + (45)(3) = d$$
$$165 + 135 = d$$
$$300 \text{ miles} = d$$

9. **(C)** The least common denominator for all fractions is 12.

$$5\tfrac{1}{4} = 5\tfrac{3}{12}$$
$$7\tfrac{3}{4} = 7\tfrac{9}{12}$$
$$+\,2\tfrac{1}{3} = 2\tfrac{4}{12}$$
$$14\tfrac{16}{12} \longrightarrow \text{reduced to } 14 + 1\tfrac{4}{12} \longrightarrow 14 + 1\tfrac{1}{3} = 15\tfrac{1}{3}$$

Subtract $15\frac{1}{3}$ from 16:

$$16 \longrightarrow \text{borrow 1 from 16} \longrightarrow 15 + \tfrac{3}{3}$$
$$-15\tfrac{1}{3} \qquad\qquad -15 + \tfrac{1}{3}$$
$$\tfrac{2}{3}$$

10. **(D)** The area of the square minus the area of the circle equals the shaded area.

$OA = 3$
$2OA = 6$ = diameter = side of square
area of square = s^2 area of circle = πr^2
$A = (6)^2$ $A = \pi(3)^2$
$= 36$ $= 9\pi$
$36 - 9\pi$ equals shaded area

11. **(C)** The depth of the South China Sea is $3\frac{1}{2}$; the depth of the Red Sea is $1\frac{1}{2}$.

$$\frac{3\frac{1}{2}}{1\frac{1}{2}} = \frac{\frac{7}{2}}{\frac{3}{2}} = \frac{7}{2} \times \frac{2}{3} = \frac{7}{3} \text{ or } 7:3$$

12. **(D)** Each unit stands for 1000 feet. The length of the bar graph for the Caribbean Sea is 6.5.

$$\begin{array}{r} 1000 \\ \times \ \ 6.5 \\ \hline 6500.0 \end{array}$$

13. **(E)** Since the area of the square is K^2, each side is K. The area of rectangle I is $8K \rightarrow$ width is K; length is 8. The area of rectangle II is $4K \rightarrow$ width is 4; length is K. The area of rectangle III is $32 \rightarrow$ width is 4; length is 8.

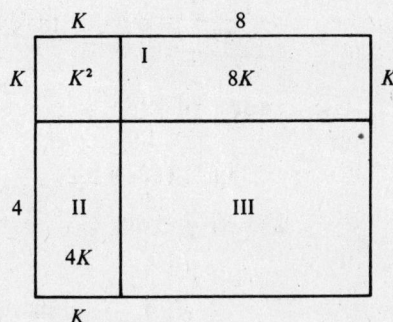

	K	8	
K	K^2	I $8K$	K
4	II $4K$	III	
	K		

14. **(E)** If DE is parallel to AC, similar triangles ABC and DBE are formed. Corresponding sides of similar triangles are in proportion. Hence

$$\frac{DE}{AC} = \frac{DB}{AB}$$

Substitute and cross-multiply:

$$\frac{x}{6} = \frac{10}{15}$$
$$15x = (6)(10)$$
$$x = 4$$

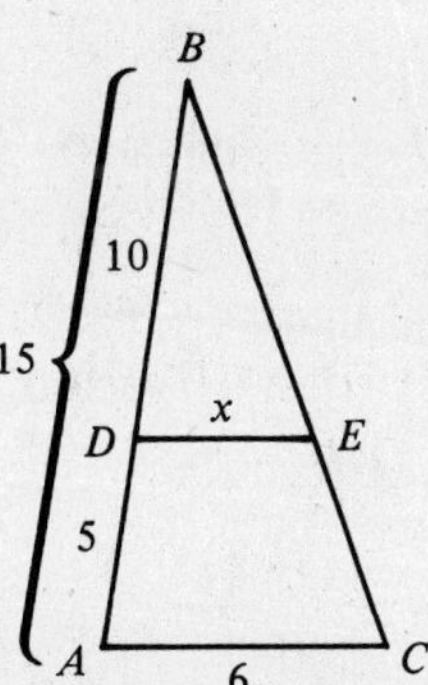

15. **(E)** Let

x = first consecutive integer
$x + 1$ = second consecutive integer
$x + 2$ = third consecutive integer

$$\begin{aligned} x + x + 1 + x + 2 &= 33 \\ 3x + 3 &= 33 \\ 3x &= 30 \\ x &= 10 \\ x + 1 &= 11 \\ x + 2 &= 12 \end{aligned}$$

16. **(E)** Find the ratio

$$\frac{\text{Time required to complete job}}{\text{Time to do whole job}} = \text{part of task not done}$$

$$\frac{Y - 2}{Y} = \text{part of task not done}$$

17. **(B)** Substitute in the formula. Use a radius of 1.2.

$$\begin{aligned} V &= \frac{4}{3}\,\frac{22}{7}\,(1.2)(1.2)(1.2) \\ &= 7.2 \text{ cu ft} \end{aligned}$$

18. **(B)** $OA = OB$ because the radii in the same circle are qual. The triangle AOB is a right triangle. By the Pythagorean theorem:

$$\begin{aligned} a^2 + b^2 &= c^2 \\ (\text{leg})^2 + (\text{leg})^2 &= (\text{hypotenuse})^2 \\ (10)^2 + (10)^2 &= c^2 \\ 100 + 100 &= c^2 \\ 200 &= c^2 \\ \sqrt{2 \cdot 100} &= \sqrt{c^2} \\ 10\sqrt{2} &= c \end{aligned}$$

19. **(D)** In any triangle, the sum of any two sides must be greater than the third side. Only example **(D)** is true: $5 + 6 > 10$.

20. **(C)** Altitude CD is drawn, forming right angles: $\measuredangle CDA = \measuredangle CDB = 90°$. Hence $\measuredangle x + \measuredangle A + \measuredangle CDA = 180°$. Also, $\measuredangle Y + \measuredangle B + \measuredangle CDB = 180°$. Substitute $\measuredangle x + \measuredangle A = \measuredangle Y + \measuredangle B$.

21. **(A)** Combine $\frac{x+y}{3}$ and $\frac{x-y}{3}$ into a single fraction. The least common denominator is 12. Change each fraction into an equivalent fraction.

$$\frac{x+y}{3} = \frac{4x+4y}{12}$$

$$\frac{x-y}{4} = \frac{3x-3y}{12}$$

Combine like terms in the numerator:

$$\frac{4x + 4y + 3x - 3y}{12} = \frac{7x + y}{12}$$

22. (A) Point D is vertically aligned with A's x-coordinate, 1, and horizontally aligned with C's y-coordinate, 4.

23. (C) Invert the divisor so that the fractions can be multiplied:

$$\frac{x^2-9}{x} \cdot \frac{5x}{x-3}$$

Factor: $x^2 - 9 \rightarrow \dfrac{(x-3)(x+3)}{x} \cdot \dfrac{5x}{x-3}$

Cancel out any common factors:

$$\frac{\cancel{(x-3)}(x+3)}{\cancel{x}} \cdot \frac{5\cancel{x}}{\cancel{x-3}}$$

Multiply: $5(x+3)$

24. (A) Solve the inequality:

$$\begin{aligned} 3x - 4 &> 8 \\ 3x &> 8 + 4 \\ &> 12 \\ x &> 4 \end{aligned}$$

25. (D) A line joining the midpoints of the two sides of a triangle is equal to one-half of the third side. In triangle ABD, $EF = \frac{1}{2}BD$. Substitute:

$$8 = \frac{1}{2}BD$$
$$BD = 16$$

SECTION TWO: VERBAL

1. **(B) INDUBITABLE: incontestable, indisputable**
2. **(D) UNGAINLY: clumsy, awkward**
3. **(C) ENNUI: torpor, lethargy**
4. **(C) SUBJOIN: affix, add**
5. **(A) CAPRICIOUS: fickle, vacillating**
6. **(C) EXPIATE: atone, do penance**
7. **(B) CAPTIOUS: hypercritical, carping**
8. **(A) LASSITUDE: weariness, apathy**
9. (A) IMPUTE: ascribe, charge
10. **(C) WINSOME: attractive, charming**
11. (A) Man's desire for wealth (or cupidity) leads to avaricious (not noisy) acts.
12. (B) This is the only choice that makes sense.

13. **(E)** Scholarship and intelligence are a positive combination.

14. **(E)** Childish remarks sometimes are silly.

15. **(B)** Wit usually wins the interest of others.

16. **(D)** The halo around the moon was a favorable sign.

17. **(E)** Her poetry was commonplace and unexciting.

18. **(E)** Caret refers to this sign.

19. **(A)** The troops on horses appeared over the hill.

20. **(D)** Only D describes the major characteristic of the first word in the pair.

21. **(D)** This answer is borne out by the allusion to the "grub" that becomes the "winged thing," and by the reference to "cosmic destinies" that man does not comprehend. *(A)* While this statement is implicit in the author's thought, his own not being witness to what may happen is not the reason for his calm demeanor. *(B)* Again, it is the vision of things to come—the "dreaming glimpse of peace" that enables him to overcome the fears and prejudices of his youth. *(C)* He recognizes that challenges to his way of life and culture may come from "other races," but he does not *fear* this. *(E)* Rather than being indifferent, he is actually hopeful and optimistic.

22. **(A)** This is in direct opposition to the author's assumption that civilization may progress "perhaps with smaller numbers," although possibly with increased stature. Each of answers *(B), (C), (D),* and *(E)* is either directly stated or implied in the selection.

23. **(C)** This is specifically stated—"competition from new races." *(A)* The competition from new races will "cut deeper than working men's disputes." *(B)* Such an apprehension is not indicated nor mentioned. *(D)* This possibility is not presented at all. *(E)* This threat from "outer space" is not indicated.

24. **(D)** The references to Pennsylvania Avenue, the Treasury, and Sherman's statue all imply residence in Washington D.C. Locations *(A), (B), (C),* and *(E)* are not indicated.

25. **(B)** Specifically stated, "I do not pin my dreams for the future to my country or even to my race." *(A), (C), (D),* and *(E)* become irrelevant because of the specific statement indicated in *(B)*.

26. **(B)** The main idea must include all other ideas in the selection. The author indicates that some people take pills to be sure of getting enough vitamins and minerals. *(A)* is not the main idea. The emphasis in this passage is on vitamins and minerals. *(C), (D)* and *(E)* discuss some of these minerals, but are too specific to be considered main ideas.

27. **(D)** Other vitamins are measured in milligrams (thousandths of a gram). Vitamin B_{12} is measured in micrograms (millionths of a gram). Therefore, each molecule has to "work" 1000 times as hard.

28. **(D)** I and II. Calcium moves in and out of cells, as well as inside cells. Sodium ions bathe the cells on the outside. Vitamin C helps hold cells together.

29. **(D)** We eat food in large quantitities. Since 90% or more of our diet is carbohydrates, fats and proteins, that is what is needed to produce, maintain, and repair cells. *(E)* is wrong. Calcium triggers the function of muscle cells. It is a mineral, needed in small quantities.

30. **(E)** People take vitamin pills because they think processed foods have lost some vitamins and minerals. *(A), (B), (C)* and *(D)* are wrong. They may be true but there is no reference to them in the passage.

31. **(C)** Bacchus is the god of wine; Diana is the goddess of the hunt.

32. **(C)** The head of a nation is a president. The head of a city is a mayor.

33. **(D)** Tepid is moderate; boiling is extreme. Similarly, cool is moderate; freezing is extreme.

34. **(D)** Friction leads to war. Discontent leads to a strike. Both indicate conflict.

35. **(C)** Depression may lead to suicide. A sufferer of paranoia may have delusions. These are both mental disorders.

36. **(D)** A caterpillar becomes a butterfly. A tadpole becomes a frog.

37. **(D)** North America is the continent where Canada is found. Europe is the continent where France is found.

38. **(D)** Rustic is the opposite of urban. Country is opposite to city. Also "rustic" is associated with "country" as "urban" is associated with "city."

39. **(D)** Pediatrics deals with children; geriatrics deals with the aged. Similarly, obstetrics deals with birth and thanatology deals with death.

40. **(D)** A bookkeeper works under an accountant as a typist works under a stenographer. All are involved in office work.

SECTION FOUR: VERBAL

1. **(E)** PROLIX: verbose, loquacious
2. **(C)** PARITY: equality, analogy
3. **(D)** BUCOLIC: rustic, rural
4. **(E)** CATACLYSM: catastrophe, calamity
5. **(A)** PRIMORDIAL: primitive, indigenous
6. **(B)** ONEROUS: laborious, toilsome
7. **(B)** NEBULOUS: vague, inexact
8. **(A)** MUTATION: innovation, change
9. **(C)** CATEGORICAL: dogmatic, certain
10. **(C)** AGGLOMERATE: unite, amalgamate
11. **(E)** INVIDIOUS: disliked, resented

12. (E) VENAL: mercenary, corrupt

13. (A) REPREHENSION: reprimand, rebuke

14. (D) EPITOME: digest, synopsis

15. (A) REPUDIATE: disclaim, refuse

16. (C) "Powerful" and "kindly" are characteristics of an effective ruler.

17. (E) A stingy man is concerned with finances.

18. (B) Since we don't have an overabundance of energy sources, we must conserve what we have.

19. (E) This pair best describes good directions.

20. (A) Abstruse means difficult to understand.

21. (D) "Obsolete" means out of use.

22. (E) Both of these have to do with the art of dance.

23. (C) Only this pair makes sense.

24. (B) People sometimes demonstrate a strength of character during a long illness.

25. (C) Care during pregnancy often prevents complications during birth.

26. **(C)** This conclusion is strongly indicated by the sentence that includes the phrase "... and not at all by the practical interests of the period. . . ." *(A)* This is contradicted by *sentence 2,* which states the direct opposite. *(B)* The statement is made that the "... homogeneous, energetic social culture that collaborated with the great Victorian writers. . . ." *(D)* This is contrary to the notion implied in the previous statement about the "collaboration" of the age and the authors. *(E)* In *sentence 2* the reference is made to "both England and America."

27. **(B)** The concluding statement of the selection states that the creeds have the effect of setting "the individual artist apart from the community in the popular opinion." *(A)* There is an allusion to this idea with reference to "artist groups," but it is not reflected as an overall feeling of the selection. *(C)* This is neither stated nor implied in the selection. It may actually appear to be contrary to the intent of the author. *(D)* This is not indicated; there is no mention of patrons and the artists' responsibility to them. *(E)* Again, this is neither developed nor indicated.

28. **(A)** This is specifically stated: "The eighteenth-century poets did not call themselves classicists, nor did the nineteenth-century poets call themselves romanticists." The implication however, is that the terms *classicist* and *romanticist* were *applied* to the artists of these centuries. Neither *(B), (C), (D),* nor *(E)* can be right, since the correct answer was specifically stated.

29. **(C)** The sense of the entire selection and certainly the implication of the statement that "Art had begun to be created for Art's sake" (especially with the capital *A)* indicates the author's feeling that art must be related to people — hence, to society. *(A)* Actually, the opposite of this is indicated, especially in the discussion of the richness of the Victorian period in its art as well as industry. *(B)* There is no indication of such "plotlike" activity either among the artists or in society in general. *(D)* This is a matter of semantics; the term *critical* usually implies some condemnation or disapproval. Actually, the author is discussing art and culture in a historical context. *(E)* Again, the use of the difference between the small *a* and the capital *A* implies a critical comment that is not warranted here.

30. **(D)** This is a specific conclusion of the author, indicated in his final statement. *(A)* This is neither

indicated nor suggested in the selection. *(B)* There is no indication that this is historically so, and such a conclusion is unwarranted simply because the selection deals with relatively modern times. *(C)* The statement is made that such groups provide "artistic" creeds. *(E)* This is neither stated nor alluded to in the selection.

31. **(E)** is correct. This is found by a careful reading of the first paragraph.

32. **(B)** is correct. The clue to this answer is at the end of the third paragraph. When the author writes "It is not what they think *it* is" the *it* refers to the way people think about art and intellect.

33. **(E)** is correct. The answer is found in the last paragraph. *(A)* is the opposite of what the author says. *(B)* The author feels intellectual training has become too important. *(C)* is stated by the author. However, this does not indicate that it is an "unfortunate result." *(D)* is wrong because the author states it is taken too seriously.

34. **(A)** is correct. The answer is found in the first paragraph. *(B), (C)* and *(D)* contradict the essay, and *(E)* is irrelevant.

35. **(A)** is correct. This is indicated by the last paragraph. *(B), (C), (D)* and *(E)* are not supported by the essay.

36. **(C) An angle is measured by degrees. A line is measured by inches.**

37. **(B) Blades make up grass as grains make up sand.**

38. **(E) One who is deaf cannot perceive tone; one who is blind cannot perceive color.**

39. **(D) The radius is half the diameter of a given circle. Similarly, 5 is half of 10.**

40. **(C) An oak grows from an acorn; a tulip grows from a bulb.**

41. **(D) 12½% is equal to ⅛ as 66⅔% is equal to ⅔. Both are fractions.**

42. **(D) Fur is made into coats; silk is made into blouses.**

43. **(D) Polyester is a synthetic cotton as acrilan is a synthetic wool.**

44. **(D) Bacon is sold by the pound; eggs are sold by the dozen.**

45. **(D) A horn is blown; a harp is plucked to make music.**

SECTION FIVE: MATHEMATICS

Part A

1. **(B)** 15

This is clearly a problem in division.

$$14.4.\overline{)216.0.}\quad 15$$

2. **(D)** $(3a + 5)(2a - 3) =$ [(3a)(2a)]

$$\text{(first term)(first term)} = (3a)(2a) = 6a^2$$

Add inner and outer products:

$$(3a + 5)(2a - 3) = (3a)(-3) + (5)(2a) = -9a + 10a = 1a = a$$

[(3a)(−3) outer; (5)(2a) inner]

$(3a+5)(2a-3)$ = (last term)(last term)
5(−3) = (5)(−3) = −15

Now add: $6a^2 + a - 15$.

3. **(B)** 1 dollar = 100 cents

n = number of articles; each cost 5 cents; then
total cost = $5n$ cents
change from 100 cents − $5n$ cents: $c = 100 - 5n$

4. (B) 5

To solve equations use inverse operations. First add 3 to both sides.

$$\begin{aligned} 4x - 3 &= 17 \\ +3 &= +3 \\ \hline 4x \quad &= 20 \end{aligned}$$

Then divide both sides by 4

$$\frac{4x}{4} = \frac{20}{4}$$

$$x = 5$$

5. (E) none of these

First find variable expressions to represent the three consecutive odd integers.

Let n be the 1st odd integer. Then $n + 2$ is the 2d and $n + 4$ is the 3d.

Now translate ". . . whose sum is −57" into an equation. Then solve the equation.

$$\begin{aligned} n + (n+2) + (n+4) &= -57 \\ 3n + 6 &= -57 \\ -6 &= -6 \\ \frac{3n}{3} &= \frac{-63}{3} \\ n &= -21 \end{aligned}$$

Finally, find the other two odd integers and check.

$$n + 2 = (-21) + 2 = -19$$
$$n + 4 = (-21) + 4 = -17$$

Check:

$$(-21) + (-19) + (-17) = -57$$

It would have been easier to answer this question by eliminating the solutions given. *B, C,* and *D* could have been eliminated since none of these answers were 3 consecutive odd integers. Then, by adding the integers in answer *A,* we can eliminate this possibility.

6. **(A)** A whole quantity is equal to the sum of its parts.

$$\measuredangle FBC = 90$$
$$\measuredangle EBF + \measuredangle FBD = \measuredangle FBC = 90$$
$$5x + 4x = 90$$
$$9x = 90$$
$$x = 10$$
$$\measuredangle EBF = (5)(10) = 50$$
$$\measuredangle EBD = 90$$
$$\measuredangle EBA + \measuredangle EBF = \measuredangle EBD = 90$$
$$\measuredangle EBA + 50 = 90$$
$$\measuredangle EBA = 40$$

7. **(A)** Let

x = number of degrees in smallest angle
$3x$ = number of degrees in second angle
$5x$ = number of degrees in third angle

$$1x + 3x + 5x = 180$$
$$9x = 180$$
$$x = 20 \quad \text{(smallest angle)}$$

8. **(B)** Draw ΔABC such that $AB = AC$. $\measuredangle B = \measuredangle C$ since base angles of isosceles Δ are equal.
Let x = number of degrees in $\measuredangle B$
$2x$ = number of degrees in $\measuredangle A$

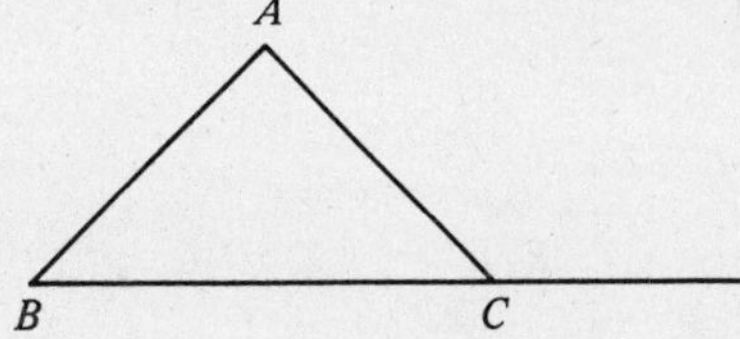

$$\measuredangle A + \measuredangle B + \measuredangle C = 180$$
$$2x + x + x = 180$$
$$4x = 180$$
$$x = 45$$
$$\measuredangle C = 45$$

The exterior angle at C is supplementary to $\measuredangle C$. Hence,

$$\measuredangle C + \text{exterior angle} = 180$$
$$45 + \text{exterior angle} = 180$$
$$\text{Exterior angle} = 135$$

9. **(D)** Draw a vertical line from 84° down to time; the two lines intersect at 4 P.M. and 6 P.M.

10. **(C)** Draw a horizontal line across from 76°. At the points of intersection with the curves, draw vertical lines down to the time axis. The two lines intersect at 10 A.M. and 9 P.M.

11. **(D)** 32 in.

Using the Pythagorean theorem,

$$\begin{aligned} a^2 + b^2 &= c^2 \\ a^2 + (24)^2 &= (40)^2 \\ a^2 + 576 &= 1600 \\ -576 &= -576 \\ \hline a^2 &= 1024 \\ a &= \sqrt{1024} \\ a &= 32'' \end{aligned}$$

12. **(A)** 28 in.

Use the formula,

$$\begin{aligned} C &= \pi d \\ &\approx (3.14)(9) \\ &\approx 28.26'' \end{aligned}$$

13. **(B)** $C = 2\pi r$
$= 2\pi(4)$
$= 8\pi$ inches in one revolution
$(8)(8\pi) = 64\pi$ inches

$5\frac{1}{3}$ ft $\rightarrow$ $5\frac{1}{3}\pi$ ft

$$\begin{array}{r} 12\overline{)64} \\ \underline{60} \\ 4 \end{array}$$

14. **(D)** Replace the value of x in the ratio:

$$\frac{8}{3-x} = \frac{8}{3-(-1)} = \frac{8}{3+1} = \frac{8}{4} = 2$$

15. **(D)** The reciprocal of any number is a new number which, when multiplied by the first, yields 1:

$$\frac{5}{x-2} \cdot \frac{x-2}{5} = \frac{5(x-2)}{5(x-2)} = 1$$

Part B

16. (A) $\sqrt{2}$ is approximately 1.414. $\sqrt{5}$ is approximately 2.236.

$5 \times 1.414 = 7.07$ $\qquad$ $2 \times 2.236 = 4.47$

17. (D) Simplify: $4m - 3n - (3m + 2n)$

$= 4m - 3n - 3m - 2n$

$= 4m - 3m - 3n - 2n$

$m - 5n$ and $m + 5n$ cannot be compared since m and n have no numerical values.

18. (C) $4{:}6 = m{:}15$

$\frac{4}{6} = \frac{m}{15}$ cross-multiply (product of extremes equals product of means)

$4 \cdot 15 = 6 \cdot m$

$60 = 6m$ divide by 6

$10 = m$

19. (A) Multiply:

$(5 - \sqrt{3})(5 + \sqrt{3})$

First term = $(5)(5) = 25$

$5(\sqrt{3})$

$(5 - \sqrt{3})(5 + \sqrt{3}) = 5\sqrt{3} - 5\sqrt{3} = 0$

$(-\sqrt{3})(5)$

$(5 - \sqrt{3})(5 + \sqrt{3}) = (-\sqrt{3})(\sqrt{3}) = -\sqrt{9} = -3$

SOM = $25 - 3 = 22$

$22 > 16$

20. (B) Solve:

$$\begin{array}{r} x^2 + 3x + y^2 = x^2 + 2y + y^2 \\ -x^2 \quad\quad - y^2 \quad -x^2 \quad\quad - y^2 \\ \hline \end{array}$$ (additive inverse)

$\frac{3x}{3y} = \frac{2y}{3y}$

$\frac{x}{y} = \frac{2}{3}$ divide by $3y$

$x{:}y = 2{:}3$ $\qquad$ $y{:}x = 3{:}2$

$\frac{2}{3} < \frac{3}{2}$

21. **(B)** Since $a > 0$, $\frac{1}{a}$ becomes a very small fraction as a gets larger and larger. Hence $1 - \frac{1}{a}$ becomes less than 1 and $1 + \frac{1}{a}$ becomes greater than 1.

$$1 - \frac{1}{a} < 1 + \frac{1}{a} \text{ when } a > 0$$

22. **(A)** Solve: $\sqrt{.09x^2} = 81$

square root of $.09 = .3$

square root of $x^2 = x$

Hence $\sqrt{.09x^2} = 81$

becomes $.3x = 81$

Divide by .3: $x = 270$

$270 > 250$

23. **(A)** If $\frac{1}{2}x = \frac{7}{6}$, solve for x by multiplying by 2:

$$2\left(\frac{1}{2}x = \frac{7}{6}\right)$$

$$x = \frac{7}{6}\left(\frac{2}{1}\right)$$

Cancel out 2's:

$$x = \frac{7}{3}$$

If $\frac{2}{3}y = \frac{7}{6}$, solve for y by multiplying by $\frac{3}{2}$:

$$\frac{3}{2}\left(\frac{2}{3}y = \frac{7}{6}\right)$$

$$y = \frac{7}{6} \cdot \frac{3}{2}$$

Cancel out 3's:

$$y = \frac{7}{4}$$

$\frac{7}{3} > \frac{7}{4}$ If the numerators are the same, the smaller the denominator, the larger the fraction.

24. **(C)** $s = 4p$ and $s = \frac{3}{2}m$; let $4p = \frac{3}{2}m$.

Divide by 4: $p = \dfrac{\frac{3}{2}m}{4}$

$p = \frac{3}{2}m \times \frac{1}{4} = p = \frac{3}{8}m$ invert divisor and multiply

Divide by m: $\frac{p}{m} = \frac{3}{8}$.

25. **(B)** Let x = price of 32 envelopes.

$\frac{2}{32} = \frac{5}{x}$ product of extremes equals product of means

$2x = (5)(32)$

$= 160$

$x = 80$ cents divide by 2

Divide: $\dfrac{\$3.30}{3\frac{2}{3}}$

Invert divisor and multiply: $\dfrac{3.30}{\frac{11}{3}}$

$$3.30 \times \frac{3}{11} = \frac{9.90}{11} = 90 \text{ cents}$$

80 cents < 90 cents

26. **(C)** A parallelogram has four sides, hence two diagonals. A trapezoid is also a quadrilateral with four sides, hence two diagonals.

27. **(A)** A hexagon is a six-sided figure with nine diagonals. A rhombus is a quadrilateral with four consecutive equal sides, hence two diagonals.

28. **(B)**

$C = 2\pi r$ Area $= \pi r^2$

$9\pi = 2\pi r$ $25\pi = \pi r^2$

Divide by 2π: Divide by π:

$\frac{9\pi}{2\pi} = r$ $\frac{25\pi}{\pi} = r^2$

$\frac{9}{2} = r$ $25 = r^2$

$4\frac{1}{2} = r$ $5 = r$

29. **(B)** Area of triangle $= \frac{1}{2}bh$

$$A = \frac{1}{2}(6)(8)$$
$$= 3(8)$$
$$= 24$$

$12^2 + 16^2 = c^2$ (Pythagorean theorem)

$$144 + 256 = c^2$$
$$400 = c^2$$
$$20 = c$$
$$p = 16 + 12 + 20$$
$$= 48$$

30. **(A)**

$$A = s^2$$
$$64 = s^2$$
$$8 = s$$
$$s^2 + s^2 = \text{diagonal}^2$$
$$(8)^2 + (8)^2 = D^2$$
$$64 + 64 = D^2$$
$$128 = D^2$$
$$\sqrt{128} = \sqrt{D^2}$$
$$\sqrt{64 \cdot 2} = D$$
$$8\sqrt{2} = D$$
$$8\sqrt{2} = 8 \times 1.414 = 11.312$$

Diagonal > side

31. (B) The hypotenuse of a right triangle is always larger than either of the sides.

32. (B)

$$\begin{aligned} \text{Sum of angles} &= 180^\circ \\ \angle A + \angle B + \angle C &= 180 \\ \angle A + 90 + 37 &= 180 \\ \angle A + 127 &= 180 \\ \angle A &= 53 \end{aligned}$$

$AB < BC$ because if two sides are unequal, the greater side lies opposite the greater angle.

33. (C) $\angle A + \angle C = 90^\circ$ since $\angle B$ is a right angle. Hence $\angle A$ is $90 - \angle C$, or the complement of C.

34. (A) Perimeter of $ABDE = 2l + 2w = 2(17) + 2(16)$

$$= 34 + 32$$
$$= 66$$

Area of triangle $BDC = \frac{1}{2}bh$

$$\text{Area} = \tfrac{1}{2}(3)(16)$$
$$= 24$$

35. (B) $(BD)^2 + (DC)^2 = (BC)^2$ (Pythagorean theorem)

$$\begin{aligned} (16)^2 + (3)^2 &= (BC)^2 \\ 256 + 9 &= (BC)^2 \\ 265 &= (BC)^2 \\ \sqrt{265} &= \sqrt{(BC)^2} \end{aligned}$$

$16 < \sqrt{265} < 17 = BC$ (BC lies between integers 16 and 17)

$\sqrt{256} < \sqrt{265} < \sqrt{289}$ Hence $BC < 17$.

SECTION SIX: VERBAL

1. (C) **SEDITION**: insurrection, rebellion
2. (B) **INTREPID**: valorous, heroic
3. (A) **EFFRONTERY**: audacity, boldness
4. (A) **TURBULENT**: disorderly, unruly
5. (C) **PIQUANT**: pungent, spicy
6. (D) **EFFULGENT**: incandescent, illuminated
7. (B) **VACUOUS**: vacant, blank
8. (E) **ABERRATION**: madness, mania
9. (C) **JOCOSE**: humorous, merry
10. (A) **RETICENT**: taciturn, reserved

11. **(B)** Only *(B)* contains a relationship between the first and second word in the pair.

12. **(D)** Only this pair makes sense.

13. **(C)** Part of the price of losing a battle is to pay the winner for losses.

14. **(E)** All the mixed weather conditions mentioned are forms of precipitation.

15. **(A)** A prim and proper person is easily offended.

16. **(B)** Mental aspects may cause stress because of worry, tension, frustration, fear, etc. *(A), (B), (D)* and *(E)* are wrong. All are causes of disease, but even in these cases the cure is helped by the mental attitude, "the doctor within."

17. **(A)** The main idea must include other ideas in the passage. The mind helps in cures. *(B), (C)* and *(D)* support the main idea that the mind can help in all cures. Even herb doctors, *(E)*, may help through a placebo effect.

18. **(E)** All three are correct because they help produce a good mental reaction. I. A hypnotist, like a doctor, can give confidence to a patient. II and III. A placebo can be made of any harmless substance.

19. **(C)** Pituitary sends hormones to all parts of the body and affects all glands that produce hormones.

20. **(A)** No experiments have proved Laetrile to be effective against cancer cells. The cures may be a result of the placebo effect on some types of cancer that have been known to be cured "spontaneously." Perhaps the minds of some patients can cure these types of cancer even without drugs.

21. **(C)** The article indicates that Cerro Tololo is an observatory located in Chile and that the astronomers there "promptly turned their powerful 158-inch telescope on Pluto. . . ." *(A)* The implication is that the Kitt Peak Observatory is American; therefore, it would not be *international* cooperation. *(B)* This is an irrelevant fact with regard to the statement. *(D)* There is no indication that this is either true or relevant. *(E)* This is a false statement.

22. **(C)** This is borne out by specific statements in the second paragraph. *(A)* This is true and is mentioned in the selection, but it is only part of the required answer. *(B)* There is no necessary point made of this conclusion. *(D)* This assumption is not sustained by any implications or statements within the selection. *(E)* This is true, according to the selection, but it does not establish the relationship between the two names.

23. **(D)** This is stated as fact in the opening sentence of the second paragraph. Since the fact is mentioned in answer *(D)*, all the other answers are not applicable.

24. **(D)** This is directly stated in the paragraph discussing Charon's orbit as being "only 12,000 miles above the surface of Pluto. . . ." *(A)* There is nothing to indicate that this is either true or claimed. *(B)* This is actually contrary to what is stated: "An observer on the far side of Pluto would never see it at all." *(C)* No such claim is made nor implied; actually, the contrary seems true. *(E)* This is contrary to what is stated.

25. **(B)** This is stated in the topic sentence of the third paragraph: ". . . thirty-three known moons and three suspected ones." *(A)* See answer *(B)* above. *(C)* This is not a factual statement; it represents a possible hypothesis. *(D)* Actually a moon *is* a planet's satellite. *(E)* This is contrary to the assumption indicated in the selection.

26. (B) is correct. *(A)* and *(C)* are contradicted by the selection. *(D)* and *(E)* are not mentioned.

27. (A) is correct.

28. (B) is correct. This main idea is found in the second paragraph. *(A), (C),* and *(D)* are details relating to the main idea, and *(E)* is too general.

29. (C) is correct. This is stated in the second paragraph. *(A)* is contradicted in the same paragraph. *(B)* is contradicted by the selection. *(C)* does not make sense, and *(D)* is a misreading of the last paragraph.

30. (D) is correct. This bird is referred to in the last paragraph as one which "nests in bird boxes."

31. (D) Gold was the most important thing to Midas. Wisdom was most important to Athena.

32. (C) Antonyms and adjectives are needed as answers.

33. (E) Lung is related to air as heart is related to blood.

34. (A) Feathers cover birds as scales cover fish. Although a jacket covers a man, it is not a part of the body and a cake is not a living thing.

35. (D) A limousine is a luxurious car as a mansion is a luxurious home.

36. (D) A diamond is a precious "rock" as gold is a precious metal.